DISCOVER
SOUTHERN AND
EAST AFRICA

PUBLISHED BY THE READER'S DIGEST ASSOCIATION LIMITED
LONDON   NEW YORK   SYDNEY   MONTREAL

DISCOVER SOUTHERN AND EAST AFRICA

Translated and edited by Toucan Books Limited, London
for Reader's Digest, London

Translated and adapted from the French
by Michael Kerrigan

For Reader's Digest
Series Editor: Christine Noble
Editorial Assistant: Caroline Boucher
Production Controller: Martin Hendrick

Reader's Digest General Books
Editorial Director: Cortina Butler
Art Director: Nick Clark

Discover the World: SOUTHERN AND EAST AFRICA
was created and produced by
AMDS (ATELIER Martine et Daniel SASSIER), Paris for
Selection Reader's Digest S.A., Paris, and first published
in 2000 as *Regards sur le Monde: L'AFRIQUE DES GRANDS PARCS*

©2000 Selection Reader's Digest, S.A.
212 boulevard Saint-Germain, 75007, Paris

CONTENTS

UGANDA

KENYA

RWANDA

BURUNDI

TANZANIA

SEYCHELLES

COMOROS

MALAWI

MOZAMBIQUE

MAYOTTE

ZAMBIA

MADAGASCAR

ZIMBABWE

NAMIBIA

MAURITIUS

BOTSWANA

RÉUNION

SWAZILAND

SOUTH

LESOTHO

AFRICA

INTRODUCING
SOUTHERN
AND
EAST AFRICA

From the snows of Kilimanjaro to the searing
sands of the Namib Desert, from the limpid
blue lagoons of the Seychelles to the wild
savannah of the Serengeti, Southern and East
Africa offers a world of variety in a single region.
Vast herds of wildebeest graze the open plains;
shy gorillas haunt remote upland forests;
sly-looking crocodiles patrol for prey in sluggish
river reaches. Here, too, precious stones and
hominid fossils lie as yet undiscovered in the
virgin strata of untrodden hillsides.

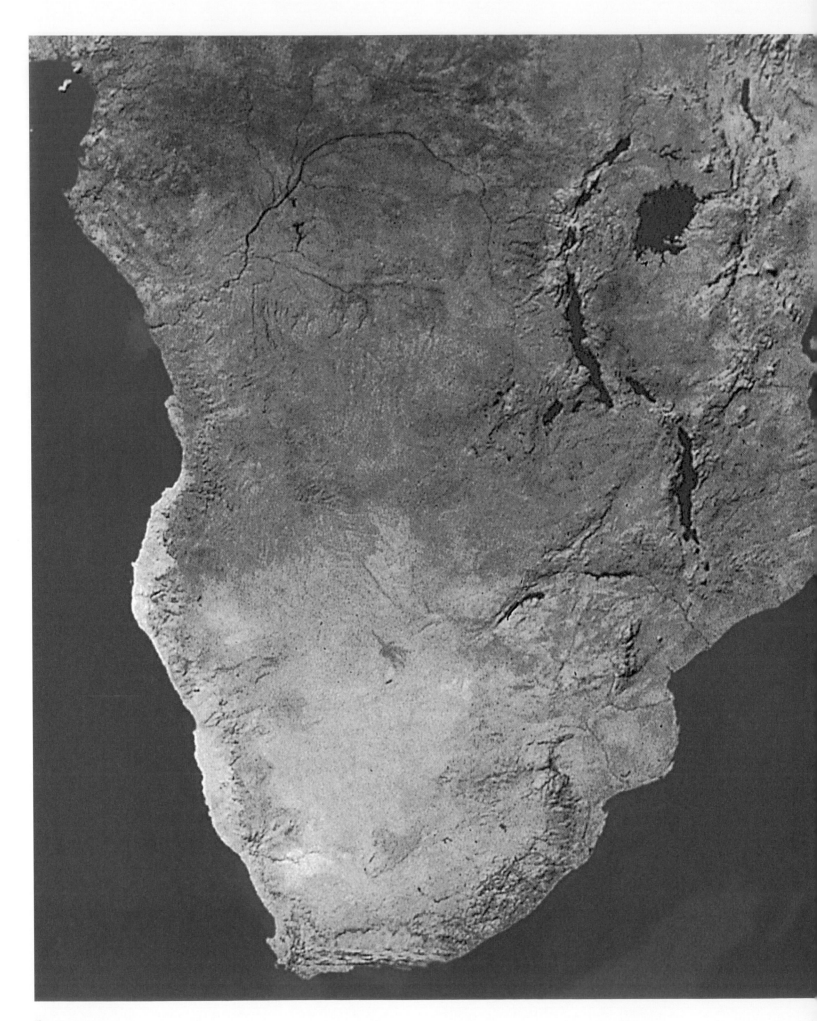

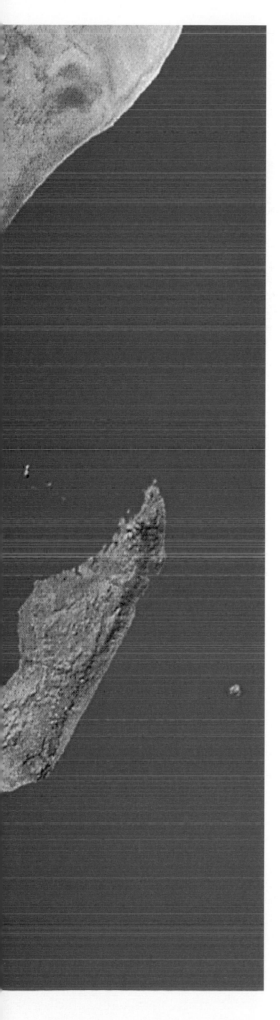

Traces of time

A huge geological fault, the Rift Valley, gashes the east of the African continent. Its formation threw up a mountain barrier that slopes in a series of plateaus towards the Indian Ocean. This is the birthplace of humanity, the place where, some 3-4 million years ago, the first bipeds stood up to survey the surrounding countryside. It was also here that, from around 3000 years ago, the peopling of modern Africa began, as communities from the Nile came together and interbred with Bantu tribes from the valley of the Niger.

Trading up and down the continent's eastern coast from as early as the 8th century AD, Arab traders changed the region's cultural, religious and economic face. Southern and East Africa possesses some of the richest mineral reserves in the world. In the 15th century, spurred on by tales of gold in Monomotapa, the great Bantu kingdom of Zimbabwe, European adventurers set forth for these distant lands. In the following centuries they were rewarded by the discovery of rich deposits, including gold, gems, coal and oil. In the resulting rush to extract and exploit these finds an entire industrial infrastructure sprang into being, with railway lines and port facilities to transport the treasures of the African interior to a covetous outside world.

Mineral and agricultural wealth was accumulated under the aegis of the great European powers, who carved the region up into colonial 'countries' with little regard for demographic divisions. The Africans themselves were very much the losers in a colonial system that weighed upon them ever more oppressively as the decades passed. From the 1960s onwards one colony after another shook off the yoke of European rule – but the 'national' boundaries drawn by the Western powers remained and proved a source of continuing tension as time went on.

The islands of the Indian Ocean, off Africa's eastern coast, are historically where Asia and Africa met. Long before its inhabitants came into regular contact with the African mainland, Madagascar was settled by migrants from Indonesia. Many more arrived in modern times to work on the huge sugar and coffee plantations that the Europeans established on Mauritius and Réunion. At first slaves were used, seized from local settlements; thereafter, as demand for labour soared, workers were shipped in from the Indian subcontinent. Today these islands have a mixed population and a rich and vibrant hybrid culture that is all their own. The islanders themselves are as remote from continental Africa in spirit as they are different in their facial features.

The Indian Ocean has many natural splendours of its own to offer – from the plateaus of Madagascar to the dizzying ravines of Réunion and the ravishing beauty of the lagoon that wraps Mauritius in blue tranquillity. On the mainland an immense belt of wildlife reserves stretches all the way from Kenya to Namibia, providing sanctuary for wild animals increasingly under threat from human encroachment. Lions, elephants, leopards, giraffes, rhinoceroses, hippopotamuses, zebras, antelopes, wildebeest and many other species range free in their natural habitat. Visitors flock from all over the world to see these incalculably rich reserves of the Earth's living natural heritage, and provide much-needed foreign currency.

The more curious Western visitors will not be content to confine themselves to the exploration of such natural treasures, for there are human mysteries to be fathomed, too. African society is rich in variety and colour and – despite the difficulties of its turbulent history – possesses a truly remarkable vitality.

Space-age view In this satellite photograph the long lakes of the Rift Valley look like torn lengths of blue ribbon. Madagascar, attached to the continent in ancient times, has slowly drifted away.

A natural hunter   A lioness approaches prey from downwind so as not to give away her presence by her scent. If the vegetation does not provide a dense enough screen, she hunts under cover of darkness. Ambushing prey around waterholes, lionesses working together may take on quarry as large as water buffaloes.

Perfect partners   The giraffe and the acacia tree (below) have a mutually beneficial relationship. According to legend, the tree has grown higher and higher down the ages in an attempt to outstrip the ever-extending neck of the browsing giraffe. The acacia is the staple diet of the giraffe, which can reach the spreading branches easily enough. The giraffe has thick saliva that enables it to cope with the tree's dry and prickly spines. This natural pruning benefits the tree, the roots of which benefit from the giraffe's dung.

Thud of feet   An elephant herd on the move past a giant acacia. In the background, the dazzling, snowy summit of Mount Kilimanjaro towers over the scene. Elephants coat themselves in a layer of mud and dust, which helps them to stay cool and protects against biting insects.

Mountain of the gods   *Kilimanjaro, a volcano, appears to prop up the sky, supporting the clouds over Tanzania. At 19 340 ft (5895 m), the mountain is the highest peak on the African continent. It is topped by a mantle of snow and ice, which never thaws even in the most searing summers. Kilimanjaro looms large not only in physical form, but in local mythology. Seen from the surrounding plains, it serves as a landmark, even a reassuring presence. From its slopes and the crater rim, however, the mountain takes on a more menacing character: a dormant gaint that could suddenly awake.*

Hell's kitchen   *Like some infernal cauldron, the crater of Mount Nyiragongo simmers, still actively shaping the landscape. As in Hawaii or the Indian Ocean island of Réunion, the lava from this volcano on the border of Rwanda and the Democratic Republic of the Congo continually wells up and cools to form new rock. All along the Great Rift Valley, two geotectonic plates pull inexorably apart – the opposing shores, perhaps, of some great ocean of the distant future. Africa may have some of the world's most ancient landscapes, but this boiling lava testifies to an Earth seething with creative fire.*

Tortured landscape The swirling patterns of these lava flows from the crater of Lengaï are visible evidence of the titanic forces and subterranean pressures still at work in this part of northern Tanzania. On the other side of the Rift Valley from Nyiragongo, the scene testifies to the existence of similar subterranean pressures: this region is still in the throes of being born.

Fantastical forest Equatorial East Africa is relatively dry and rises inland to cloud forest that cloaks the upper slopes of the great volcanic peaks of Kenya and Tanzania. It is in Uganda, in the Ruwenzori Mountains (left), that this mysterious landscape finds its most spectacular expression. In scenes of gothic extravagance, gigantic ferns and flowers strike outlandish poses, while trees stand draped with moss, and festooned with luxuriant creepers. The wildlife in these strange woodlands is appropriately unusual, pride of place being taken by the reclusive mountain gorilla.

Land of lakes Whether formed by a dam, like Zimbabwe's Lake Kariba (left), by subsidence along the Rift Valley (like Lakes Malawi and Tanganyika) or, like Lake Victoria, by the drowning of a low-lying basin, the great lakes of Southern and East Africa are stunningly beautiful additions to the landscape and greatly add to the variety of life in the region.

Falls that thunder Wrenched this way and that by the forces beneath the Earth's crust, East Africa's lakes and rivers have never had a chance to find their own level. Vast heads of water build up behind geological obstacles to burst forth in mighty torrents. Thus the formidable, mile-wide River Zambezi finds its easy meanderings through Zimbabwe interrupted by a sudden faultline. Abruptly forced into a deep and tight rocky gorge, the river drops 295-354 ft (90-108 m) in a single headlong plunge. Though twice the height of North America's Niagara, the Victoria Falls (right) yield the continental record to South Africa's Tugela Falls, a series of five falls whose waters drop a total of 3110 ft (948 m) including a single breathtaking fall of 1345 ft (410 m).

Desert features Up by the northern border of Namibia, the aridity has given rise to rugged wastelands marked at intervals by wide depressions known as 'frying pans' (above). The name comes from their roughly circular shape, the streams that run in after an occasional rainfall carving out indentations that look a little like handles, while the saline deposits left behind by evaporation resemble the whites of frying eggs. Add to that the blazing heat of a region whose rocks do indeed get almost hot enough to cook on in the midday sun, and the term begins to seem a good deal less fanciful. Similar features can be found at the head of the Rift Valley, in a desert zone where the temperatures soar even higher.

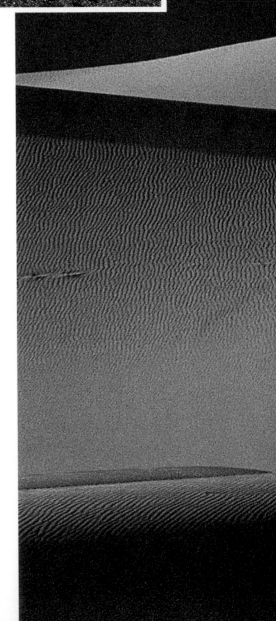

Chameleon scene The semiarid grassland that covers so much of Southern and East Africa may take on a strikingly different appearance with even the slightest variation in climatic conditions. This corner of the Kalahari (left) is seared to such yellow brittleness in the dry season that it could be mistaken for true desert, but the least rainfall brings forth lush greenness in a matter of hours. A real storm may take things still further, the new-sprung savannah promptly disappearing beneath the waters of a lake. Within a few weeks, however, the transformation will reverse itself and the landscape will once more look like desert.

A land on the move The purest, sandiest desert in Southern Africa extends along the Atlantic coast from South Africa's Orange Estuary to Walvis Bay, Namibia. The great dunes that are a feature of this part of the Namib Desert (right) are formed from an ochre sand borne towards the coast by a wind that blows from well inland. Its comings and goings, which ripple the dry sand, can be traced in the complex forms of these mobile dunes, whose grain-by-grain displacement is actually audible as a rustling sound.

A tale of two seashores The islands in the south of the Seychelles archipelago, like Mahé (below) are formed of solid granite. Essentially, they are a chunk of the African plate that came adrift from the mass of the mainland. Here a rough, craggy coastline is littered with boulders, and what sand there is is heavy and coarse-grained. The islands to the north, by contrast, have low-lying coastlines with endless fine, white sand beaches: these are classically formed tropical islands, their sand the ground-down shells of creatures from coral reefs.

Every kind of coast Madagascar has a wonderfully varied coastline. At the northern tip of the island (right) the volcanic slopes of Mount Ambre meet the sandy beaches of Antseranana Bay. To the east the island ends abruptly, its coast cut off short and uncannily straight by a geological fault, though the effect has been softened down the centuries by the formation of a great reef fringed by sparkling coral sands. To the west the land shelves gently seawards and alluvial mudflats have accumulated over time. Here there are sticky wetlands, narrow creeks and dense mangrove swamps.

Land's end At the Cape of Good Hope (right) the waters of the Indian Ocean and the South Atlantic swirl and mix around the southern tip of Africa. Here, Table Mountain and the city of Cape Town provide one of the world's most recognisable views.

A brief history

The 19th-century naturalist Charles Darwin outraged many in his day by suggesting that the first bipeds – our forefathers – were descended from the great apes. In the 1950s, palaeontologists Louis and Mary Leakey made bone discoveries that bore out Darwin's theories. Modern research suggests that protohuman 'hominids' did indeed evolve from early apes, and that the development took place on the high plateaus of East Africa.

A difference of opinion

In 1974 a team of American and French researchers working in south-eastern Ethiopia discovered the fossil remains of 'Lucy', estimated to be 3.2 million years old. Some anthropologists are certain this is a specimen of one of our earliest hominid ancestors; others give that title to a different, and slightly older species, *Australopithecus africanus*. Still other experts believe that the vital 'missing link' has yet to be found. All agree, however, that the various different australopithecenes whose remains have been found in the Rift Valley belong to the same general family of species, forced into periodic migration by climatic changes.

The first humans *The fossil finds of Mary and Louis Leakey in the Olduvai Gorge of Tanzania support the theory that East Africa was the cradle of humanity. Here Mary, pictured in 1978, pursues her painstaking researches in Laetoli.*

The cradle of humanity

Between 4 and 3 million years ago the first true hominid, *Australopithecus*, emerged in Africa. The fossil record shows that these protohumans were small-brained, but walked upright on two legs. Australopithecenes are of crucial significance, as they belong to a time when our distant ancestors had only just made the decisive break with ape evolution to follow a path of separate development as hominids.

It was also in East Africa 2 million years ago that *Homo habilis*, or 'handy man' emerged – so-called because of the ability to use simple tools. Then, 1 million years ago, *Homo erectus*, 'upright man', appeared. Although evidence of *Homo erectus* is found around the world, the oldest fossil specimens come from East Africa, suggesting that this was where the species first lived. Then, 100 000 years ago something like a modern human first appeared: in all physiological essentials, *Homo sapiens*, 'thinking man', was identical to us.

Hunter-gatherers

The lifestyle of our first fully human ancestors resembled that of the Bushmen, or !Kung San nomadic hunter-gatherers, who still range the scrubland of South Africa's Kalahari Desert. The more settled Hottentot society emerged about 10 000 years ago: rather than hunting, they relied for food on domesticated livestock. By 7000 BC people had begun to grow crops. Throughout this period climatic change caused the arid belt to the north (the Sahara) to expand. The desert reached its present dimensions around 2500 BC, dislodging farming peoples from what had previously

Fossil finds *Evidence of hominids has been found around Lake Turkana and in the Omo valley.*

Valley of Man

SUDAN

Nile

Omo

ETHIOPIA

UGANDA

Lake Turkana

KENYA

Equator

Lake Victoria

A precious inheritance *Time has taken its toll on the Bushmen's rock art. A team from the University of Johannesburg has visited all South Africa's sites and compiled a record of photographs and tracings to conserve these amazing paintings for future generations.*

been fertile land. Many tribes moved southwards in the quest for life-giving water. Settling along the valley of the Niger, they established the Nok civilisation, the first in Africa to master metalworking skills and the region's first agricultural society.

The Bantu on the march

It was from such beginnings that the Bantu culture arose, slowly spreading from one valley to the next as groups of nomadic hunter-gatherers settled down in villages. Around 2500 years ago, Bantu tribes in search of new territories skirted the equatorial rain forest to reach the area north of the Great Lakes. There they came into contact with pastoralist peoples who spoke the

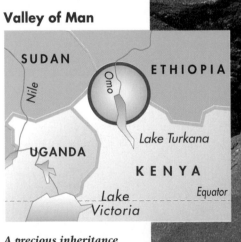

Nilotic languages – descendants of races that had sprung up along the valley of the Upper Nile. Like the Bantu, they had been driven out of their homelands by the steady desiccation of the Sahara: they struck southwards from what is now Sudan in the hope of finding fresh grazing for their livestock.

For 2000 years Kenya was the scene of an intense coming and going of population groups as new plots were brought under cultivation by the Bantu, and new areas of pastureland opened up by the

African pastoral
An anonymous 19th century painting of Bantu farmers on the banks of the Zambezi.

Ethnic groups

▦ Hamitic	▨ Bushman-Hottentot
▦ Nilotic	▦ Malay
▢ Bantu	▢ Indo-European

Nilotic herdsmen. The pastoralists' entire existence revolved around their livestock, which they grazed across the grasslands of the high plateaus. Their villages were lightweight, temporary affairs, their huts thrown together from branches and leaves at a moment's notice: they could be dismantled just as easily and carried to the next encampment. The Bantu farmers, by contrast, confined themselves to the valley bottoms, whose rich, damp soils were far more fertile than those on the surrounding hilltops. They spread rapidly along the region's riverbanks and round its lakes,

developing strategies for surviving seasonal floods and immunity against insect-borne diseases. They lived by the cycles of the growing season, and learned to lay by any surplus in dug-out stores or granaries.

Although their different patterns of land-use helped to minimise potential conflicts between farmers and herdsmen, both groups encroached on areas occupied by the Bushmen (San) as they expanded southwards. The San had by now been roaming the open plains of Southern Africa for 40 000 years; their Kung descendants still pursue their traditional lifestyle in the arid Kalahari.

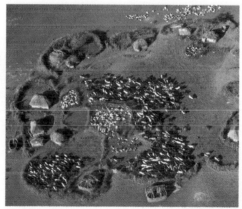

Communal living Pastoralist peoples like the Masai share their living space with their livestock.

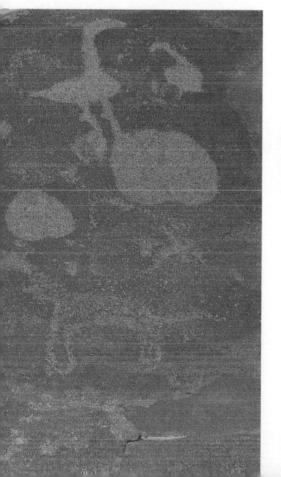

The doomed dodo The large, flightless dodo was a source of easy meat and eggs for early settlers on the Mascarenes.

The Mascarenes

The Mascarenes – Réunion, Mauritius and Rodrigues – were named after the 16th century Portuguese explorer Don Pedro Mascarenhas. In 1598 a Dutch squadron landed on Mauritius and named it in honour of Prince Maurice Van Nassau, 'Stathouder' of Holland, but they did not settle there until 1638. In 1652 the Dutch established Cape Colony and, when it was a success, they abandoned Mauritius. By the end of the 18th century, the French East India Company had set up outposts on the islands and the days of the dodo, indigenous tortoise and other species were numbered. When Louis XIV's attempt to found a 'France of the East' in nearby Madagascar failed, the Mascarenes became home for a motley crew of smugglers and buccaneers.

19

Nomadic hunter-gatherers, the Kung San move about from place to place in search of food, the men hunting game with poisoned arrows, while the women scratch for roots and bulbs with stone-tipped digging sticks. Erecting an impromptu shelter in the shade of a fruiting tree, or camping on the trail of migrating game, they supplement a diet of roast meat and ostrich with roots, herbs, nuts and berries.

At home *This Himba girl, a native of Kaokoland, Namibia, looks out at the landscape her ancestors have inhabited for untold generations.*

Irreconcilable differences

The distinctions between the farming, pastoralist and hunter-gathering lifestyles were not as clear-cut as they may sound, for farmers often kept a few cattle or supplemented their diet with hunted meat from the bush, while their womenfolk took time out from tending their cultivated crops to forage for natural produce. Each group forged its own links with the land, developing its own distinct system of traditions and taboos, its own kinship structures and dietary regime. But the hunter-gatherers were gradually absorbed into, or displaced by, the larger, more tightly organised farming communities. A people who had once been masters

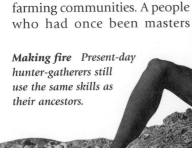

Making fire *Present-day hunter-gatherers still use the same skills as their ancestors.*

of much of Southern Africa found themselves restricted to an ever smaller area: the San only endured in the Kalahari because the land there is agriculturally worthless. As the population grew and land resources became short, competition between pastoralists and farmers could no longer be avoided. If the tightly organised farming communities put down their own deep roots in the land and defended it fiercely, the pastoralists were well able to look after themselves, acquiring extra livestock by force from neighbouring communities. Wars flared up over land or water holes: in the 14th century Tutsi pastoralists, of Nilotic origin, drove their flocks southwards into the lands of the Hutu, a Bantu farming people, and the resulting conflict smouldered on for generations, to erupt with a vengeance in the 1990s.

Realm of gold

The Bantu peoples expanded into the heart of the continent, spreading slowly along the open corridors of the great river valleys. One group of migrants, making its way up the Zambezi, established the kingdom of Monomotapa, with its capital city Great Zimbabwe built around a citadel of stone. In the 14th century, with 10 000 inhabitants, Zimbabwe grew rich on gold and ivory. The Bantu excelled in the discovery and extraction of minerals and in metalworking, becoming skilled in the handling not only of gold but of copper and pewter, too. There were some 60 000 mines between the Zambezi and Limpopo river basins, testimony to the stupendous resources of this East African El Dorado.

The riches of Zimbabwe exercised a strong fascination on the outside world. In 1417 and 1433 China sent expeditions to East Africa in the hope of bringing back some of the fabled

Trading nation *To their surprise, the first white explorers found significant settlements and a well-organised African economy already in place.*

Africans from Asia

From a cultural point of view, Madagascar belongs just as much to Asia as to Africa. Driven west and south by surging monsoon winds, the island's first inhabitants arrived from Indonesia, bringing with them such un-African plants as the banana, coconut and yam. These errant seafarers stayed on to take part in the thriving Indian Ocean trade, running incense, shells and slaves to Arabia and beyond. Nowadays the descendants of those first Madagascans live in the upland areas of the island's centre, their language and culture displaced around the coast by that of more recent immigrants from the mainland of East Africa.

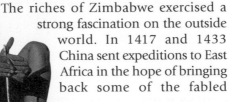

Swahili woman in Zanzibar

The turbulent history of Zanzibar

This little island off the African coast was known to Persian seafarers as early as the 6th century. By 730, Arab merchants had established operations there and by the 10th century had built up a prosperous trading city. In 1503 Zanzibar was sacked and its merchant fleet scuttled by the Portuguese. Two centuries later the inhabitants rose to expel their European masters, their rebellion encouraged and assisted by the Sultan of Oman. In 1832 his successor, Seyyid Said, transferred his court to the island from Muscat, and by 1856 it had become an independent Sultanate. But Zanzibar soon became absorbed into the British Empire, Britain's concern was to curtail the power of Germany, already well-established in mainland Tanganyika. In 1963 Zanzibar gained independence and in 1964 joined Tanganyika to form Tanzania.

the interior. Called 'Swahili' from the Arabic *sawahil*, meaning 'coast', it was a rich and exotic mixture of languages, customs and ideas, based not only on Bantu and Arabic models but also on those of other nations involved in the African coastal trade. Thus distinct Persian and Indian elements were also incorporated into one of the richest cultural complexes the world has ever seen.

The luxury trade

Colonies were first established on coastal islands such as Zanzibar and Pemba, but soon the merchants were setting up shop on the mainland in bases such as Malindi, Mombasa and Kaloua. Then their dhows ventured further, to the Comoro archipelago – the 'Islands of the Moon'. The Swahili sphere of influence extended to include Madagascar: enterprising traders landed all around the coast, exchanging goods with the natives. A network of mercantile cities developed, all politically independent yet in constant communication with one another. Remote as it may have been in European terms, East Africa was actually

The ivory trade Tusks were brought to the coasts in large numbers by long columns of native slaves.

treasures. The stories were just as attractive to Europeans: by the end of the 15th century Portuguese navigators had established the first outposts of European colonisation in the region. But the first foreigners to discover East Africa's mineral wealth had actually stumbled upon the secret centuries before. Arab traders had been travelling

Sail power Stately symbols of an ancient trading tradition, dhows like this have sailed the east coast of Africa for 14 centuries.

this coast since the end of the first millennium. Not only did they establish ports at the mouths of the mainland rivers, but they also instituted a thriving commerce with the outlying islands.

Arab outposts

The Arab merchants who traded along the East African coast were some of the most accomplished seafarers in history. In their distinctive dhows, 'lateen-rigged' vessels, they had plied up and down the East African coast since the 8th century. What may have been an unknown region to Europeans had, thanks to the Arabs, long been in commercial contact with India and the Orient.

Some of these merchant princes married the daughters of local chiefs and established a distinctive coastal culture very different from that of

Arab influence Swahili culture is a fusion of Arabic and African influences.

very much in the swim, one end of a continuous commercial and cultural zone that extended as far as Muslim India.

Seashells for gold

A steady flow of cowrie shells from the Maldive Islands and fine cottons from India were brought southwards on the dhows to meet demand in Swahili Africa. The merchants used these commodities as currency in their

The first European Portuguese explorer Vasco de Gama made landfall in East Africa.

dealings with the tribes of the interior, from whom in return they obtained gold, ivory and giraffe skins as well as slaves. Luxuries were brought from Asia too: spices, silks and porcelains from China, and precious stones from Thailand. By the 10th century, Arab economic dominance in the Indian Ocean was so strong that the only coinage recognised in the region was the dinar.

The coming of the Europeans

Arab supremacy in the region lasted until 1498, when Vasco da Gama discovered the sea route round the Cape of Good Hope. With their superior firepower and swift caravelles, the Portuguese easily overpowered the Arabs. Their cities sacked and their merchandise plundered by Portuguese adventurers, the Muslim traders also found themselves threatened by inland tribes, who sensed the opportunity to shake off an irksome authority – though the Portuguese replaced Swahili dominance with their own monopoly maintained by naval power.

The first European outpost in Africa was established by the Dutch in 1652, when Protestant settlers from the Netherlands and France founded black Africa's first white colony at the Cape of Good Hope. Situated at the southernmost tip of the continent, Cape Colony asserted the

Portuguese expansion in the 16th century

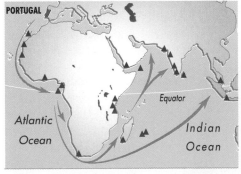

PORTUGAL

Atlantic Ocean

Equator

Indian Ocean

■ ▲ Portugal and areas under Portuguese control
→ Portuguese expeditions

Unavoidably detained

The English sea captain Matthew Flinders is famous for charting the Australian coastline in two expeditions between 1795 and 1803. His second venture completed, he was heading homewards across the Indian Ocean when his ship, the schooner *Cumberland*, began leaking badly. Rather than brave the stormy Cape in an unseaworthy vessel, Flinders decided to put in to French Mauritius for repairs, unaware that his country was at war with France. As he neared the coast, he saw a smaller vessel hurrying in before him and presumed it was a pilot boat – but it was in fact fleeing from what it took to be an aggressor. The French did not believe that Flinders' small schooner had come all the way from Australia: he was arrested and interned for the duration of the war.

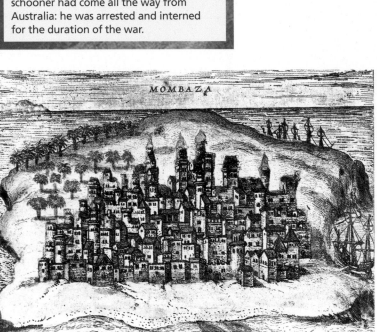

MOMBAZA

Netherlands' African presence as well as providing a convenient waystation for ships en route to the Dutch East Indies.

Islands claimed by France

The French had set up their first colonies in the region at the start of the 17th century: these were offshore, on the Mascarene Islands, where they started extensive coffee plantations. An abundant supply of slaves ensured cheap labour and the introduction of the steam engine in the 19th century made production even more economical. The planters on Bourbon (now Réunion) persuaded France to send out forces to claim Madagascar, and in 1839 a French colony was established on the island of Nossi-bé, just a few miles off the northern tip of Madagascar.

Human cargo At the height of the East African slave trade more than 50 000 unfortunates are thought to have passed through Zanzibar annually, to be sold overseas for their labour on plantations.

Trading centre This engraving of Mombasa is the earliest representation of the great Swahili city. The square-riggers show that Europeans have already arrived.

The abolition of slavery in the mid-19th century posed problems for the planters, who still needed enormous quantities of labour to exploit the opportunities opened up by a boom in demand for cane sugar in the industrialising countries. They therefore turned to India, bringing in contract labourers who, when their term of service was over, were free to return, if they so wished, to their homeland.

The slave trade

The slave trade was not the invention of Europeans: from the end of the first millennium the enslavement and exchange of black African populations were essential elements of the Swahili economy. Slaves were sold throughout the East, from Arabia to China, but the biggest market was Iraq,

Arab alliance Long before the coming of the Europeans, Arabs and Africans formed strong bonds, relating as equals at higher levels of society. This engraving by the French artist Philippe Simonneau dates from the early 18th century.

A republic of rogues

A History of the Most Notorious Pyrates published in 1728 tells how, towards the end of the 17th century, a French sailor named Misson turned to piracy in the Indian Ocean. He married a princess from the Comoros, for whom he built a city at Diego-Suarez in the north of Madagascar. This was for a brief period the capital of the Republic of Libertalia, where a multiracial population of pirates and other assorted misfits lived in liberty, equality and fraternity with the princess's retinue of Comoran ladies. Any shortage of wives was made up by snatching Arab women from the pilgrim ships that plied to and from Mecca. Whether fact or fiction, Misson's Republic has been a source of interest ever since.

where slaves were put to work on the Caliph of Baghdad's cotton and sugar-cane plantations. History records an insurrection among Iraqi slaves that began in 898 and lasted for 15 years until quelled by the Caliph's forces.

Back in Africa, the trade brought violence: the demand for slaves was a catalyst for war, as tribes sought to enrich themselves by capturing their neighbours to sell to the Swahilis. To begin with, the slavers' operations were centred on the coast, but their influence soon spread inland. In their search for labour, the Swahilis also scoured the Comoros islands for slaves, and established a base at Majunga, on Madagascar's west coast.

In the 19th century, Seyyid Said, Sultan of Zanzibar, seized control of the main trafficking routes into the African interior, through his principal agent, Hamed bin Muhammad or

'Tippu Tip'. A wealthy potentate in his own right, Tippu's quest for the choicest slave stock took him to the shores of the Rift Valley lakes, and Zanzibar became Africa's leading centre for the export of slaves. A feared yet all too familiar figure among the native tribes, Muhammad met Livingstone in 1867: where the white 'explorers' went, Arab traders had been long before them.

A lucrative business

The arrival of Europeans escalated a trade that had been going on at a more or less constant rate for several centuries. In the Mascarenes in particular a new breed of Creole colonists – born in the islands, but of European descent – was crying out for

Royal agent Tippu Tip (1837-1905) extended the slave trade into the African interior.

Chained like beasts *This image seems shocking now, but was surprisingly slow in stirring the European conscience.*

labour to work their coffee plantations. A rabble of European buccaneers, often married to local women, responded to this need by putting to sea and raiding both the coast and outlying islands for slaves, rounding up even the Swahili populations that until now had been in the ascendancy. As the demand in Europe grew for all sorts of tropical produce, from sugar cane to coffee, the clamour for slaves intensified. As the slavers went flat out to meet it, the effects on a war-ravaged African society were far-reaching: it would be no exaggeration to say that this appalling trade tore the heart out of East Africa, with consequences that the region must wrestle with to this very day.

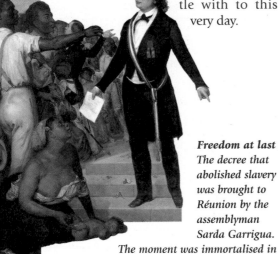

Freedom at last *The decree that abolished slavery was brought to Réunion by the assemblyman Sarda Garrigua. The moment was immortalised in 1848 by the painter Alphonse Garreau.*

A living death

Ships from Liverpool and Bordeaux took charge of the East African slave trade to begin with, though these were supplanted by vessels owned by the Creole islanders themselves. For the hundreds of thousands of slaves ferried in inhumane conditions, ownership was a matter of complete indifference: their bodies weighed down by heavy chains, their necks, wrists and ankles rubbed sore by tight-fitting collars and clamps, they were caged in like animals, crammed into fetid holds where they were forced to wallow in their own bodily wastes. Once arrived at their destination, they were sold to the highest bidder, wives and husbands parted, whole families broken up. On the plantations they were forced to work themselves into the ground on starvation rations. That, in such circumstances, the transplanted slaves maintained any sort of cultural identity at all is testimony to the amazing spirit of Africa and its endurance through adversity.

Mozambique, mine of men

As they set about the business of colonising Brazil, the Portuguese found themselves needing labour in vast quantities: without it they would not be able to exploit their new possession. In the early years of the 17th century they carried off many thousands of slaves from Angola – only to find that the Dutch were also taking advantage of this rich source of manpower. It was to Mozambique, therefore, that they turned to make up the deficit: a development that blighted the country's history from that time forward. By the beginning of the 19th century, the traffic in slaves was worth more than that in ivory: between 1800 and 1842, it is thought, some 40 000 were exported. Arab slavers, Portuguese colonists and native chiefs were all complicit in this trade.

The runaways

The more slaves were shipped in to the islands of the Indian Ocean to work the plantations, the more the islands' demographic balance became skewed: soon black slaves outnumbered their white masters. Emboldened by their majority, more and more slaves were prepared to face the hazards awaiting them in the forests – and the vicious punishments meted out to any absconder unfortunate enough to be apprehended. Known as maroons, these runaways came together to form little outlaw bands living deep in the interior, emerging at times to raid outlying plantations or lend encouragement to any slave unrest that might be brewing. Punitive expeditions were sent out to hunt them down, but many managed to elude capture for years, a constant thorn in the side of the Creole authorities. But time was running out: in

Anchaing, first of the free

Scarcely had the first consignment of slaves been landed on Réunion than one of their number escaped, taking refuge in the dense forests of the island's interior. Holing up in a cave high on a rugged mountain, Anchaing, by birth a Madagascan, found himself the pre-eminent figure in a growing community of fugitive maroons. With his wife Héva he started a distinguished outlaw dynasty: his most famous daughter, Marianne, became the companion of the celebrated marron freedom-fighter Cimendef. Anchaing's story ended in tragedy when the great manhunter Touchard tracked him down to his mountain hideaway and killed him near his cave. The remote valley of which Anchaing was for so long king has since been named after him.

Britain a law forbidding slave trading was passed in 1807, and in 1833 slavery was abolished in all British colonies. Today, over a century and a half later, slavery has by no means been forgotten: the slaves' descendants still celebrate the abolition of one of the great crimes against humanity.

The great explorers

One of abolitionism's most eloquent 19th-century advocates, David Livingstone is now more famous as a great explorer. His reports shed light on what had hitherto been – for Europeans at least – the Dark Continent. Starting out from the southern Cape in 1841, this Scottish doctor and missionary travelled with his wife Mary to spread the Word of God. Striking north and east into the interior, along a route that skirted the major areas of Dutch settlement, the couple confined themselves as far as possible to regions where white Christians had not yet penetrated, eventually finding their way across the Kalahari to the Zambezi. That they unwittingly opened up what Cecil Rhodes would afterwards describe triumphantly as a 'British Suez Canal' into Central Africa was incidental as far as the Livingstones were concerned.

African encounter Stanley (left) finds Livingstone, and catches the world's attention.

Livingstone met Tippu Tip, and his subsequent denunciation of the slave trade still persisting under the Portuguese helped galvanise public opinion at home.

By now Livingstone had not been heard from for several years, and an American reporter, Henry Morton Stanley, was sent out to find him. At Ujiji, by the shores of Lake Tanganyika, he found an old, sick white man. 'Doctor Livingstone, I presume', said Stanley – and his presumption turned out to be correct: he had pulled off one of the great scoops of the century.

Determined to discover the source of the Nile, a goal in which Burton and Speke had failed, Livingstone stayed on in Africa despite failing health. Within a couple of years he was dead: porters bore his body down to the coast, and he was taken back to London and buried in Westminster Abbey.

African hospitality The first white explorers were at times treated to the most elaborate ceremonies of welcome, which may merely have heightened European arrogance.

The travels of Livingstone and Stanley

Livingstone ····· 1841–51   Stanley —— 1871–72
          –·–· 1853–56   —— 1874–77
          —— 1866–73   ‑‑‑ 1887–89

☆ Meeting of Livingstone and Stanley, October 1871

In a second expedition, Livingstone found a route from the upper Zambezi to the Atlantic coast at Luanda, before retracing his steps and following the Zambezi down to the Indian Ocean. In the process he became, in 1855, the first white man to see the great waterfall that he named after his monarch, Queen Victoria.

'Doctor Livingstone, I presume'

In a third expedition a decade later, Livingstone set off through new territories farther north, following a tributary of the Zambezi to Lake Nyasa, then heading on through the Great Lakes region. This area was relatively crowded with European pioneers, including Richard Burton and J.H. Speke, then exploring the shores of lakes Tanganyika and Victoria. The region was also well-populated by slavers: it was here that

The Zulus

The first white explorers went into the African interior convinced they were opening up a savage wilderness, yet time and again they encountered long-established civilisations. The hills of Natal, in south-eastern Africa, had been occupied by the Nguni-speaking peoples for 200 years before the region was officially 'discovered' by the white man. The traditional Nguni tribe was really no more than an extended family. Around the figure of the chief clustered a small community of dependants: his wife, and his sons with their wives and children. These groups existed in close alliance with others that shared a common ancestor.

The Nguni tribes were fortunate in having a homeland that, though watered by regular rain, was well-drained, and free of malarial mosquitoes and the tsetse fly. Agricultural and stock-rearing skills provided the economic basis for a society to develop and thrive. But the Nguni became a victim of their own success: as their numbers grew, some tribes started to extend their lands at the expense of others. Tribesmen armed themselves to defend their territory, and in the wars that followed, no tribe was more feared than the Zulus, who under their chief Shaka fashioned something very like an empire in Natal, transforming Nguni life and culture in the process.

The tribal village   This Zulu kraal near Umlazi in Natal was sketched by George French Angas in 1849: by now this proud warrior people had been forced back into more peaceful ways.

Bloody battle   *Ambushed at Blauwkrantz in February 1838, a party of Boers is massacred by Zulu warriors: the tables were turned at Blood River just a few months later.*

The rise and fall of Shaka

Though Shaka was born the son of a chief, his mother was expelled from her husband's *kraal* on account of her temper and sharp tongue. He grew up among strangers, who mocked his pretensions to chiefdom. These experiences left their mark on a young man determined to let nobody hinder his path, a warrior of reckless bravery and a politician of ruthless cunning. Seizing the leadership of the Zulus on his father's death in 1816, within two years he had made himself lord of all the Nguni.

Shaka changed Nguni society by turning a farming people into an army of full-time warriors. He changed the face of warfare in Southern Africa, too: the iron discipline he imposed on his forces enabled him to develop an altogether new style of combat. Whereas warriors had once hurtled pell-mell into battle, yelling bloodcurdling threats and hurling spears, Shaka's men marched forwards in tight for-

mation behind big oxhide shields. Their shortened assegais were ineffective as javelins: instead they were used for cutting and thrusting at close quarters. The 15 000 warriors Shaka had under arms by 1824 were worth many times that number of untrained men: these were soldiers in the European sense, a true war machine. No other nation could match the Zulus now: Shaka's realm soon stretched all the way up to the Tugela River. But in 1828 Shaka was killed in a coup.

The Zulus now found themselves facing the rifles and cannons of the Boers, who were pushing up-country to find new territories out of reach of the British Cape authorities. Descendants of the first Dutch settlers, these independent-minded farmers had been finding British rule increasingly

Prophet of empire

As prime minister of the Cape Colony in the 1880s, Cecil Rhodes dreamed of far greater things: to him it was the racial destiny of the Anglo-Saxons to rule all Africa from the Cape to Cairo. The railway he envisaged supporting his great vision petered out in Zambia, yet even so it opened the way to untold riches. Rhodes made his fortune in gold and diamonds and in 1889 was awarded the title to Rhodesia (now Zimbabwe) and Northern Rhodesia (Zambia), where he brought settlers to create a very British colony.

White leader   *Unimpressed by Zulu strength, Rhodes had no doubt of his racial destiny.*

White inroads *European settlement in South Africa extended north and eastwards from the Cape: this picture dates from 1849.*

Reluctant recruits *Africans were often forced to enrol in the armies of the white colonists.*

irksome: finally, united in determination, they uprooted and made the 'Great Trek' northwards. At Blood River in 1838, they found their way blocked but, arranging their wagons around them in a barricade or *laager*, they poured gunfire into the advancing waves of warriors: the Zulu forces – and the myth of their invincibility – were shot to pieces. More than 3000 Zulus fell, for only two casualties on the settlers' side: modern firepower had prevailed in the most dramatic possible manner. Though the Zulus kept their kingdom, they did so only by arrangement with their Boer overlords: Shaka's dream had died, and with it any possibility of resistance to white rule in Southern Africa.

Colonial empires in 1914

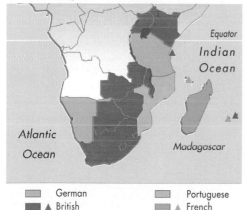

Equator

Indian Ocean

Atlantic Ocean

Madagascar

| | German | | Portuguese |
| | ▲ British | | ▲ French |

Carving up the continent

At the start of the 19th century, several factors came together to influence European attitudes. The industrial revolution gave rise to a voracious hunger for raw materials – especially the mineral wealth found here in such abundance. For these resources to be worked, an adequate infrastructure

would have to be built, which required the pacification of the native peoples. The colonial powers – Britain, Portugal, Germany and France – recognised the need to reach an accommodation with one another: they could not afford to be fighting both African and European enemies. So they confined operations to their own separate spheres of influence, in an implicit understanding that was ratified by treaty in 1885. Black Africa had its own ideas about white domination, but, as the Zulus had found, the most determined warriors could hardly hope to prevail against men armed with rifles and heavy artillery. By the end of the century the marks on the map had become reality, Britain seizing the lion's share.

The independence struggle

It took more than half a century for Africans to free themselves from the colonial yoke. While the missionaries did much to inculcate the values of empire, they also created a class of educated Africans increasingly inclined to question their subjection. As unrest grew, the European powers disengaged from a colonial system whose

time had clearly passed – despite protests from the white settlers. In some cases the Africans had to fight for their freedom: Kenya's struggle took several years as Mau-Mau rebels waged a guerrilla war that was brought to an end in 1960. But there was no way of putting back the clock: as Britain's prime minister Harold Macmillan said , a 'wind of change' was blowing through the African continent. In 1963 Kenya became a fully independent country.

Spreading the Word *The missionaries played a vital, if often underestimated, role in white colonisation.*

The imperial bandwagon

By the beginning of the 19th century, Portuguese rule in East Africa had reached its fullest extent: only France and Britain were actively engaged in occupying what was still regarded as the Dark Continent. As the 'scramble for Africa' intensified, Léopold II of Belgium raised the stakes in 1879, when he embarked on the colonisation of the Congo. Not to be outdone, Germany followed suit, though the scepticism of 'Iron Chancellor' Bismarck meant that Europe's pre-eminent power was a latecomer to the imperial party.

Not only governments were involved: missionaries also had their role to play, sometimes going against the directives of those in power. Members of the London Missionary Society were invading what was nominally French territory when they preached Protestantism to the peoples of Madagascar, their schools helping to spread not only the Word of Christ, but the British way. Meanwhile, the Catholic White Fathers, founded by the French Archbishop Lavigerie, were making their own distinctive mark in British Uganda.

The socialist mirage

In the dawn of independence, everything seemed possible, but the old empire-builders haunted the new nations like the ghost of past oppression, their influence apparent in the boundaries of the countries. In Europe, nation-states had taken shape over centuries of European history:

Partners in power *The support of the army has remained crucial to President Robert Mugabe's continuing rule in Zimbabwe.*

'Cover up, or I resign'

Campaigning for the Kenyan parliament in 1977, MP John Keen issued an astonishing ultimatum to his country's Masai people: 'Cover up your bottoms within six months,' he told them angrily, 'or I resign.' This controversial intervention from a man who was half-Masai himself, on his mother's side, went right to the heart of the African dilemma and opened up a debate that has yet to be satisfactorily resolved. Can Africa participate fully in a wider modern world and still retain its unique identity?

here they had been conjured out of nothing around the conference table. Imposed without regard for the realities of demography on the ground, their frontiers cut indiscriminately through tribal homelands. Colonists had always taken advantage of their ability to divide and rule their African subjects: for the newly independent states the situation could only end in chaos and bloodshed. Hence the appeal of a centralising system of government that rejected Western capitalism and promised to transcend tribal differences, while remaining responsible to the African people.

Throughout East Africa Marxist leaders came to power, including Julius Nyerere in Tanzania and Didier Ratsiraka in Madagascar. The victory of the radical Robert Mugabe in the Rhodesian elections of 1980 marked the birth of a new – and distinctly left-wing – independent state of Zimbabwe. But socialism was no better adapted to the political and economic needs of a complex continent than the capitalism that had preceded it. Not only this, but Africa was fast becoming the Cold War cockpit for a series of proxy wars in which guerrilla forces backed by Soviet and Western powers fought each other to a standstill.

Yet if America and Soviet Russia had made a bloody battlefield of many of the newly independent states, their rivalry had also brought its benefits; for the superpowers had fought just as fiercely to win hearts and minds. The end of the Cold War brought with it the end of the massive aid projects with which the two sides had sought to woo their African clients. Their debt liabilities soaring as their prestige plunged, many African governments found themselves becoming ever more impotent, and without a strong, centralising state, ancient ethnic enmities began to resurface.

Reconquest of the south

South Africa, meanwhile, had been following its own historical path: its white community was not only large and long-established, but crucially divided. The descendants of the first Dutch settlers, the Afrikaaners, or Boers, feeling that their British rulers had never really

A new role *Once subservient wives and mothers, African women are increasingly demanding a voice of their own.*

Guerrilla warrior *The Mau-Mau rebels of Kenya fought a long and bitter war from 1952, it was not until more than a decade later that the country became fully independent.*

Face of freedom *Nelson Mandela has become an icon throughout the world, but nowhere more so than in his native South Africa.*

Whites only The sign is in three languages to avoid misunderstanding: such notices now belong to South Africa's history.

Britain and the Boers

In 1652 the Dutch established a colony in the Cape. They pushed into the interior in the decades that followed, displacing Hottentots and Bushmen to the north, and driving out Bantu in the east. But after 1815, when the British occupied the Cape, the settlers' descendants, the Boers, found themselves marginalised in their turn. The 'Great Trek' of the late 1830s took these proud settlers into the uplands of the interior, where they established the independent Orange Free State and Republic of Transvaal. The British attempt to annex the Transvaal resulted in the First Boer War in 1880. War broke out again in 1899 and the British finally prevailed in 1902. They had earned the enmity of a bitter Afrikaner population, however – particularly through their use of concentration camps – with lasting consequences for the history of South Africa.

In action Neuman's painting of the Boer War.

protected their interests, came to power in the (white-only) elections of 1948 in uncompromising mood. By 1958 Hendrik Verwoerd had realised his dream of a racially segregated South Africa, enshrined in law as 'apartheid'. Under the banner of 'separate development', South Africa's black, white and 'coloured' (largely Asian) communities would remain apart: there was little pretence that 'separate' should mean 'equal'. African populations in the countryside were confined to 'tribal homelands' or 'Bantustans', outside which they were forced to carry identity cards and travel permits. In urban areas blacks were crowded into squalid townships with inadequate amenities. Any black who set foot in a white area risked being picked up by the police as a potential criminal.

The British Government's disapproval of apartheid led to South Africa's ejection from the Commonwealth in 1961. The plight of black South Africa met with some sympathy in the West in the years that followed, but the concerns of the Cold War muddied the waters. Trade sanctions introduced to marginalise the apartheid regime were routinely circumvented by those Western powers who saw in South Africa a vital ally in the war against communism.

Resistance

Black opposition to white rule in South Africa had been mounting steadily since the late 19th century. Now, an educated élite emerged who were influenced by radical African-American thinkers. From 1952 Albert Luthuli, the son of a Zulu chief, was leading a nonviolent campaign against apartheid. The angry young men of the African National Congress (ANC) – men like Nelson Mandela, Oliver Tambo and Walter Sizulu – scorned such gradualist measures, demanding more aggressive action. In the wake of the Sharpeville Massacre of 1959, the ANC despaired of peaceful progress and embarked on what it acknowledged was to be the 'armed struggle'. The government responded by declaring a state of emergency and imprisoning the ANC leaders as terrorists: they were locked up for almost three decades.

Years went by without apparent change, any expression of black feeling quickly and brutally suppressed. Yet South Africa was increasingly feeling the chill of international disapproval. Attempting to defuse the criticism, the government introduced a new constitution in 1984, yet its 'reforms' were dismissed with contempt by a still-disenfranchised black majority.

As elsewhere in Africa, the end of the Cold War had its implications here: no longer could the apartheid state expect Western backing on account of its anti-communism. Under President De Klerk real liberalisations were introduced, and in 1990 Nelson Mandela was released from prison, to become, in 1994, his country's first black president.

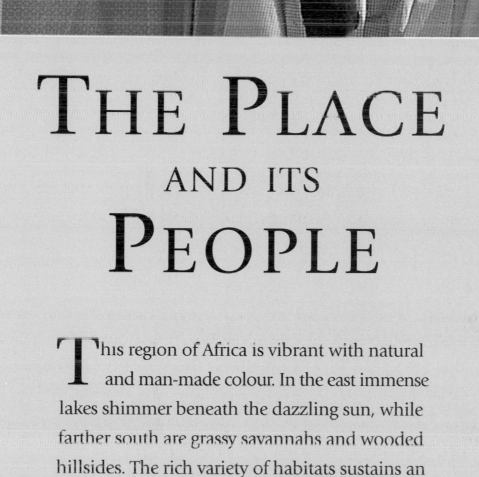

THE PLACE
AND ITS
PEOPLE

This region of Africa is vibrant with natural
and man-made colour. In the east immense
lakes shimmer beneath the dazzling sun, while
farther south are grassy savannahs and wooded
hillsides. The rich variety of habitats sustains an
incomparable range of flora and fauna, and the
human inhabitants and their lifestyles are no less
diverse. The region is home alike to Masai
herdsmen and Bushmen hunter-gatherers, to the
traditional seafarers of Zanzibar and to the
commuters of the modern Cape.

CHAPTER 1

THE MAJESTY OF NATURE

owhere is the power of nature more apparent than in Southern and East Africa, a region cleft by the great Rift Valley. Here, pushed and pulled by immense forces, the Earth's crust buckled and cracked, producing a corrugated country where cataracts cascade over clifftops and lakes and marshes lie in deep recesses. Vast plateaus stand proud of a landscape riven with faults, their courses marked by the massifs of active volcanoes, the smoking vents of a subterranean furnace. Biology has taken its cue from geology here: the region's diversity of habitat is a direct consequence of its geological history. To the north misty forests cloak the hillsides; to the south the open savannah stretches away, its lush parkland shading imperceptibly through thorny scrub to sandy desert. Out on the islands the story is the same – a breathtaking range of scenery formed by the force of shifting plates or spuming craters.

The inland delta of the Okavango river may be grassland, marsh or lake according to the season.

The Rift Valley: a mighty trench

Taking the form of a gigantic 'Y', the Rift Valley runs through the whole of East Africa, its deep fractures marking out what is still an area of great geological instability.

Standing sentinel *Rising from the Rift Valley's eastern edge, Kilimanjaro and Meru (left) flank the great wildlife sanctuaries of Tanzania and Kenya.*

At the beginning of the 20th century a railway was inaugurated to link the Indian Ocean port of Mombasa with the head of Lake Victoria. Crossing the full width of East Africa, the new railway highlighted the significance of the Rift Valley, one of the deepest and most dramatic fissures in the Earth's crust. To negotiate the eastern arm – the narrower and less deep of the Rift's two branches – it was necessary to uncouple every train and haul its carriages one by one up specially constructed slipways. The top engineers of Britain and France, with viaducts to their credit all over the world, had baulked at the challenge of bridging the valley more conventionally. Humans might have tamed much of the Earth, but this was one African possession that European colonists would never truly conquer.

Great gashes *The two branches of the Rift Valley cleave the East African landscape.*

Future destiny *Scored with fissures and lined with volcanoes, the Rift Valley expands each year. The arid region of Kenya along the eastern branch of the 'Y' (below) will eventually become an ocean.*

Wider and deeper

Some 4000 miles (6500 km) in length, the Rift is the longest of the three great fault-lines by which the first continents were divided when the Earth's landmasses parted company many millions of years ago. And the valley is still growing wider and deeper, its two sides separating at a rate of $^1/_{32}$ in (1 mm) each year. Though wind and occasional rain have taken their toll, wearing away at the Rift's rocky walls and the surrounding areas, erosion has not been swift or severe enough to cancel out this overall expansion, or to soften the steepness of escarpments that in places reach heights of hundreds of metres.

Abruptness is the hallmark of this landscape, which is still in the process of formation. Violent movements of the Earth are still pushing up great blocks of stone, and also have a cataclysmic effect on the region's rivers and lakes. Here, its bed having dropped away, a sluggish stream becomes a roaring waterfall; there, a lake takes shape where a river finds its way barred by a new rock formation.

A long groove down the continent's eastern side, the Great Rift Valley has served as a sort of gutter: A string of lakes now stretches out along the bottom of its western section. Lake Tanganyika is the biggest of these, but it is dwarfed by the expanse of Lake Victoria, shaped by the slight depression between the Rift's twin arms.

An exceptional area in every way, the Rift Valley revealed in the 1940s that it had been keeping one last surprise in store: it was here that the first traces of our hominid ancestors were uncovered.

Cradle of humanity

A thick layer of volcanic cinder mixed with alluvial sands forms a carpet across the dusty bottom of the Rift Valley. A similar soil lines the deeper indentations in the plateaus: it could not have been a better environment for the preservation of fossils. Since 1948 the English palaeontologists Louis and Mary Leakey have made a series of spectacular finds in this area – discoveries that between them have helped delineate human evolution in unprecedented detail. Spanning more than 18 million years, their findings at Tanzania's Olduvai Gorge, and around lakes Victoria and Turkana, have established the Rift Valley's claim to be the 'cradle of humanity'.

Gondwanaland: fragmented continent

Shards of the same splintered red granite plate form both East Africa and its offshore islands. It continues to break up into blocks that drift off in the direction of Asia.

Wave worn   The northern Seychelles are made up of gigantic crags of hard red granite, eroded into skeletal shapes by the unremitting ocean.

An interrupted continent   The rugged red granite of Madagascar's central upland betrays the island's origins as part of the mainland shelf.

Less well-travelled chunks of Gondwanaland that split off from what is now East Africa are the northern Seychelles and Madagascar. With their rock formations and red soils, both recognisably belong to Africa. And like the East African mainland, their faulted landscapes bristle with vigorously active volcanoes and with mineral veins: both areas bear the geological scars of the continental break-up that brought them into being.

Built as it is on such unstable geological foundations, Southern and East Africa could hardly be anything other than a place of diversity and change, as much in its human cultures as in its landscape, and its flora and fauna. The sense of a continent still actively taking shape can be disorientating, but it is essential to the vigour and excitement of the region.

Some African origin myths place the birth of humankind on the slopes of Kilimanjaro; other equally ancient tales evoke a far distant time when all lands were grouped together in a single place. Now, after more than half a century of research, science is lending credence to what once seemed fanciful stories. Most palaeontologists now agree that the African Rift Valley is where human life began.

Geologists, meanwhile, believe that, some 250 to 200 million years ago, today's continents constituted a single enormous landmass. Known as Pangaea, this super-continent then broke apart. The theory of continental drift, rejected with scorn when first suggested more than 100 years ago, has achieved general scientific acceptance. It proposes that the solid plates upon which the continents are built 'float' on molten rock or magma. Welling up through the gaps between the plates, more and more magma has solidified, causing them to drift farther and farther apart.

A landscape of change

Africa was at the centre of the Pangaean landmass, until the super-continent split into two sections now known as Laurasia and Gondwanaland. The former, lying to the north, comprised what we now think of as North America and Eurasia; the southerly half subsequently split up to form South America, Antarctica, Australia and India. Inching its way northwards and eastwards, India finally collided with the southern edge of Asia, locking on to the northerly landmass, and in the process forcing up the ridge of the Himalayas.

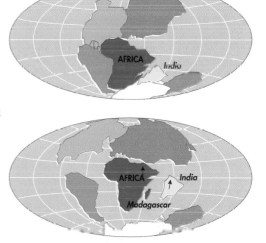

Continental drift
Once clustered together around Africa (above), India, America, Antarctica, Australia and Madagascar began to part company around 200 million years ago. By 65 million years ago (below), Africa was in its present position.

Drifting rocks, migrating people

The Madagascan story is one of to-ing and fro-ing traffic across the Indian Ocean. First, through the aeons of geological time, came the slow but steady sliding away of Gondwanaland's coastal sections. What we now know as India and Indonesia ended up thousands of miles away. Madagascar's subsequent journey was short by comparison, though it followed a similar north-eastward path. Much later, people migrated in the opposite direction from Indonesia and southern India, bringing back to Madagascar plant species and traditions that evolved in far-off Asia. The resulting exchange has enriched the life of the African island, and has had far-reaching implications for the region as a whole.

Azure jewels of the Rift Valley

Jarring breaks in the continental plate have interrupted what was once a gently shelving plain, forming steps down which waterfalls spill, and deep cavities where lakes have gathered. Such a landscape has engendered a biological diversity that is unparalleled elsewhere.

For an area that spans the Equator, East Africa is surprisingly short of water, with no more rain than one might typically expect in England. What moisture there is evaporates quickly at these latitudes: for the most part, this is an arid landscape. Yet there is water to be found, some of it locked up in the snowcaps of high mountain summits, while more has accumulated in the chain of enormous lakes that runs right down the region. The greatest of these, Lake Victoria, lies between Uganda, Kenya and Tanzania: second only to Siberia's Lake Baikal in size, it occupies an area as large as Ireland. Lakes Tanganyika and Malawi are the second and third biggest lakes in Africa: each would easily cover the entire land area of Belgium. But the gutter-like groove of the Rift has squashed and stretched them into thin shapes, long enough to reach from the Channel Islands to Rotterdam.

Rich margins *Although plumbing great depths, Lake Tanganyika's shores are often shallow and full of aquatic plants.*

The incomparable Lake Victoria

Lake Victoria is Africa's largest freshwater lake, and the second largest in the world. It is unique among the Great Lakes in not lying in the Rift Valley. Instead, it occupies a vast hollow in the high plateau between the arms of the great 'Y', and is roughly circular, rather than elongated. It is much shallower, too, with a maximum depth of 270 ft (82 m) compared with Lake Tanganyika (4600 ft/1400 m) and

Lake Malawi (2300 ft/ 700 m). Whereas the other lakes are confined by the Rift Valley, Lake Victoria lies in a shallow upland basin and sprawls across the marshy hinterland when swelled by seasonal rainfall. This has a negligible effect on water levels, but an extraordinary one on surface area – it grows from 26 000 sq miles (68 000 km²) to more than 32 000 sq miles (83 000 km²).

East Africa's great lakes

Deceptive calm
Nestling between the two arms of the Rift, Lake Victoria can be as smooth and unruffled as a garden pond, but its ferocious storms would not be out of place on an ocean.

Climate and communication

East Africa's great lakes play an active role in the ecology of the region. They are the headwaters of the Zambezi and the Nile rivers, so their impact is felt many hundreds of miles away, as well as on the immediate hinterland. Their moderating effect on temperature helps to reduce both daytime heat and overnight chill; it also gives rise to winds that lash their waters into ferocious storms. The lakes are a fertile breeding-ground for wildlife – including microorganisms that spread disease.

The lakes provided the first white explorers with a means of bypassing some very difficult terrain, but constant fluctuations in water levels and frequent storms have limited their usefulness as water highways, and it is impossible to travel by boat from one to another. The folds and fissures in the Earth that produced the lakes have made the terrain between them particularly difficult: this is no place for a Suez Canal or St Lawrence Seaway.

Lake Victoria, once envisaged as the communications crossroads for a highly developed and productive region, has never quite lived up to expectations. It has remained – quite literally – a backwater, but its exquisite beauty has encouraged a thriving tourist trade.

The Tugela Falls

Africa's highest waterfall is not in the Rift Valley: it forms where an otherwise insignificant South African river, the Tugela, plunges down the steep face of the Drakensberg Mountains into the coastal plain of Natal. Rising on Mont aux Sources, one of the highest points in the Drakensberg mountains, the river plunges through a wooded gorge, dropping 3110 ft (948 m) over a series of falls. Almost half of that drop is accounted for in one single leap of 1345 ft (410 m). At the foot of the escarpment the river heads generally east, before turning south-east into its main valley and crossing the narrow coastal plain to the Indian Ocean.

Murchison Falls   The headwaters of Lake Victoria surge into the Nile.

make matters more confusing, there is a second Murchison Falls (now often known as Kholombiozo Falls) at the other end of the Rift Valley, on the Shire River below Lake Malawi. These awesome waterfalls exemplify the titanic forces that have shaped East Africa, and that are still pushing and pulling at the region's geological construction.

The great escarpment

Like a billowing wave set solid in stone, a great escarpment rears up along Southern Africa's eastern side, interrupting what might otherwise have been gently undulating countryside. Rising slowly at first, but climbing steadily to the south, the escarpment reaches its highest point in South Africa's Drakensberg Mountains, towering 11 500 ft (3500 m) above the coastal plain at Durban. Running west across Cape Province, it reaches the Atlantic at the Cape itself, though a spur, the Roggeveldberg, then promptly peels off northwards. On the inland side the descent is gradual, across the grassy plateaus of the South African interior, from Transvaal in the north through the Orange Free State goldfields to the kingdom of Lesotho. To seaward the plunge is precipitous, a vast and forbidding wall of rock down which streams rush helter-skelter.

Though thrown up by the same cataclysmic forces that created the South, the great plateaus of East Africa have nothing comparable: there is no single escarpment to match the Drakensberg in dramatic scale. Instead, a line of volcanoes dominates the horizon, of which Mount Kilimanjaro at 19 340 ft (5895 m) is the highest, with Mount Kenya (17 057 ft/5199 m) coming close behind. Amongst these peaks, mountain-sized blocks of stone stick up apparently at random, squeezed out of the ground by the pressure beneath them. Ruwenzori is one such block: standing at the astounding height of 16 794 ft (5174 m), it is easily the highest non-volcanic mountain in Africa.

In leaps and bounds

Despite a corrugated, uncooperative landscape, the rivers somehow find a way to flow, tumbling down over rocks and rushing through narrow gorges. In November 1855 the Makololo guides who conducted David Livingstone down the River Zambezi showed him a spectacular waterfall. Livingstone was strongly tempted to give the falls their local name *Mosi oa tunya*, 'the smoke that sounds'. In the African language the name evokes a rumbling, grumbling conflagration, its swirling spray as dense as the smoke from a great forest fire. But in the end politics won the day and Livingstone took the opportunity of flattering the imperial power whose support he needed to continue his explorations. So he called the roaring *Mosi oa tunya* Victoria Falls, in honour of his monarch, Queen Victoria.

Seven years later and 930 miles (1500 km) away, Livingstone's fellow British explorer John Speke dedicated to the queen the huge lake he discovered at the source of the Nile – Lake Victoria. Other falls were also given English names, including the Owen Falls at the head of the Nile, and the Murchison (now Kabalega) Falls farther downriver at the entrance to Lake Albert (it has since been renamed Lake Mobutu Sese Seko). Just to

The smoke that roars   At the Victoria Falls the great Zambezi River pours into a narrow gorge – a trench of spray and roaring, white water

Towering heights *The Drakensberg (above) rises to 11 500 ft (3500 m), the highest and best known section of the escarpment that runs the whole length of Southern Africa.*

Rocky outcrop *Mount Ambalavao rises high above the rice fields of Madagascar's south-eastern plateau.*

Island outcrops

The offshore islands also have rocky outcrops, which are often sheer on one side but dipping away more gently on the other. Madagascar's continental origins are evident in the escarpment that runs down the east coast, reaching a height of 9442 ft (2878 m) in the northern massif of Tsaratanana. Réunion was formed by volcanic activity and seems to erupt from the sea, rising swiftly to 10 068 ft (3069 m) in the giddying peak of the Neiges.

Altitude affects climate everywhere, with the paradox that there is perpetual snow at tropical latitudes and plants are adapted for aridity in a region where one might expect equatorial rain forest.

Environmental threat

The forests of Southern and East Africa may seem untamed and abundant, but many of them are in fact under grave environmental threat. The great plateaus of the region rise high above sea level, and scored by deep rifts and gullies where waters gather into lakes, they lend themselves more readily to open savannah grassland than to forest – but where forests do flourish, there is an amazing diversity. This cannot be attributed to climate alone: patterns of human land-use over many millennia have also had their impact.

Those parts of Africa that are described as 'virgin' lands have generally been kept in their natural state by the hunter-gatherers who inhabit them. By setting fire to large tracts of land, these peoples have prevented forests from maturing: the new scrub that rises from the scorched earth is often ideal for game. Pastoralists, too, have burned what they consider to be useless woodland, while Bantu farmers have cleared plots more permanently.

In recent times, however, human intervention has been getting out of hand, accelerated by the rising demand for timber for both domestic and industrial use. All the states in the region have now realised that positive action is needed to conserve their

A botanical wonderland

When Italian naturalist Filippo de Filippi joined the first expedition up the Ruwenzori in 1906, he was astonished by the scenes that awaited him. High above the surrounding savannah, at an altitude of 6500-10 000 ft (2000-3000 m), flourished the most untypical equatorial flora he could ever have imagined. He wrote of 'grotesque, leprous' mosses that seemed to cover every surface and hang from every tree like untended beards; he marvelled, too, at the 'monstrous' lobelias and groundsels he found growing at higher levels. Just below the snowline, at a height of between 11 500-13 000 ft (3500-4000 m), plants had to contend with freezing night-time temperatures and blazing hot days. He could only wonder at the resilience of these shrubs and flowers, clinging to existence at the Earth's harshest outer limits.

Saving the forest The dry Madagascan forest is home to many rare plants and endangered animal species. Vast tracts have been burned down for agriculture, but it endures thanks to government protection measures and the support of foreign conservationists.

precious natural heritage. Preservation of the forests is not just about plants and animals: the region's soils and climate, and the traditional lifestyles of the inhabitants, are also under threat.

It seems likely that equatorial East Africa was once completely covered by forest. Patches can still be seen around lakes and along river valleys. But throughout the high plateaus trees have been felled by farmers, or simply displaced by the ever-advancing grasslands of the savannah. Those pockets of woodland, or *miombo*, that have remained on the open plains are regarded as unhealthy because of the tsetse fly, which is responsible for transmitting the parasites that cause sleeping sickness.

Cloud forests and mangrove swamps

High up where the northern peaks of Kenya and Tanzania thrust through the clouds, ferns and mosses flourish in the eerie atmosphere of the cloud forest. Climb still higher, and the topmost slopes are cloaked in thickets of waving bamboo.

Meanwhile, down at sea level, in the coastal lowlands, the twisted roots of mangroves poke grotesquely out of the mud. At high tide, the roots are inundated with salt water, a physiological stress that would kill any other tree. The mangrove swamps have the primeval air of a scene that has remained unchanged since the Earth's infancy. Ironically, though, no landscape in Southern and East Africa has been more threatened in recent times by human activity: the trees have been felled for timber, and the land reclaimed for more apparently productive agricultural and industrial uses. Unless dramatic steps are taken to preserve them, the mangrove swamps look set for imminent destruction.

A conservation quandary

More densely populated than the mainland, the offshore islands have been more affected by human activities such as herding and farming. Madagascar has been badly scarred by such pursuits, with only 23 160 sq miles (60 000 km²) of woodland still remaining. What may sound like a significant area in fact accounts for only 15 per cent of the land thought to have been covered by forests 2000 years ago. The island authorities are now making a stand against deforestation, and are putting a stop to *tavy*, the deliberate burning down of wooded areas to leave cleared areas rich in leafy compost and ashes. In doing so, however, they are jeopardising a traditional lifestyle that has been followed for centuries – and to which many people are clinging with determination and defiance.

Shades of green The quintessential equatorial scene is surprisingly difficult to find in tropical East Africa, surviving only in the most inaccessible or best-protected areas. This pocket is under the protection of the Ugandan government in the Mburo National Park.

Down the Zambezi

The Zambezi is one of the world's greatest rivers, flowing 1650 miles (2660 km) from Zambia to the Indian Ocean. Making its way across many different terrains, it encompasses a wide diversity of natural and human life.

Water babies *The Zambezi is a source of water for many animals, such as these hippopotamuses.*

Lazy river *Where the gradient is low, the Zambezi meanders slowly between the sandy banks. Its waters are diminished after passing through hydroelectric turbines, as here below the Kariba Dam.*

An animal paradise

A bright silver strip across the Kalahari sand, the Zambezi opens out into exquisite water gardens, where blue-footed lilytrotter birds cross from pad to fleshy pad like tightrope-walkers. A floating log, its wood decaying rapidly in the warm humidity, is still solid enough to take the weight of a keen-eyed fish eagle. Local inhabitants avoid these banks, which are liable to flood, leaving them to the hippos that emerge from the water to sunbathe on sandbanks. They share the banks with crocodiles, which need to bask in the sun to boost their body temperature and generate energy.

Several hundred miles downstream, where the river flows through Botswana, herds of elephants crowd its muddy banks, along with other game seeking drinking water. The river is joined here by two tributaries, bringing so much water that they form one of Southern Africa's widest wetlands, the Caprivi Marshes. Soon, though, the Zambezi follows a less leisurely course.

Search for the source of the Zambezi and you find yourself in an upland forest in the north-west corner of Zambia. The forest floor lies thickly carpeted with decomposing leaves, and a tiny trickle of water steals through the undergrowth, widening only occasionally to become a stream. From such unlikely origins springs the full flood of the great Zambezi, Africa's fourth longest river after the Nile, the Congo and the Niger.

Cutting across the continent as it winds its way from west to east, the Zambezi traverses six countries: Zambia, Angola, Namibia, Botswana, Zimbabwe and Mozambique. In places it meanders across wide plains; in others its waters abruptly plunge down deep gorges as roaring rapids, or spill suddenly over rocky shelves as thundering waterfalls.

The upper reaches

Some 43 miles (70 km) downriver from its source the river is already 80 ft (25 m) wide. It leaves Zambia to cut across a corner of Angola, and by the time it re-enters Zambia 125 miles (200 km) later it has grown enormously in volume and the constricting rocks of the Chavuma Gorges raise a roaring head of raging water. After that the river settles down, winding sluggishly along between sandy banks. Bridges and ferries are few and far between, so travellers must choose which bank to take before they start their journey up here, in what remains one of Africa's least-travelled and most mysterious regions. Untouched by outside influences, the landscapes and lifestyles encountered here today have prevailed without interruption since prehistoric times: stone-age fishermen drive dugout canoes through the tepid waters.

White waters *Below the Victoria Falls the tumultuous waters of the Zambezi make it the perfect place for white-water rafting and kayaking.*

The Okavango delta

With a length of 800 miles (1300 km), the Okavango is the third greatest river of Southern Africa. Rising in Angola, it heads southwards, cutting across the Caprivi Strip in north-eastern Namibia before continuing into Botswana and the northern Kalahari. There it spreads out across the desert sand, forming a gigantic delta criss-crossed by channels and lagoons and studded with low-lying islands. Covering an area of 5800 sq miles (15 000 km²) at its outermost limits, the delta simply ceases to exist, its shallows evaporated by the fierce sun or soaked up by the sand. The Okavango River never reaches the sea, but ends here at this inland estuary. This peculiar geography has given rise to an extraordinary natural heritage. Visitors to the area must travel by *mokoro*, a dugout canoe carved from a trunk of ebony wood: these are shallow waters, but they are infested by hungry crocodiles.

Raging whiteness

To describe the impact of the Victoria Falls, just a few miles down-stream, one cannot do better than quote David Livingstone. 'Fancy the Thames leaping bodily into the gulf,' he wrote, 'and forced there to change its direction, and flow from the right to the left bank, and then rush boiling and roaring through the hills.' Only then, said the ecstatic explorer, would his readers have some idea of the scene at this, 'the most wonderful sight I had witnessed in Africa'. Around a core of raging whiteness the sunlight casts an iridescent curtain, in which every colour of the rainbow shimmers.

The Zambezi

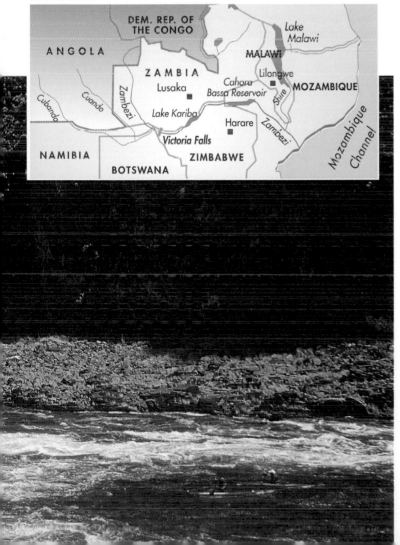

No need to hurry For centuries time has moved sluggishly on the Zambezi, following the same slow rhythm as the river.

More than 1 mile (1.6 km) wide, in places the falls drop 354 ft (108 m). Even in the driest season 700 000 cu ft (20 000 m³) of water plunges down this cataract every minute, but this increases to 17 657 500 cu ft (500 000 m³) at the wettest time of year. Then the falls disappear, drowned by the surge of water: all that can be seen is an impenetrable cloud of spray that soaks onlookers to the skin.

A source of energy and a frontier

When the rapids have calmed down, the river resumes its silent progress to Lake Kariba. Since 1960 this man-made lake has provided a rewarding livelihood for local fishermen. They have to take care, though, because Lake Kariba has its own idiosyncratic microclimate: storms can get up suddenly here, raising waves up to 6 ft (2 m) high. Tumbling down through Kariba's hydroelectric turbines, the river flows peacefully once more, making a natural frontier between Zambia and Zimbabwe.

On entering Mozambique, the river is dammed again at Cahora Bassa. Water levels fluctuate dramatically down here, the lake varying between 26-46 ft (8-14 m) in depth. In the dry season drowned treetops, incongruously bedecked with water hyacinths, protrude from the surface of the reservoir.

Journey's end

South of Sena the Zambezi joins the Shire, which flows south from Lake Malawi with all the waters from the Great Rift Valley. The huge river that results is navigable for large ships. It soon separates into hundreds of smaller branches in an enormous triangular delta 7000 sq miles (18 000 km²) in area.

By the time it finally reaches the Indian Ocean, spread out across a 75 mile (120 km) front, the Zambezi flows sluggishly, as though exhausted, all energy spent. Here the river lays down its alluvial deposits in a mosaic of muddy islets and oozing creeks where mangroves grow, their roots submerged at each high tide by the lapping of the ocean waves.

The man-made savannah

A vast expanse of natural grassland studded with acacia trees, the East African savannah seems unchanging, but this 'virgin' land has to a large extent been shaped by human intervention.

Not quite natural *Like an island in a sea of swaying grass, the massif of Isalo rises above the wide savannah of south-east Madagascar. It may look like an untouched wilderness, but this is an environment influenced by humans.*

In his book *Dimbili: The Story of an African Farm*, Errol Whittal wrote of Africa's 'great plains of scorched grass and thorn'. The plains are not only seared by the sun, but burnt more literally. Fire is almost a part of the weather on the savannah, coming unfailingly with each dry season: it is certainly taken for granted by the region's animal inhabitants. Conservationist George Schaller, recalling a savannah fire he had seen in Kenya, described how 'one male lion

Plant that defines the plains

Elephant grass, *Pennisetum purpureum*, is the champion plant of the savannah. What other species could provide such sustaining fodder for Africa's elephant herds? Its exceptional resistance to fire and aridity enable it to thrive in places where other grasses could never hope to flourish. Its long, luxuriant, fast-growing, fleshy leaves make it the ideal foodstuff for both wild herbivores and domestic cattle. So quickly does it grow to

maturity, die and replenish itself – with or without fire – that it is continually laying down nutritious compost for its own regeneration. Elephant grass is also the savannah's best check against desertification and erosion, its roots binding the soil and storing moisture every bit as effectively as the densest forest. Africa's flora includes many species stranger, bigger or more beautiful than elephant grass, but none to match it for sheer adaptability.

fed on a warthog, seemingly oblivious to the line of flames that crackled towards him through the grass. At last, with the fire only three feet from his paws, so close that I was afraid his mane might ignite, he reluctantly dragged his meal to a safer spot.'

Schaller also observed how marabou storks stood calmly before the advancing front of the flames, waiting to catch the mice, snakes and lizards that sped in panic from the burning brush. What might have seemed an extraordinary event had, in short, been accepted as just another part of the seasonal round, no less natural than a fall of rain – and perhaps more common.

Regenerating flames

Not so much a sea of grass, then, as dry kindling: for much of the year the savannah is a brush-fire just waiting to happen. Often it ignites spontaneously in the sun; elsewhere dry lightning strikes and sets the grassland blazing. The flames spread so quickly that they barely singe the trees in their path; the roots are left undamaged. Burrowing creatures remain safe underground, while birds and larger mammals usually manage to flee to safety. When the flames have died and the smoke has cleared, the savannah will look like a blackened waste. But appearances are deceptive: fresh shoots will spring from the scorched earth, taking vital nutrients from the charred plant remains. A new savannah will rise, phoenix-like, from the ashes of the old.

But nature has not been the sole influence at work here: for countless generations hunter-gatherers, herdsmen and farmers have

the Transvaal, to the bushy scrub of the South African Karroo and the baobab-studded steppes of Madagascar's Savoka. As the savannah merges into semidesert there is a wide spectrum of vegetation, ranging from woodland, through thorny thickets to stony wasteland.

A delicate balance

All savannah landscapes remain poised in a precarious equilibrium. The slightest over-exploitation by farmers or herdsmen – even visits by tourists if these are not carefully controlled – runs the risk of destroying a habitat that is far more fragile than it may at first appear. A balance needs to be struck between the demands of nature and those of humanity; between traditional local lifestyles and the modern tourist trade.

All the nations of Southern and East Africa face this challenge and have responded in different ways. Kenya has turned over large tracts to conservation and carefully controlled tourism, while graduates of Tanzania's famous Wildlife College now work in reserves throughout East Africa and beyond, developing African solutions for African conservation problems. Madagascar, meanwhile, is attempting to preserve only its most important, unspoilt areas.

Most states in the region have yet to resolve the dilemma and still hesitate, uncertain how best to proceed. Such indecision risks jeopardising the region's most invaluable asset – the incomparable natural beauty and range of wildlife. International efforts on Africa's behalf have of course been appreciated, but increasingly Africans themselves have felt a need to 'Africanise' development. Reacting to the failure of 'modern' methods of cultivation in largely arid areas of Southern and East Africa, teams of African agriculturalists have been working to find ways of adapting indigenous traditions to today's conditions.

understood the regenerative properties of fire. Their intervention over a period of thousands of years has produced the savannah that we see today. a landscape that is 'natural' only in its appearance.

Ever-changing landscape

Once an endless expanse of thick woodland and scrub, this zone was home only to those rare animal and plant species that could cope with repeated fires: only very gradually did it give way to today's parkland. Cleared by burning, and grazed away by livestock over generations, the present prairie of elephant grass, interrupted by occasional clumps of acacia trees, is to a large extent the conscious creation of human herdsmen, as artificial an environment in its way as any in Europe or North America.

Natural or not, the East African savannah is breathtakingly beautiful: the Masai country of Kenya, in particular, is an example of what man can achieve in cooperation with nature. In some of the great game parks, meanwhile, a fascinating experiment is being attempted: the savannah is being allowed to return to its original, wooded state.

In Southern Africa the savannah takes on a different character according to the predominant type of vegetation or climatic condition, ranging from the grassy veldt of

Good grazing Midway between treeless grassland and true forest, this acacia-flecked area near the foot of Mount Ngorongoro, in Tanzania, is home to a wide range of herbivores.

Stately progress Like a fleet of tall ships under sail, a herd of giraffes makes its way across Kenya's wide savannah.

Fragile Edens: the isles and archipelagoes

With their diverse geological origins, contrasting scale and individual character, the islands of the Indian Ocean add a dash of spice and colour to the African pot.

Ocean jewel *As enchanting as anything in Polynesia, the Isle of Cerfs lies off the east coast of Mauritius.*

Are we in Africa or Asia? The Indian Ocean or the South Pacific? Visitors to the offshore islands have good reason to be confused: the northern Seychelles, white coral paradises, might just as well be in Polynesia; Réunion could easily be in the Antilles. This *is* Africa, but not as we think we know it.

The islands add a flourish of tropical luxury, an exotic touch of Asia: for all its infinite variety, Africa would be a duller place without them. And a world of difference marks the islands out from each other, a diversity that matches anything on the mainland. Zanzibar and Madagascar, for example, could hardly be more different, the former Arabian in culture, the latter Indonesian.

Beside the sea *Long stretches of Tanzania's idyllic coast are the sole province of fisherfolk.*

Africa's children

Despite their cosmopolitan qualities, the islands clearly belong to Africa: the mainland is their geological mother. Beneath the cultural diversity that now enriches them, the original connections remain, although they have been disrupted by seismic shifts and violent eruptions. The same interplay of faults and volcanoes that characterised the formation of East Africa formed the islands, too. The same great forces that scored East Africa with the Great Rift Valley detached Madagascar and the southern Seychelles from the continent: their angular shapes bear witness to the manner of their formation. The eastern coast of Madagascar runs in a virtually straight line for 300 miles (500 km), and the shape of the western coast reveals the island's origins as part of the mainland.

Save the mangroves!

The mangrove swamps around the islands are threatened by development and pollution. They suffer from the disadvantage of not being a tourist attraction – a trip to a muddy wetland where tangled trees grow out of brackish water has none of the appeal of an excursion to a coral reef. There is also the difficulty of getting around: neither walking nor swimming are advisable because of the climbing crabs, walking fish and swimming snakes. Add to that the stinging insects and the generally unhealthy air, and you can see why the swamps are not popular with tourists. Yet they are an important habitat, making a unique contribution to world biodiversity, and they are in need of urgent help: it looks likely that intervention from an international organisation such as the Worldwide Fund for Nature, which has helped to save the swamps in Madagascar, will be necesssary to avert an ecological disaster.

Surfers' paradise *At the foot of the Drakensberg mountains lies a wild coast, where the sea erodes the rocks and casts them back up the beach in the form of sand, so keeping wear and repair in constant equilibrium. Cliffs and gently shelving sands are common to long stretches of the coastlines of South Africa and Madagascar. Surfers come to these shores for the waves, but tourism remains limited.*

The volcanic action that exploded along the edges of the Rift thrust up compact little islands such as Njazidja (formerly Grand Comoro), Réunion and Mauritius. Other volcanic peaks have been worn away, but sometimes the coral reefs that they sustained have survived them, forming the beautiful islands of the northern Seychelles and the eastern Mascarenes.

Sometimes faults and volcanoes have both played a part in an island's formation. Madagascar falls into this category: its coastline may have been caused by the cracking of the continent, but the inland landscape owes much to volcanic activity.

Individual identity

Apart from the broad differences in construction, there are other features that give each of the islands its own specific identity. For example, the astonishingly delicate lacework structures of light volcanic ash that characterise the tiny island of Ronde set it apart from its sisters in the Mauritian archipelago. Then there are the black corals of Réunion, the mangroves of Pemba and Zanzibar, the giant tortoises of Aldabra, the strange little lemurs of the uninhabited islets in the Mozambique Channel, and the sheer size of Madagascar – the fourth biggest island in the world. All these features add to the extraordinary variety and appeal of these offshore islands.

While these features make each island individual, there is another side to the coin: each one is irreplaceable, its uniqueness making it particularly vulnerable to the pressures of the modern world. It is difficult for such scattered lands to act together for their own protection, though they have done their best to coordinate appeals for international aid.

The Réunion rush hour

Réunion Island rises to two central volcanic peaks, the aptly named Piton des Neiges ('Peak of Snows'), a dormant volcano 10 068 ft (3069 m) high, and its active twin, the still more accurately named Piton de la Fournaise ('The Furnace'), which stands at 8632 ft (2631 m). Because of its conical shape, the best way to see the island is to travel around its circumference. This may be easier said than done, owing to an unusual form of congestion on the island's ring road. These are not the kind of traffic jams that are a feature of city life, but drivers may well find themselves having to share the road with a lava flow, or swerving to avoid a sudden swelling in the carriageway or a micro-seismic crack. The island authorities do their best to maintain the road, but cannot keep pace with the constant volcanic activity. Drivers on Réunion would be well advised to prepare for bottlenecks.

Pebble shore *The island of Réunion has a variety of shore types, their colours often wild and starkly contrasting. Here, where a river of hot lava has met the sea, giant pebbles of polished basalt have formed.*

Deforestation is a problem shared by all the islands; its impact is intensified by the confined land space. There is also the question of how the islands' tiny populations might best prepare themselves against volcanic eruptions, earthquakes, cyclones and other natural disasters. The protection of coral reefs and other wildlife habitats is another common challenge. Conservation of the environment is an important matter of principle, but where the only significant industry is tourism, it also becomes a matter of economic survival.

A programme of assistance that was started in Madagascar, said to be one of the top conservation priorities in the world, has now been extended to embrace many of the other islands. Several important international organisations, including the United Nations Environment Program and the Worldwide Fund for Nature, have been helping to develop a general strategy for conservation. The policy of creating wildlife sanctuaries and national parks, which has achieved such success in mainland Africa, is now increasingly being adopted in the offshore islands.

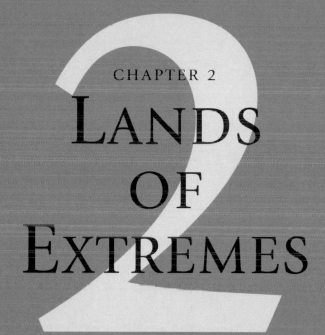

CHAPTER 2

2 LANDS OF EXTREMES

Southern and East Africa contains an amazing range of natural wonders: a red lake, a lava cauldron, a whispering dune, a desert drowned in water – these are just a few of the surprises the region has in store. This is a landscape of extremes: more than 30 active volcanoes still heave and splutter, plus a hundred or so lie dormant. Some peaks, like the incomparable Kilimanjaro, stand out on account of their sheer size and beauty; others, like Nyiragongo or Lengaï, are known for their irascible energy. This region of Africa is also remarkable for its strangely coloured lakes and spontaneous savannah fires, as well as for geographical eccentricities that have inspired a rich traditional folklore. This is a land that seems to defy scientific understanding. Perhaps it belongs in a different world – the weird and wonderful Namib and Kalahari deserts would not look out of place as a stage set for Mars.

Mount Lengaï volcano towers over Lake Natron in northern Tanzania.

Life cycle of the volcanoes

Mount Kilimanjaro, one of Africa's great emblems, belongs to a series of volcanoes that has endowed the surrounding region with some of the most striking scenery in the world.

Nourishing food *Volcanic mud produced by Mount Mogado, Kenya, is rich in bacteria – and eaten with relish by the region's herbivores.*

The Chagga people, who for generations have lived at the foot of Mount Kilimanjaro, have a strange tale to tell about its formation. The story dates back to an age when nobody had yet scaled the mountain, yet it describes exactly what its first climbers discovered. The snowcapped top of this great volcanic mass seems flat and even, but in fact there are three distinct peaks, which are invisible from below. Kibo, the highest and youngest peak, is perfectly conical in form; Shira, to the west, and Mawenzi, to the east, have been badly eroded.

The battle of Kilimanjaro

Curiously, current scientific evidence seems to bear out the Chagga legend. Once upon a time Mawenzi, and not Kibo, was the highest peak. One day, running out of fire, Mawenzi asked his younger brother to help him out, offering some of his spare bananas, as was customary, in return. Next day, Mawenzi had to ask again, for his hearth had again become exhausted; young Kibo obliged once more, but not quite so graciously this time. The following day, when the old volcano had to ask yet again, his younger brother lost his temper: he roared, hit him with his bananas, and erupted into flames. Spitting cinders and spluttering with rage, Kibo swelled up in his ungovernable fury; seizing Mawenzi, he shook him so hard that Mawenzi started falling to pieces. By the end of the day, young Kibo had made himself king of Kilimanjaro, while Mawenzi was the merest shadow of his former self.

The Furnace *Piton de la Fournaise on Réunion lives up to its name, spouting red hot magma and spewing out lava, and is still active after 2 million years. Réunion is the youngest in a series of volcanoes that has sprung up along an ocean-floor fault, the foundation of the entire Mascarene archipelago.*

Fiery beginnings

It may seem like an eternity in human terms, but Réunion is very young in geological terms – just 2 million years old – indeed, there is a strong case for saying that the island is still in the process of being born. Réunion is the latest in a series of volcanoes that has sprung up along the line of the Mascarenes since the island of Mauritius erupted out of the ocean 3 million years ago. The island's active peak, the Piton de la Fournaise ('The Furnace'), has minor eruptions as a matter of course, throwing up cinders and spilling lava down the hillsides. The island's inhabitants are so familiar with volcanic explosions that they have to be reminded by their own government to take the situation seriously. Their *sang froid*, though impressive, may be misguided: La Fournaise still has the potential to erupt on a much larger scale, as it has done from time to time – most recently in 1977. Concerted efforts are now being made to put effective safety procedures in place: these include a watchtower that will enable islanders to be warned of eruptions.

Snowcapped peaks

Apart from Ruwenzori and the peaks of Kenya's Aberdare Range – both sections of the continental plate pushed upwards by colossal forces – the major mountains along the edges of the East African Rift have their origin in volcanic activity. With its seething lakes of lava, Mount Nyiragongo, on the Zairean side of the Virunga Range, vividly illustrates just how ongoing the process is. Close as they are to the Equator, the highest peaks are capped with perpetual snow, deposited by the lashing blizzards that have eroded their less lofty neighbours. Around Mount Kenya, for example, the covering strata have been slowly worn away to leave massive peaks of lava, reflected in lakes of the purest water. This starkly beautiful scene is enhanced by the swirling mists that swathe Mount Kenya's summit.

A youngster The deeply etched valleys in the foothills betray the comparative youth of Mount Lengaï in Tanzania. During its short lifetime – less than 370 000 years – the cone has hardly been scored by the run-off of water.

The volcanoes

Just dozing Despite the ice, Kilimanjaro still smokes gently from hot cavities. The mountain may be dormant, but it is sleeping only lightly.

Bananas apart, that seems to have been pretty much how it really happened: analysis of ash deposits and lava beds has broadly concurred with Chagga tradition. But the cataclysmic dethroning of Mawenzi took place around 36 000 years ago: it has thus remained in folk memory since prehistoric times. Human memory may on occasion be as reliable as the record of the rocks – which is, in any case, open to only a handful of specialists. Since its first appearance, the form of the mountain has been continually modified by a series of eruptions and lava flows, its growth to 19 340 ft (5895 m) outstripping erosion by rain and wind.

Comings and goings

The volcanic belt of Africa is still in a youthful stage. It was created some 30 million years ago, when a series of violent seismic lurches cracked and shifted the existing strata, and hot magma from the Earth's core welled up to fill the fissures that appeared along the fringes of the Rift Valley. Weathering has worn away innumerable cinder cones and lava beds, but the pressure inside the Earth has continued, pushing more matter upwards to replace them.

Kilimanjaro and its giant cousins, Meru and Elgon, will in time collapse into their own craters, undermined by the same surging, seething magma that brought them into being. Then, as has happened with Mount Kenya, their outer covering will wear away to reveal the hard, inner core: what are now their bases will eventually become their summits. But the region will retain its dramatic topography, however much the individual details may change: long before these great peaks have vanished, others will have emerged to take their place.

Two main types of volcanic structure testify to this process of constant renovation. First, there are those volcanoes being born and reborn along the continent's great faultlines, either obliterating or coexisting with those that came before them. Then there are those taking form where the oceanic plate, still sidling slowly yet unsteadily eastwards, has allowed hot magma to bubble up – at times erupting with explosive force – from the ocean floor. Along this latter line, some of the youngest and highest volcanic peaks have formed: they are still spectacular, despite much of their mass being concealed by water. Kartala and others of the Comoros chain come into this second category, as do the northern Seychelles, and the Mascarenes. From Réunion to Rodrigues, the whole volcanic life cycle can be seen in this archipelago: the former still under (often violent) construction, the latter all but worn away – the part that still appears above the waves is not the peak at all, but an edifice built by the encrustation of corals over passing centuries. The northern Seychelles, too, owe their existence to volcanic activity, yet show no sign of it in their immediate physical fabric.

The influence of volcanic activity extends far beyond the relief of the region. Climate is affected by hot springs and warm water currents in the oceans. Volcanic soils, rich in mineral nutrients, sustain a rich and distinctive flora and fauna, which in turn has had an impact on human lifestyles. And in the past few decades it has been the basis of a thriving tourist industry, bringing in vital revenues for communities that may be lacking in other resources.

The lakes of many colours

Volcanic minerals and algae able to tolerate hot springs and extreme salinity colour many of East Africa's lakes gaudy, improbable hues.

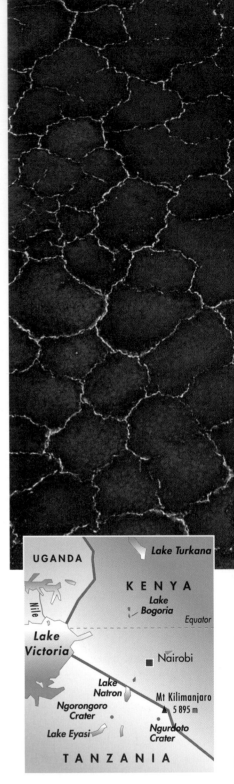

Struck dumb at finding themselves in what seemed like a dreamworld, the Europeans gazed down incredulously into Tanzania's great crater-lake Ngorongoro. It was not the sight of so many flamingos that transfixed them, but the bright red colour of the water in which the birds waded. The two were associated, their native guides told them, the flamingos' white plumage stained a stunning pink by splashes from the lake. Why the water should be red in the first place, though, they did not think to explain: perhaps it did not seem to need explanation. Here in the Rift Valley, after all, multicoloured lakes were practically the norm.

A sea of jade...or blood

Down the long, dry, diagonal strip that is the eastern arm of the East African Rift Valley runs a line of luridly coloured lakes and saltpans. Rainwater running over volcanic rocks has dissolved minerals, and the solution has been concentrated by an endless cycle of evaporation and replenishment. As a result, the lakes and dry flats of this region boast a spectrum of improbable colours – green, yellow, violet, white, and even black.

Lake Turkana (formerly Lake Rudolf) is also known more poetically as the 'Jade Sea'. The title comes from the vivid green colour of its highly sulphurous waters. In the crater-lake of Ngurdoto, in Tanzania's Arusha National Park, metallic chlorates have stained the water a weird, vibrant blue. Meanwhile, the red salt lakes of Bogoria in Kenya, and Ngorongoro and Natron in Tanzania, owe their colouring not only to chemical but also to biological influences. The micro-algae that swarm here protect their precious

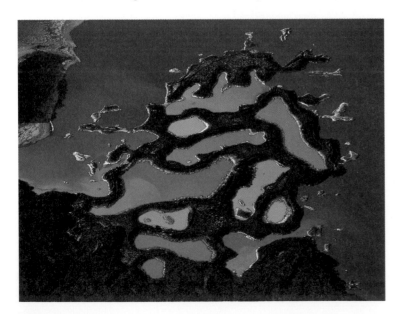

The haunted lakes of Madagascar

The cult of the dead has always been important to Madagascans: many lakes and pools are said to be haunted by the departed. The crocodiles in Lake Antanavo are thought to be the reincarnated spirits of dead humans. The waters of the lake appeared suddenly out of nowhere one day, so the story goes, drowning the village in the valley bottom. Local people still throw hunks of meat to their erstwhile neighbours. At the centre of the island, the crater-lakes of Andraikiba and Tritiva are said to be haunted by a pregnant woman and two young lovers who drowned there. Similar stories are told, with minor variations, of many lakes in Madagascar and the Comoros.

Crimson lake With soaring temperatures, salt-laden waters and a rich variety of algae and bacteria, East Africa has all the ingredients required for an alchemy of exotic colours. Though it takes its name from the sodium salt that abounds there, Lake Natron (above) derives its extraordinary colour from the microorganisms that swarm in its waters.

Jade Sea The varied shades of green in Lake Turkana (left) are created by a complex process involving the evaporation of salt solutions from volcanic sources in combination with the growth of certain algae.

chlorophyll from the sun by secreting an opaque red masking substance that gives the water the colour and viscosity of fresh blood. Strong concentrations of sodium chloride trace swirls of white on the crimson surface of Lake Natron, lending it the appearance of a bowl of tomato soup into which a generous spoonful of cream has been stirred. Rich as the region is in active volcanoes, such as the boiling cauldron of Mount Nyiragongo, a sight like this can be disconcerting. A visitor may wonder whether the red liquid spread out before him is really only coloured water – or whether it might be glowing magma, molten stone.

Slow death *Over-exploited by irrigation schemes, Lake Victoria's levels have dipped. Its waters are clogged by plants that are slowly strangling the lake, reducing oxygen and impoverishing its waters as a living environment.*

The changes in colour in the Madagascan crater-lake Andraikiba, by contrast, take place at disorientating speed, moving from blue to green, through violet to grey or even black. These transformations are caused by the sudden welling up from the crater's depths of hot water laden with mineral deposits, which then disperse by convection through the lake as a whole. At the island's northern tip, Lake Texier occupies the massive volcanic crater of Mount Ambre. Here strong-smelling, sulphurous salts come bubbling up from thermal vents deep down at the heart of the volcano: small wonder that the lake is also known by the name of 'Hell'.

For most of these phenomena, however strange, scientists have been able to come up with convincing explanations, but one has so far succeeded in eluding their best efforts. Near Dilolo, in a remote area where Zambia, Angola and the Congo meet, lies a lake with quite extraordinary properties. Draining a largely flat area of savannah, its level seems to fluctuate disproportionately according to the season. But this, though eccentric, is by no means its most peculiar feature. Following some secret logic of its own, it may choose to channel its surplus waters either of two ways: down the Congo, Atlantic-bound, or eastwards down the Zambezi to the Indian Ocean. The science of hydrography, advanced though it is, has yet to fathom how this apparent choice is made: even now, it seems, Africa retains some of its natural mystery.

Similar sights can be seen in the islands. The Salt Lake on Njazidja (formerly Grand Comoro) gets its bright green colour from the volcanic sulphurs it contains. The green tinge of Madagascar's Lake Anranotsara, on the other hand, is algae, while the white, milky appearance of Lake Tsimanampetsotsa comes from the thick bed of kaolin, or china clay, on which it lies.

Strange waters

Some of the region's lakes actually change colour – in some cases by slow and subtle degrees, but in others quite abruptly. Satellite photographs show that Lake Victoria's green waters are growing darker year by year. This is caused by the lake's progressive colonisation by water hyacinths, which threaten to crowd out other plants. Their eventual decomposition will deprive the lake of life-supporting oxygen. And to make matters worse, the two species that are thriving under these conditions are the malarial mosquito and the blood-flukes that cause bilharzia.

Filter feeders *Beyond the hot springs and geysers that feed Lake Bogaria, in Kenya, flocks of flamingos feed in the shallows, filtering algae from the warm, salty water.*

The unreliable road

Fresh from their conquest of the Sahara, the drivers of the 1924 *Croisière Noire* (Black Cruise) expedition felt that their cars were ready for anything: the customised Citröen halftracks had taken the desert in their stride. Seeing the saltflats of the Rift Valley stretched out before them, the drivers' spirits rose: these were surely the ideal surface for motoring at speed. Their confidence was misplaced, however, for much of the flats are composed of mud and the cars got stuck. Fine dust blown over the valley's shallow waters takes up just enough moisture to come to ground here, where it forms a distinct layer that is half mud, half salt crystal. Rather than compacting under pressure, it becomes more fluid, while any vibration also causes the surface to puddle.

Punishments and gifts from the gods

Water, sand, meteorites, thunderbolts, storm-blown debris and volcanic ash … all sorts of things can come hurtling out of the African sky.

Two legends, from two very different traditions, agree on one crucial point: that all the waters of the islands came down in one single rainstorm. Mauritians say the deluge that filled the vast Indian Ocean and the islands' many lakes was the work of the god Shiva. With loving patience, over a whole season, he emptied the great River Ganges, ladling out its waters over the ocean and the islands as a mark of his divine favour. Every year since then Hindu believers have given thanks to him, processing around the crater-lake of the Great Basin in pilgrimage to commemorate this first great blessing.

In contrast, the prophet Muhammad's purpose was altogether sterner, according to the Muslim inhabitants of Madagascar and the Comoros. He unleashed a terrible storm that within seven days drowned much of the region, sparing only those faithful few who had kept to the path of piety and justice.

Life-giving waters   Mauritians give thanks to Shiva for bringing water from India.

Good and bad rains

These tales highlight the difference between 'good' and 'bad' rains in the region's folklore; between the benign monsoons of winter and the brutal summer cyclones. The monsoons are indeed borne on gentle breezes from the direction of India, while the cyclones

Raining blood

If UFOs have neglected Southern and East Africa, that may be because of the difficulty of navigating an already crowded sky. 'Rains of blood' from Africa are familiar to people living in southern Europe, where globules of ochre sand carried north from the Sahara on the dry sirocco wind fall as red 'rain'. In Southern and East Africa, there are at least three different versions of this phenomenon. First, the southerly equivalent of the red sirocco showers falls on the dry grasslands of Namibia and the Kalahari Desert. Then there are the rains that wash away the red earth of the Madagascan hillsides, producing red rivers that course down to the Indian Ocean. Third, there are those showers which, though to all appearances conventional, stain some of the lakes of the Great Rift Valley a startling red. Here the colour is produced by microorganisms that, exploding into reproduction at the very first splash of rain, secrete a red substance as protection against the scorching sun.

East Africa or the Antarctic?   Tanzania's Lake Natron is named for the concentrations of sodium chloride it contains. Sudden winds can whip up fierce white blizzards here, but they are storms of salt, not of snow.

Cyclone damage   Though the lashing rain blots out the sun, there is still enough light left in the sky to see the devastation wrought by one of Réunion's fearful cyclones. This picture was taken in January 1993, and it is a scene with which the islanders are only too familiar.

Storm warning

The cyclones that batter the islands off East Africa have their origins far out in the Indian Ocean. Between latitudes 5° and 20° south the summer sun overheats the sea, creating convection currents in the air above. These currents spiral out to a diameter of up to 620 miles (1000 km) before finally exploding with all the whirling force of a cyclonic storm. Carried along curving paths to north and south by the rotation of the Earth, the cyclones for the most part attack the islands from a northerly direction. Once they hit land, however, their course becomes erratic and unpredictable. No island can expect to escape their attention for very long, experiencing on average at least one major storm every 15 years. The damage caused is proportionate to their strength: in April 1984, for example, tropical storm Kamisy was estimated to have destroyed some 80 per cent of the crops under cultivation on the Comoran island of Mayotte. Then in February 1992 Geralda ravaged

Réunion before claiming 70 000 casualties on the eastern coast of Madagascar. Réunion was hard hit again in February 2000, when Eline rushed through the island, with wind speeds of 155 miles (250 km) per hour. The storm also created havoc on the mainland, high winds compounding the misery of a Mozambique already under water from several days of torrential rain.

Even now the traditional distinction between 'good' and 'bad' rain holds, and there is one respect in which modern meteorology concurs with ancient folklore. Ancestral sources agree that the 'good' rains come from higher up in the sky than the 'bad', originating as they do in more exalted celestial regions. Today's scientists have meanwhile come to believe in the existence of 'bad winds' that blow through the lower reaches of the atmosphere, disrupting normal weather cycles to prolong droughts or intensify flooding.

Other hazards from the sky

Worse things than rain come from the sky, including red hot drops of lava or glowing cinders, a serious hazard around active volcanoes. Plagues of tsetse flies sweep down on herds of cattle, bringing the deadly sleeping sickness, and bloodthirsty leeches drop down from trees to hook into the flesh of unfortunate travellers.

The region has also had more than its fair share of giant meteorites. A meteorite that struck in prehistoric times was found in the Hoba district of Namibia, in 1920. It is one of the largest objects to survive its impact, and weighs some 60 tons.

The sky can shower benefits, too: not only life-giving rain, but solar energy and fresh air. Bolts of lightning hurled down during dry thunderstorms can set the savannah ablaze, causing destructive – but also regenerative – conflagrations. All in all, it's probably true to say that the best and worst of things can fall from the African sky.

come tearing down the Swahili coast from the north, just as though they are vengeful emissaries from Mecca. In fact this is somewhat unfair, as the apparent northerly origin of the cyclones is an illusion – they have generally spiralled around from the south, far out in the Indian Ocean.

The two stories underline cultural and demographic differences between the Arabic traditions of the mainland seaboard and the Asian antecedents of many of the islanders. Many East Africans are descended from nomadic herdsmen who feared floods, while island rice growers were more frightened of drought. The mainland interior is arid by equatorial standards and largely unaffected by the cyclones that afflict the coast. Yet even in such semidesert landscapes the threat of flooding exists: flash floods can suddenly surge down from the mountains without notice to inundate the savannahs. Not only the nomads are affected: so, too, are the plantations and the modern tourist industry.

Regeneration or destruction?
Fire helps regenerate the savannah, but it can create havoc on farms and plantations.

Enchanted deserts

Southern and East Africa is fringed with deserts. These are not just geographical frontiers, but the limits of life: no harsher environment could be imagined. Yet the Kenyan Chalbi, the Namib and the Kalahari hold many unexpected delights.

In the 1920s the European empires competed bitterly for influence in the Sahara. At that time there was only one African desert, as far as Westerners were concerned. As for the deserts of the South and East, few even knew of their existence: for those who did, the Chalbi and Kalahari were just empty wastes, with none of the Bedouin romance of their North African counterpart. The only thing that could be said in their favour was that they were not quite as irredeemably drear as the 'frightful Namib' described by Ernest Grangier in his *Universal Geography* of 1922.

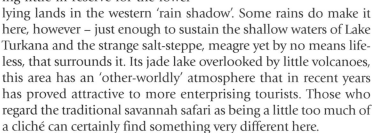

The first explorers at the end of the 18th century responded with enthusiasm to the deserts' austere beauty. But their successors, driven by more economic motives, could see no value in these wastes of land. Yet in recent decades the deserts have come into their own, their ecological complexity an object of intense fascination to scientists; their scenery a magnetic draw for foreign tourists.

Back to life *Apparently dead after two years of drought, this tree in the Kalahari will revive quickly when the advancing storm breaks.*

Consciously or not, visitors are moved by the paradoxical appeal of these strange locations, none of which is quite what it seems, or apparently 'ought' to be. Not only are there astounding flora and fauna, flourishing in what appears to be a barren, inhospitable landscape, but there are also deeper contradictions. The Chalbi, given its latitude, should by rights be an equatorial rain forest, while in the Namib, the arid desert lies adjacent to the rolling sea.

Confined by contours

The Chalbi and Kalahari owe their peculiarities to the great mountain ranges that hem them in. The Chalbi is squeezed between the Rift Valley's northern heights and the Ethiopian Highlands. Rain-bearing winds from the eastern ocean are forced upwards over Ethiopia and cool to shed their moisture, leaving little in reserve for the lower-lying lands in the western 'rain shadow'. Some rains do make it here, however – just enough to sustain the shallow waters of Lake Turkana and the strange salt-steppe, meagre yet by no means lifeless, that surrounds it. Its jade lake overlooked by little volcanoes, this area has an 'other-worldly' atmosphere that in recent years has proved attractive to more enterprising tourists. Those who regard the traditional savannah safari as being a little too much of a cliché can certainly find something very different here.

A desert besieged

In comparison with the Chalbi, the Kalahari lies in a more obvious place for a desert: it is the southern equivalent of the spreading sands of the Sahara. The paradox here is the desert's size: it is relatively small and stuck in the continent's centre, whereas the Sahara sweeps majestically from coast to coast. The great mountain ranges that run down the length of southern Africa cut the Kalahari off to

Chatterboxes *Famous for their upright posture and animated 'talk', these meerkats abound in desert areas of South Africa.*

The white bushman

Why excavate old ruins in search of our ancestors, asked South African writer Laurens van der Post, when they are walking round in our midst? In the bushmen of the Kalahari, he reasoned, modern city-dwellers could glimpse what their own remotest forebears had been. Rather than speculate on what was fundamental to human nature, why not simply ask the men and women who knew?

His experiences in a Japanese prisoner-of-war camp in the Second World War afforded him an all too tangible insight into humankind's capacity for cruelty, van der Post found in the hunter-gatherers a dignity and spirituality which more advanced societies seemed to have lost along the way of 'progress'. The author of unforgettable studies of Kalahari life, he was much more than an academic anthropologist: lyrical in his love for the desert and its people, he was a poet, a mystic, a philosopher, a psychologist and sage.

Fight for survival In northern Namibia, in the region known as Kaokoland, the vegetation is too sparse to provide much protection against evaporation. Between these scraggy tussocks a dense tissue of roots extends just below the surface, to take advantage of the slightest trace of morning dew. Though little rain falls here, the breezes are often cooled and condensed by cold currents pushing northwards up the Atlantic coast.

the east before swinging north along the Atlantic coast to hem it in on that side, too. The green hills of the Great Escarpment are high enough to catch clouds scudding in off the Indian Ocean, and even in the western ranges Mediterranean rainfall levels prevail.

Though imprisoned on every side, the Kalahari is not quite as arid as it looks: it is effectively a basin, and has accumulated its own underground reserves of water. And while the desert may be lower than the hills that surround it, the average altitude of more than 3300 ft (1000 m) means that it loses comparatively little of its moisture to evaporation.

The Kalahari is a more stable environment than the Sahara: it has neither the Sahara's temporary standing pools, nor its completely arid seas of shifting dunes; rather, patches of sand are interspersed with tussocky grass and scrubby thickets. There are even clumps of trees in the low-lying areas closest to the water table, as well as in the north along the damp fringes of the Oka-vango delta. Not just a wonder, but an outlandish eccentricity of nature, the Okavango is a wetland in one of the world's great deserts. The presence of so much water helps to moderate conditions in the Kalahari hinterland, which never quite attain the arid near-sterility of some parts of the Sahara.

A place apart

Isolated in its setting, the Kalahari also stands apart in the richness of its natural and human heritage, its incredible flora and fauna and its indigenous people, the !Kung San Bushmen. The two are, of course, intimately associated, the !Kung San still to a great extent upholding a Stone-Age hunter-gatherer lifestyle in close harmony with nature – a way of life the rest of us can barely imagine.

That this fascinating place has managed to maintain its unique character for so long is in large part due to its setting. The uplands that imprison the Kalahari have also discouraged incursions from the world beyond, and tourism has had little impact here – 'thank heavens', some conservationists would say. Yet outside support will be needed to save the Kalahari and its culture in the long term: the great challenge will be to strike the right balance between access and protection. Though the Kalahari and its people have much to teach us, our enlightenment must not be achieved at the expense of their traditional way of life. A nation that knows how to hunt big game with a bow and arrow, and how to suck water through a straw from the desert sand, has clearly learned a great deal about survival. But it is one thing to survive the rigours of the wild, quite another to withstand the seductive ways of Western 'civili-sation': the Bushmen's way of life could yet be killed with modern material kindness.

Watering hole The word vley is used in Southern Africa for those more or less permanent water holes in the desert where animals, like these oryx, can find refreshment.

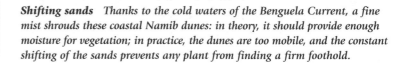

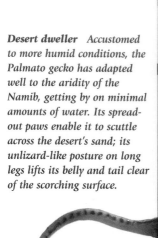

Desert dweller *Accustomed to more humid conditions, the Palmato gecko has adapted well to the aridity of the Namib, getting by on minimal amounts of water. Its spread-out paws enable it to scuttle across the desert's sand; its unlizard-like posture on long legs lifts its belly and tail clear of the scorching surface.*

Shifting sands *Thanks to the cold waters of the Benguela Current, a fine mist shrouds these coastal Namib dunes: in theory, it should provide enough moisture for vegetation; in practice, the dunes are too mobile, and the constant shifting of the sands prevents any plant from finding a firm foothold.*

'Nor any drop to drink'

'Water, water everywhere, nor any drop to drink', wrote poet Samuel Taylor Coleridge, which pretty well describes the situation all the way up the Atlantic coast of Southern Africa, where the ocean waves break on the arid edges of the Namib Desert. Far from easing the desert's dryness, proximity to the ocean seems to intensify it: paradoxically, the farther inland you go, the more evidence of moisture you come across. Like Chile's Atacama Desert, which it resembles in conditions and relief, the Namib owes its existence to a cold-water ocean current forced to make its way to the surface because its path is barred by an underwater

Stunted growth *In the driest reaches of the desert, only the* Welwitschia mirabilis *will grow. Its long leaves spread across a wide area so as to attract every drop of dew.*

Cold current

Each second, 565 million cu ft (16 million m³) of water washes the Atlantic coast of Southern Africa between the Cape of Good Hope and the Angolan port of Benguela. Finding its way barred by the underwater Walvis Ridge, the current chops and eddies, but pushes on and does its best to continue northwards.

Though it may have produced desert conditions ashore, the current creates a bountiful harvest for fishermen: life teems in the bracing freshness of these surging waters. The sea here holds other riches, too: notably the fine diamonds found on the bed, washed away from the adjacent landmass by the ocean rollers.

obstacle. In this case the current is the Benguela, pushing northwards up the coast, and the obstruction is the long diagonal of the Walvis Ridge. The ocean surface is unusually cold for this latitude and evaporation is meagre: so, too, is precipitation onshore. It is hard to see where the beach ends and the desert begins, for both are formed from the same red sand, ground down from bedrock rich in iron ore (and, on occasion, yielding diamonds of astonishing purity). The winds mark the desert sands with ripples and heap them up into the biggest dunes in the world.

Even by desert standards rainfall is low in the Namib – perhaps half an inch (13 mm) in a good year – and droughts can last for up to five years. Only flora and fauna adapted to cope with conditions of extreme aridity can survive here, extracting moisture from the mist that comes off the Atlantic. Hence the early morning ritual of the beetle, which assumes improbable acrobatic postures in order to sip the dew that trickles down its carapace. One of the few plants to survive is the stunted-looking *Welwitschia mirabilis* – a dwarf tree with oversized leaves that trail far across the sand to garner every last trace of moisture from the widest possible radius.

The human inhabitants of this desert coast are every bit as well-adapted: adventurers, for the most part, snatching a living under the harshest conditions, from the most adverse of environments. Some collect salt, while others fish the rich but treacherous offshore waters, or dive after precious stones dumped in the sea by the advancing dunes.

Noble savages

David Livingstone's 1849 crossing of the Kalahari has rightly gone down in the annals of exploration, but an earlier visitor to the region highlighted our changing attitude to the area and its inhabitants. In 1784 François Levaillant ventured into the Kalahari's semi-arid fringes and found what he was looking for: the society of man in a state of nature. Levaillant was a great reader of the philosopher Rousseau, who had contempt for the ways of civilisation and an idealised view of the 'noble savage'. Levaillant was thrilled when he met his first desert Bushmen – tribes quite unspoiled by

any contact with European culture. They caught on to 'civilised' ways quickly, though, their petty pilferings tarnishing – but not destroying – Levaillant's romantic view of their natural innocence. For all its absurdity, this attitude seems preferable to the one that David Livingstone had to fight in his contemporaries: the assumption that Africans were fit only to be enslaved. Only in our own time have Westerners held a more balanced perspective on African people and their ancient lifestyles: neither 'better' nor 'worse', but just as good and worthy of respect.

The desert has numerous abandoned shanties – and even sizable ghost towns – which bring the gold rush of the American West to mind. But if there have been failures in the past, mining is important to Namibia in the present – and will probably remain so in the future. Another money-making activity that seems set to continue is the recently emerged tourist trade. While the driest reaches of the Namib are likely to remain off-limits to most, the less hostile conditions around the capital, Windhoek, 186 miles (300 km) from the coast, could make that city an important centre for the more adventurous sort of trekking.

Collecting its dew   Thrusting its hindquarters high in the air, this desert beetle makes its body into an ingenious water-collection system, directing downwards the dew that forms by condensation on its carapace.

A desert park

Wishing to entice tourists to the country whilst preserving many of its unique habitats and species, the Namibian government has created a wildlife park, the fourth largest in the world, around its capital, Windhoek. Not only does the Namib-Naukluft Park cover considerable tracts of the Namib Desert proper, but it extends inland to take in the dry plateaus and craggy canyon country of the Naukluft. Here live such rare species as Hartmann's mountain zebra, as well as herds of ostrich, and antelope like oryx and springbok. The park also includes the coastal wetlands around Sandwich Bay, 26 miles (42 km) south of Walvis Bay, where sea birds congregate in their millions. But pride of place inevitably goes to the coastal section, just inland, with its eerie lunar landscape of giant, drifting dunes. Those round the Sossusvlei salt pan are almost alpine in their proportions, the highest sand dunes in the world. No visitor will ever forget the contrast between the blue ocean breakers and the giant red waves of sand ashore.

The Madagascan semidesert

In the south of Madagascar – and especially in the extreme south-west – is an area of thorny bushes, alternating with patches of bare sand. This area owes its aridity partly to its tropical latitude, and partly to its situation: it is sheltered by the higher ground in whose 'rain shadow' it lies.

Some of the clouds that sweep in from the open ocean do release their water here, ensuring an average rainfall of around 20 in (500 mm) per annum. But the summer thunderstorms, driving up against the eastern face of the Isalo Massif, release the bulk of their rain on the sea. Thus, though tantalisingly close to bucketing rains, these south-western regions gasp for water, a semidesert owing to an accident of relief.

The sparsity of grass has led to the evolution of some unusual agricultural practices, notably the tradition – still followed – of rearing livestock 'in the ditch'. Instead of allowing the animals to roam and graze free, they are kept corralled in pits in the ground, and the villagers throw down to them forage that they themselves have gathered.

Red waves   Beyond the flat bed of a temporary salt pan, at Sossusvlei, south of Walvis Bay, the horizon is formed by great red dunes that can rise to a height of 1150 ft (350 m). Though eternally the same in overall effect, this part of the Namib is in fact an ever-changing landscape, its wave-like dunes driven westwards by the winds at a rate of over 65 ft (20 m) a year.

CHAPTER 3

FLORA AND FAUNA

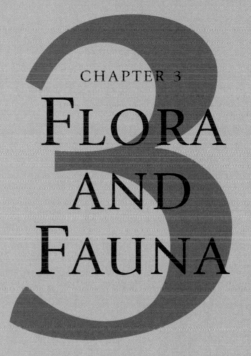

Large areas of Southern and East Africa remains more or less untouched by human activity. From the rolling savannahs to the misty mountain forests, from the rivers to the coastal mangrove swamps, nature reigns supreme and exotic flora and fauna abound. There are 30 or so different types of herbivore, a dozen primates, thousands of bird species, hundreds of fish and reptiles, and a profusion of beautiful plants. A wildlife safari takes the traveller across vast plains grazed by herds of wildebeest and zebra, by solitary rhino and groups of giraffe; past muddy water holes where antelope and buffalo drink side by side. Lions, leopards and cheetahs hunt these open parklands, along with less glamorous predators – troops of wild dogs, jackals and hyenas. The stately secretary bird, the scurrying spider, the armour-plated pangolin: life here comes in all shapes and sizes.

Each giraffe has a distinctive pattern, which enables experts to tell individual animals apart.

Plants beyond the imagination

In a region that encompasses a wide range of landscapes, plants have adapted to their individual habitats. This has produced some amazing species – trees that absorb water like sponges, plants that feed on other plants, flowers that burst into bloom in the desert.

The classic savannah landscape of waving elephant grass and acacia trees covers large areas of Southern and East Africa, but what is often loosely referred to as 'grassland' may in fact support a far more varied and complex flora, including small trees, thorny shrubs, cacti and creepers. Watercourses provide pockets of green, with ecosystems quite different from those of the more arid country all around. There may be great variety even within the same single landscape, as when sudden rains cause brightly coloured flowers to burst from the sun-scorched earth, or when a fire causes destruction yet within days nature is re-establishing itself, new plants emerging from the blackened roots of the old.

A gigantic sponge and a parasol

One of the strangest sights of the savannah is the baobab tree, which looks as though it has been thrust into the earth upside-down. Leafless for much of the year, its stunted branches protrude from an oversized, swollen trunk. The baobab is ideally adapted to semiarid conditions: the bulbous trunk – it can measure more than 26 ft (8 m) in circumference – acts like a sponge for storing water and carbohydrates, while the meagre branches and foliage reduce evaporation. Africa's indigenous peoples eat the acidic fruit,

A garden of delights

The varied landscape and Mediterranean climate of South Africa's Cape Province make it the ideal habitat for thousands of different plant species. A visit to the botanical garden at Kirstenbosch provides the perfect introduction to the richness of the South African flora.

The desert in bloom   This arid section of South Africa's Namaqualand gives some sense of the unexpected diversity and colour of the desert flora. Yet there is no mistaking the rigours of an environment whose few, deep-rooted kokerboom trees stand out starkly amid the ground-hugging vegetation.

Source of bread and water

When the indigenous peoples of Southern Africa talk of eating elephant's foot, they are not speaking literally. So called on account of its large size and bulbous shape, the elephant's foot plant is an invaluable source of nourishment and water. Its tuberous root, standing proud of the arid soil, makes the perfect source of water. Its spongy mass is also a repository of carbohydrate, hence its other name of 'Hottentot Bread'.

known as monkey-bread, which is a valuable source of refreshing water. The baobab is found throughout Southern and East Africa, wherever the savannah zone starts becoming semidesert, but the largest specimens are found in Madagascar.

With its slender trunk and graceful parasol of leafy branches, the acacia could hardly present more of a contrast, though the two trees occupy overlapping territories on the savannah. The acacia has all the height and elegance of its inseparable companion, the giraffe. Evolutionary biologists have suggested that the tree may have grown taller over time in the attempt to lift its lower branches out of reach of the steadily lengthening neck of the browsing mammal.

Other animals, too, have their own relationship with the acacia, from the bird species that nest in the tree, to the leopards that rest on its boughs between hunting expeditions.

Another world   Here, just below the snowline of the Ruwenzori, lies a zone where overnight frosts are daily burned away by the tropical sun. Its warming effects are, however, tempered for long periods by banks of cloud. These conditions support some peculiar exotic plants such as these giant groundsels.

vital deposit of general nourishment, but is also a source of water for grazing animals. The plants do what they can to protect themselves with fearsome thorns.

One desert plant, *Welwitschia mirabilis*, bucks the trend by having long, fleshy leaves that trail across the ground. 'Miraculous' indeed, the Welwitschia is technically a tree, though what ought to be its trunk is in fact no more than a few inches tall. What the Welwitschia lacks in height it makes up for in area, its long tough leaves sprawling out to a distance of up to 2 ft 6 in (76 cm). Running lengthwise inside the leaves are channels of absorbent fibres. These soak up moisture from early morning mists or dews, and transport it to the root below. Despite their strength, the leaves usually have a torn, frayed appearance due to the battering they receive from wind-blown sand. Welwitschia is slow-growing: a large specimen may be up to 2000 years old.

Water storage Baobabs are found in semiarid areas across much of Southern and East Africa, as well as in Madagascar. The tree's most distinctive feature is its water-storing trunk: the largest can hold up to 20 000 gallons (100 000 litres).

Damper by degrees

The closer one gets to the Equator, the warmer and wetter the climate becomes. In general, East Africa is an exception to this meteorological rule, thanks to local vagaries of altitude and relief, though there are some tracts of rain forest that are as moist and muggy – and as fertile – as any in the world. Here the soft light filtering down onto the mulchy forest floor gives the impression of a cathedral in which every stained-glass window is a different shade of green – though calling birds, chattering monkeys and buzzing insects keep up a cacophony that is anything but reverent.

There is far more to a rain forest than just its trees – though these can be spectacular, rising to heights of more than 130 ft (40 m). Every branch, every nook and cranny at every level, provides refuge for some species of bird, mammal, reptile or insect life, each tree becoming an ecosystem in itself. And it is not only animal life that finds a home: a rich variety of mosses cloaks trunks and branches, while ferns and orchids find a foothold in any hollow where wind-blown dirt or falling leaf mould has accumulated.

Some plants ride piggyback on other plants in order to gain access to the light. Such epiphytes, as they are known, include the liana, a creeping plant whose rope-like stalks make a trellis of any available branches. Truly parasitical plants are those that feed on the sap of their hosts, sucking them dry. The strangler fig can in time envelop its unfortunate victim from crown to roots, reducing a once-vigorous living tree to a brittle husk.

Desert plants

Water is as scarce in the desert as it is abundant in the rain forest. Those few plants that are able to eke out an existence have root systems that reach far underground, while their stems seem to cower on the surface. Creeping along the ground, keeping a low profile against the desiccating breezes, they have tiny, tough leaves that help keep evaporation to an absolute minimum. Their foliage is a

Paradise islands

On Madagascar, the Seychelles, the Comoros, Réunion and Mauritius the flora and fauna have evolved in isolation. This has protected the wildlife from genetic interference from mainland species. The giant tortoises of the Aldabra atoll, for example, are not quite the same as others elsewhere. Livingstone's Flying Fox, meanwhile, is unique to the Comoros – as are the Comoro Scops Owl and the marvellously named Mrs Benson's Brush Warbler.

Termites and giant spiders

African 'big game' represents only a small part of Southern and East Africa's remarkable fauna. Insects, arachnids and other 'bugs' are far more numerous, and every bit as vital to the ecological scheme of things.

Small but dangerous

The lion may be the king of beasts, but it is not the most dangerous: that title would have to be given to one of Africa's deadly disease-carrying insects. The tsetse fly (genus *Glossina*, pictured) is a bloodsucker which feeds on humans and livestock. It carries the deadly *Trypanosomiasis*, or sleeping sickness. The malarial mosquito *Anopheles* is another insignificant-looking creature, but when it plunges its proboscis into a victim's veins to feed, it transmits the infectious *Plasmodium* parasite. The resulting fever is at best unpleasant, at worst chronic or even fatal.

Of Africa's many thousands of exotic insect species, the termite is perhaps the most remarkable of all. Yet, to look at, this 'white ant' is quite undistinguished – which only goes to show just how deceptive appearances can be.

Termite cities

Not strictly speaking an ant at all, and in size and shape rather more like a cockroach, the termite lives in a colony of up to 3-4 million. Worker termites build nests of masticated clay, wood and vegetable matter, which dry in the sun to a concrete-like hardness. These elaborate constructions tower skywards like mini-Manhattans, rising up to 26 ft (8 m) above the surrounding savannah. Inside is a warren of interconnecting passages and cells where the whole life cycle of the colony is conducted. With different castes performing different functions, this complex society functions just like a city.

Fine web
The Nephila *spider produces the longest and finest webs.*

The colony's activities reveal an astonishing degree of interdependence between individual creatures that could not survive alone. The overdeveloped jaws of the soldier termites make formidable defensive weapons, but the soldiers are unable to feed themselves. The queen's sole purpose is to produce up to 30 000 eggs a day, but her body is too big to move of its own volition. Most of the eggs yield barren workers, whose job is to maintain and feed the colony. At intervals, however, she produces batches of eggs containing fertile males and females: they will eventually swarm, and a lucky few will found colonies for themselves.

Spider's silk

The world's greatest spinner is the spider *Nephila*, which has been known to produce continuous lengths of gossamer up to 2300 ft (700 m) long. Whereas a common European or North American spider spins its web between one twig and another,

Nephila makes a web up to 9 ft (3 m) in diameter between adjacent trees. Though fine enough to be invisible to its insect victims, the thread is still enormously strong: so strong, in fact, that in Madagascar it has traditionally been woven into a precious fabric that is softer than silk.

The scorpion's sting

With two wicked-looking claws at the front and a venom-tipped tail arching over from behind, the scorpion has a fearsome appearance. In Southern and East Africa there are scores of different species of scorpion and, while some measure less than half an inch (1 cm) in length, the largest, *Pandinus imperator*, may grow to a truly terrifying 8 in (20 cm). This little monster lives in East Africa, taking refuge in rocky crevices by day, emerging at night to hunt insects and spiders.

Termite chimneys *The constructions on top of this termite mound are vents, designed to dissipate some of the heat generated by the colony.*

Where the crocodile is king

The varied terrain supports many different species of reptiles, from darting lizards and geckos to lumbering tortoises. There are snakes – some highly poisonous – and monitor lizards 3 ft (1 m) long, but the undisputed ruler of the reptile realm is the crocodile.

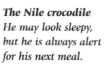

The Nile crocodile
He may look sleepy, but he is always alert for his next meal.

The Nile crocodile is not confined to the Nile River. Though hunted to extinction in some long-settled white colonial areas, and barred by waterfalls and rapids from finding its way into remote mountain lakes, the crocodile is otherwise ubiquitous, living even in the rivers and lakes of Madagascar. Every visit to a water hole or river is fraught with danger when this ferocious predator is keeping vigil.

Murderous hunter, but model parent

Though it may grow up to 20 ft (6 m) in length, the crocodile is nothing if not discreet, lying hidden with only its eyes protruding above the muddy water. Its sleepy expression and ungainly appearance are deceptive: in the water it can move with silent grace, and summon up explosive bursts of speed as it hurtles ashore to seize an unwary drinker. For, while the crocodile's staple diet is fish, it much prefers the meat of mammals, antelope and zebra being among its favoured prey.

Spit and strike *Seen here guarding her eggs, the female spitting cobra spits venom into the eyes, then follows up with a lethal strike.*

At nesting time the female crocodile scoops out a hollow in the sand, in which she lays some 30 eggs before reburying them for warmth and safety. In the three months it takes for them to hatch, she will never be far away, watching out for predators. When hatched young crocodiles are still vulnerable: measuring only 12 in (30 cm), they have to be carried to the relative safety of the water. Even then, the mother's work is not done. A doting parent by reptilian standards, she tends them closely, carefully shepherding them around for several months.

A slither of snakes

Africa is well-endowed with snakes, from venomous coral snakes and spitting cobras to coiling, crushing pythons. For all the apparent simplicity of their design, snakes are highly developed hunting animals. Climbing holds no fears for the tree-dwelling green mamba, while its cousin, the black mamba, can speed along at up to 12 mph (20 km/h), demonstrating that to creep is not necessarily to crawl.

Other snakes display different accomplishments. The spitting cobra shoots its venom with accuracy over distances of up to 10 ft (3 m), while the egg-eater's expanding jaws can accommodate an egg five times the size of its own skull. Once swallowed, the egg is crushed by specially adapted vertebrae and the shell is bundled neatly into a pellet for regurgitation. Without weapons of its own – no venomous fangs or constricting coils – the egg-eater relies on the power of fear, the pattern of its scaly skin mimicking those of its poisonous relatives.

Giant tortoises and monitor lizards

The crocodile is the most notorious of the reptiles, but there are others that reach a great size, including the giant or elephant tortoise of the Seychelles. This mild-mannered monster measures up to 5 ft (1.5 m) in length and carries a shell weighing more than 66 lb (30 kg), yet it is no more of a threat than the smaller tortoises found on the mainland. The monitor lizard is a different matter: growing up to 6 ft (1.8 m) in length, it is a surprisingly agile hunter – though it is unlikely to attack a human.

A multitude of birds

A flock of pink flamingos in flight, a solitary eagle soaring across an open sky, an egret riding serenely on an elephant's back, a heron standing sentinel in the shallows, a bird that doesn't fly… the feathered life of the region is colourful and immensely varied.

Carrion eater *Thanks to scavengers like this vulture, no part of any kill is wasted.*

A sand grouse makes its whirring flight through the desert back to its fledglings in their nest. It is carrying a cropful of seeds and termites to feed the chicks, and has also soaked the down of its breast with water for them to drink. The bird's resourcefulness enables it to thrive in an inhospitable environment. Other birds use equally ingenious methods of survival: often their individual skills and habits allow a number of different species to occupy the same living space.

A division of labour

Birds of prey are able to coexist because they have different hunting habits: peregrine falcons go exclusively after other birds, while augur buzzards will tackle small game on the ground. Eagles are even more specialised, some confining themselves to snakes, while other species scour the savannah for small mammals or fish the rivers. Griffons and vultures are content to take the leavings of other hunters: many have evolved long, bare, unfeathered necks that can be thrust deep into a carcass without becoming soiled with blood and tissue. Those that have full heads of feathers, like the hooded vulture, feed by browsing around the periphery of a kill site, picking up scattered scraps that can easily be eaten without contamination.

The bearded vulture of the Drakensberg, which gets its name from the distinguished moustache of trailing feathers on its face, has its own particular niche in the food chain. Arriving at a kill after other scavengers have finished, the bearded vulture is not in the least disconcerted at finding the flesh all gone, because it has learned how to break bones by dropping them onto rocks from a great height – and then it can get at the tasty, vitamin-rich marrow inside.

Any snakes that escape attack from airborne eagles may still fall victim to the secretary bird, which is a voracious predator. Named for the crest of dark-coloured feathers that stand out from its head – looking for all the world like a set of old-fashioned quill pens – this long-legged bird of prey can fly, but nevertheless hunts by pacing on foot through the open grassland. Flushing out rats, mice, snakes and lizards as it goes, it falls on them with carnivorous zeal. It may not match other raptors in style, but it beats them all in workman-like efficiency.

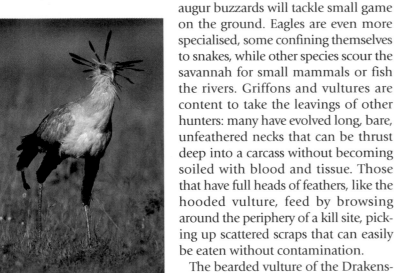

The walking raptor *The secretary bird struts through the long grass snapping up snakes, lizards, frogs and small mammals.*

Europa

The tiny islet of Europa lies in the Mozambique Channel between Madagascar and the mainland. The trade of past centuries passed it by, an oversight for which we can be grateful. Today Europa is one of the most important and beautiful bird sanctuaries in the world.

Rose island *Painting a Kenyan lakeside pink, a flock of flamingos crowds and jostles to the water's edge, while countless others swirl overhead like windblown blossom. These lesser flamingos feed on microscopic algae which they filter out of the surface water.*

A ticket to ride

See a rhino, elephant or buffalo on the African savannah, and as often as not it will be carrying a passenger. Several species of bird, including the cattle egret pictured here, ride on the backs of grazing herbivores. This lofty perch gives the bird a moving vantage point from which to survey the countryside. The herbivore disturbs the grass and shrubs as it walks, flushing out insects, snails, frogs and lizards. An alert bird can flutter down and snap up any tasty morsel it may see, then fly back on to its perch to scout for more. There are also advantages for the host in this partnership: the bird picks parasites off the animal's hide and, sharp-sighted as it is, gives warning of any potential hazard before the slower senses of the herbivore have detected danger.

Why the ostrich never flies

According to a Bushman's legend, the ostrich could fly if it wanted to. It chooses not to because it is jealously guarding a secret. Once, when the world was new, the ostrich alone of all creatures possessed the gift of fire: the bird kept it underneath its wing where nobody could see it. It was a terrible day for the ostrich when a cunning Bushman managed to steal a spark and make off with it: since then, humans have had the use of fire. Enraged by the theft, the ostrich determined that no other creature would ever share it: to this day it keeps fire bundled up tightly beneath its wing, and runs off as soon as anyone approaches.

Of fish and fowl

On the coast sea birds are able to share the same hunting grounds because of their different habits. Pelicans use their baggy bills to scoop up fish from the surface, while other birds, such as cormorants, dive down in active pursuit. Cape gannets may look ungainly ashore in their vast breeding colonies, but they move effortlessly in the air and dive with the speed of an arrow to fall upon fish in the water below. The jackass penguin, which breeds on islands off Africa's south-western coast where the cold Benguela Current flows, is the ultimate aquatic bird. It has become so sleek and streamlined for swimming that it long ago lost the power of flight.

Freshwater birds have also evolved so that they can live together in their African environment. As the fish eagle plunges into the river for the largest fish, the heron stands sentinel in the shallows, while kingfishers flash across the surface, snatching at the smallest specimens. The African jacana, meanwhile, has elongated toes that distribute its weight, allowing it to walk on floating weeds and lily pads in search of insects and crustaceans. In the shallows nearer the bank, egrets dabble for tadpoles and tiny fish, as well as any other small organisms the mud may yield. Here, too, the long-necked sacred ibis, held in veneration by the ancient Egyptians, probes the mud for molluscs and crustaceans, apparently oblivious to its exalted status.

Savannah sprinter
The ostrich can run at 50 mph (80 km/h).

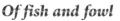

Flamingos are a stunning sight when they congregate in their thousands on the great salt lakes of the Rift Valley. The distinctive beak – which the Red Queen in Lewis Carroll's *Alice in Wonderland* thought fitted the flamingo for the role of croquet mallet – functions as a filtration system for extracting microorganisms from the muddy water of the shallows. This is just one of many unusual feeding adaptations: the shape of its beak has earned *Balaeniceps rex* the name of shoebill. This bird waits in ambush in marshes or beside slow-moving rivers and streams, and jumps in feet first when it sees a likely quarry, trapping the unfortunate fish with its claws while clobbering it senseless with its heavy, club-like beak.

In what was a uniquely varied environment to begin with, evolution has maximised diversity. Specialised adaptations allow different species to avail themselves of every conceivable source of food. Even when two outwardly similar species occupy what would appear to be identical ecological niches, a shift system may operate: the same stretch of river may, for instance, be hunted by the fish eagle by day and by Pel's fishing owl by night.

A precision instrument The beak may look big and clumsy, but the hornbill wields it with great dexterity. This red-beaked hornbill is one of several species found in Southern and East Africa.

Madagascar: a naturalist's paradise

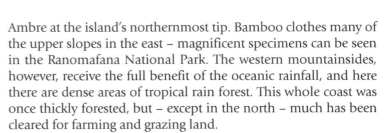

Long since separated from the mainland of Africa, Madagascar has to a large extent followed its own evolutionary path. The result is a rich and unique flora and fauna, with many species that are found nowhere else on earth.

Master of disguise *Changing colour to match the background, the chameleon is difficult for predators to detect. And by minimising movement, it makes itself even harder to spot.*

A hundred million years ago Madagascar parted company with the coast of Africa. Drifting infinitesimally out into the Indian Ocean, the plate on which it is founded has moved only 370 miles (600 km) in all those millennia. In geographical terms, the island still clearly 'belongs' to Africa. At its narrowest point the Mozambique Channel is not quite 250 miles (400 km) across, but it is wide enough for Madagascar to have developed its own unique flora and fauna, completely cut off from continental influences.

Sticky feet *The tree frog is well adapted to climbing trees in the forest – it has adhesive pads on its fingers and toes.*

Splendid isolation

Yet there is no sign of biological impoverishment here, no sense of a land marooned – if anything, evolution has gained energy in isolation. Some 120 species of birds are unique to Madagascar, while the majority of the island's mammals, reptiles and amphibians are found only here. Plants, too, have pursued their own evolutionary path: all sorts of species grow exclusively here, including several strains of bamboo and hundreds of different orchids.

The fourth largest island in the world, Madagascar is extensive enough to contain many contrasting landscapes and shorelines, from the coral reefs that fringe the rocky eastern coast to the squelchy mangrove swamps that mark the island's western edge. Inland the interior rises – shelving slowly in the west, where the Bemaraha plateau stretches out, an expanse of dry savannah with thickets of thorns and baobab forests. From the east the climb is steeper: a range of mountains runs all the way along this coast, linking the heights of Isalo in the south with volcanic Mount

The island with it all *Just about every type of tropical habitat is found on Madagascar, from dense jungle and savannah to lily ponds.*

Ambre at the island's northernmost tip. Bamboo clothes many of the upper slopes in the east – magnificent specimens can be seen in the Ranomafana National Park. The western mountainsides, however, receive the full benefit of the oceanic rainfall, and here there are dense areas of tropical rain forest. This whole coast was once thickly forested, but – except in the north – much has been cleared for farming and grazing land.

Madagascar has suffered less from human development than the neighbouring mainland, but nevertheless has experienced the destructive effects of settlement. Though no doubt easier on the environment than many more modern systems, the Madagascans' traditional methods of 'slash and burn' cultivation have had an impact over time. Yet, threatened as it is, Madagascar still possesses some of the world's loveliest, most unspoilt country, and is home to some of the strangest, most fascinating flora and fauna.

The Madagascan manikin

The lemur is Madagascar's mascot. Despite its appearance, it is not a monkey but a more primitive primate species – as such, it is a relative, however distant, of humans. There are 20 or so different species of lemur on the island. Once upon a time there were lemurs in many parts of the world, but the evolutionary success of monkeys

and apes has left them increasingly marginalised. Kindred species such as the galago are still found in the forests of sub-Saharan Africa, while loris have evolved in parts of India and South-east Asia, but Madagascar is now the last remaining home of this fascinating and charming genus.

Remote they may be from us in evolutionary terms, but the lemurs' puckish manner can make them seem more irresistibly human-like than many monkeys, while thanks to their apparently harmonious family life they are easily idealised. The best-known species, the ring-tailed lemur, is the least typical, not only on account of its black-and-white banded tail, but because of its habitat, favouring as it does the rocky slopes of the Madagascan mountains, while its relatives prefer the forests lower down. The smallest lemur, the aptly named dwarf lemur, measures only about 12 in (30 cm), much of which is its tail; but most lemurs are 3 ft (1 m) or more in total length.

The leaping lemur All Madagascar's lemurs are agile but the sifaka has to take the prize for acrobatics, covering the ground with huge leaps.

distinct species of chameleons, one giant growing up to 25 in (64 cm) long, while another species never reaches more than 2 in (5 cm) in length, even in adulthood.

Opportunist lemurs

Generally speaking, lemurs are omnivorous, eating not only fruit and buds, but also insects, eggs and even nestlings and small birds. The nocturnal avahi of the northern rain forests appears to be entirely vegetarian, but this is the exception rather than the rule. The aye-aye has evolved an elongated middle finger specifically for inserting into crevices to hook out insects and grubs. Living in the more open coastal forests of the west, the safika has learned to jump enormous distances from tree to tree. Though only about 3 ft (1 m) long, it has been recorded making leaps of up to 30 ft (10 m). Lemurs need all their agility and speed to keep a jump ahead of the fossa, a leopard-sized civet that is unique to Madagascar.

The island also has its own species of mongoose, though these are more of a threat to small reptiles than to lemurs. Chameleons and geckos are particularly numerous and varied. There are 40 or so

Plants of Madagascar's rain forest

But it is not on account of its animals, interesting though they are, that Madagascar is today attracting such intense scientific interest: rather, it is the island's plants that have been brought into sharper focus. For it has only recently been realised quite how precious and irreplaceable the biochemical bank that is the Madagascan rain forest really is. From the Madagascan periwinkle, for instance, pharmacologists have extracted a drug that has proved extremely useful in treating certain cancers. Many of the islanders' traditional herbal remedies are currently undergoing scientific analysis.

Vegetable monster Madagascar has the biggest baobab trees in the world, some with trunks 26 ft (8 m) in diameter (below)

Gifts of nature

The flowers of the ilang-ilang (right) smell too strongly to be pleasant, but the petals are distilled to obtain extracts for the manufacture of perfume, an important strand of the national economy. The traveller's tree (big picture) is a relative of the banana. It has been valued not so much for its fruit as for the water it provided travellers in the forest. The stems fan out like celery stalks, each forming a fleshy gutter down which rain falls. The water collects in clefts where the stalks meet at the bottom. Herdsmen moving their flocks, or people travelling from village to village, knew they could scoop out water from the base of a traveller's tree whenever they needed it.

The Indian Ocean: sea of life

The coast of East Africa is strewn with tropical islands and coral reefs. Here, in the warm waters of the Indian Ocean, an exotic and richly coloured fauna has evolved: garish clownfish and angelfish, the rare coelacanth, and the largest animal on Earth – the blue whale.

Along the eastern side of Africa runs what might be called the coral coast, one of the richest natural habitats on the planet. To describe the coral reef as the ocean's rain forest is not exaggerating – in fact, it fails to do justice to an environment that, as far as biodiversity is concerned, is unequalled anywhere else on Earth.

Another world

Diving into the waters of the coral reef is like entering another world much brighter and more colourful than our own. Reef species vie with one another to display the most dazzling colours, the most garish patterns, as if unsure whether they are doing it in the name of camouflage or ostentation. Down here, fish have to be outlandish to blend in: take, for example, the tiger stripes and porcupine spines of the venomous devilfish, the bright blue, black,

Protein by the ton *This shoal of silver jack is packed tightly together for protection against predators, but it is vulnerable to fishermen's nets.*

orange and white bands of the triggerfish, the wispy 'wings' of the angelfish, the bright red robes of the cardinal fish, or the garish, slapstick colouring of the clownfish.

The clownfish lives among the poisonous tendrils of the sea anemone: its scales have evolved a special coating so that it is protected against the anemone's paralysing barbs. In one of those mutually convenient arrangements that occurs so often in nature, the anemone protects the clownfish against larger predators. In return, the clownfish emerges from time to time and presents itself as living bait to a larger fish, which then rushes straight into the anemone's venomous embrace.

A living fossil

As far as science was concerned, the coelacanth died out some 80 million years ago: before that, it was found throughout the world's oceans for over 300 million years. Imagine, then, the amazement of the scientific world when a fisherman caught one in the Indian Ocean off the coast of South Africa in 1938. His catch caused an international sensation: soon palaeontologists were beating a path to his door. Later investigations indicated that this particular fish had strayed from its species home territory near the Comoros islands.

The coelacanth is of particular interest to palaeontologists because it is the only surviving species of the 'lobe finned' group of fishes. The fins of these fish are bony and have taken on some of the characteristics of a land animal's limbs – for example it can operate its pectoral and pelvic fins independently. It was another group of lobe-finned fish, the

osteolepiforms, from which the first four-legged animals evolved.

Comoros fishermen watched coelacanth mania develop with bemusement: they had been landing the fish for generations. Once alerted to its importance, they brought any further finds to the attention of the authorities, and since then several coelacanths have been found. Thanks to such discoveries, researchers have been able to learn much about the coelacanth, but one question it raises has never been answered. How did it come to hold out here so many millions of years after its extinction elsewhere?

Source of myth *The dugong or sea cow (right) of the Indian Ocean is believed to have been the original inspiration for the myth of the mermaid. Given to floating for long periods in an upright position, the sea cow can indeed take on a vaguely human shape when seen in silhouette.*

Prowlers *The triangular fins of black-tipped sharks cleave the clear Seychelles water as they search for food. The ringed octopus (below) blends in beautifully with its surroundings on the coral reef.*

Coral construction

Coral reefs are built of living organisms: they may look like lovely flowers, but they are actually conglomerations of minute polyps, carnivorous creatures that feed on microorganisms washed across them by tidal movement and ocean currents. As each generation of polyps dies, another replaces it, establishing itself on top of the hard, stone-like external skeleton left by its predecessor. Over millions of years, vast structures of stone-like material may be formed, many hundreds of feet deep and thousands of miles long.

There are three main kinds of coral reef, and East Africa has examples of them all, when the classic coral atolls of the Comoros and northern Seychelles are included. These ring-like reefs grow up around volcanic peaks, straining upwards to reach the daylight as the volcano subsequently subsides, until in many cases all that shows above the surface is the coral atoll. Barrier reefs tend to form along the leading edge of a geotectonic plate, where it drops away suddenly seawards, sometimes plunging to 3000 ft (1000 m) or more on the offshore side. Not much is known of the exterior walls, which are continually lashed by ocean breakers, but on the gently shelving landward side the reefs enclose natural paradises. Barrier reefs lie along the eastern edge of Madagascar, as well as along the mainland. Smaller ribbon reefs are also found along the mainland. These flat fields of coral grow up in shallow water and may often be uncovered at low tide.

Out to sea

Beyond the barrier reef the seabed falls away steeply, and the waters here are inhabited by shoals of bream, tuna and other deep sea fish. Flying fish swarm in, and over, the open ocean: their wing-like fins enable them to glide 300 ft (100 m) or more in a single 'flight'. This ability to 'fly' stands them in good stead when they are being pursued by dolphins, whose streamlined grace may entrance us, but spells destruction for the fish they feed upon.

Great rorquals like the blue whale present no threat to fish. The largest animal on earth – more than 100 ft (30 m) long and up to 140 tons in weight – subsists contentedly on some of the smallest creatures. Through a series of plates, or whalebone, which take the place of teeth in its upper jaw, the whale strains microscopic 'krill' from the water.

The manta ray is minuscule in comparison with the blue whale, but large enough to be intimidating. Its wing-like fins may reach a span of more than 20 ft (6 m). The manta ray swims near the surface, feeding on small fishes and planktonic animals that are funnelled into a large mouth between fleshy flaps, or 'horns' on the head, and are then filtered from the water by the gill rakers.

Smaller still, measuring up to 11 ft (3.4 m) in length, the sluggish dugong, or sea cow, is found all along the East African coast. It can remain submerged for up to ten minutes at a time, grazing on undersea grasses and algae. But, too slow and gentle for its own good, the dugong is under threat throughout its entire territory.

A world of colour *Even the tropical rain forest cannot match the coral reef for colour – a gaudy parrot fish is nothing out of the ordinary here. But, like the rain forests, the reefs are threatened, pollution and overfishing both taking their toll, while global warming may be upsetting the ecological balance.*

Sanctuaries for wildlife

The Serengeti, Masai Mara, Tsavo, Ngorongoro…huge areas of East Africa are set aside as wildlife sanctuaries. Reserves stretch across Africa from Kenya to Namibia, and down to South Africa's Kruger National Park.

Poacher's target
The white rhino has been hunted to the verge of extinction because its 'horn' – which is really cartilage – is valued as an aphrodisiac.

The African savannah has no fewer than 70 different species of antelope, ranging from the great eland – which stands at around 6 ft (1.8 m) tall at the shoulder – to the diminutive dik-dik, which only measures about 14 in (36 cm). Size is not the only variable: habitats differ, too, as does the specialised use each species makes of the land's resources.

To each his own

How does the savannah support such variety? With so many antelope species (not to mention numerous other herbivores), why has the pressure of overgrazing not destroyed it? The answer lies in the subtle complexity of an ecological order in which each animal species has its own particular niche. Among the herbivores there is a distinction between those that graze, living entirely on grass, and those adapted by evolution to supplement, or even replace, that diet by browsing on the buds and foliage of trees and bushes. The impala, for example, is a grazer and its digestion is not capable of dealing with anything but grass; but Grant's gazelle will nibble at low-hanging foliage. Larger species with a higher reach, such as the eland and kudu, are the best equipped as browsers, and both eat leaves.

There are further divisions within each main group: among the grazers, some species favour fresh young shoots, while others like tough and fibrous older growths. Biting away the tallest and toughest clumps, the buffalo clears the way for smaller, more fastidious grazers, such as the

A walking watchtower
A giraffe surveys the savannah for any sign of danger – or of fresh food supplies.

Under pressure

For the moment, conservation and its value as a tourist attraction have saved the African elephant from extinction. However, ivory poaching and human population pressures on its range still pose long-term survival problems for the species. The prospects for saving the white rhino from extinction by the poacher's rifle are bleaker.

Thomson's gazelle, which much prefers finer grasses. The zebra and wildebeest are able to coexist because the zebra's taste for drier, more mature grass complements the wildebeest's preference for moister, more succulent stalks. These two species are so much at home with one another that they often migrate together.

Migration is another of nature's strategies for sparing the savannah from over-exploitation. Each year as the dry season approaches, the wildebeest migrate in their hundreds of thousands – often attended by herds of zebra and smaller antelope – to areas where they may be sure of pasture and a reliable supply of water. This great trek of the animal kingdom is a stunning sight, but like so many other natural wonders it is being jeopardised by humans. In a bid to modernise East African agriculture and cattle-rearing, fences have been erected to enclose and 'rationalise' the open range, making a difficult and dangerous journey more demanding still.

Water hole etiquette

The ability of so many species to live side by side on the savannah in peaceful coexistence is one of the great miracles of nature. Even carnivores fit in surprisingly easily to the scheme of things: the grazing species know

Balance upset *Traditionally the elephant has played a vital role in the cycle of savannah regeneration. But as urbanisation and agriculture have squeezed the herds into smaller areas, so the vegetation has been overbrowsed.*

Fellow feeders *Zebras and black wildebeest coexist because the zebra grazes the tougher, taller grass while the wildebeest favours the young growth.*

Idiosyncratic insectivores

Few mammals are quite as strange as Southern Africa's pangolin, whose prehensile tail looks like that of a monkey or lemur, while its 'scales' give it a distinctly reptilian air. Large, overlapping plates of horn cover its back and flanks like the mail of a medieval warrior, affording all-round protection when the pangolin curls up into a bony ball. Raised up as they are in that position, the sharp edges of the plates present a sufficiently fearsome prospect to ward off predators. As its alternative name, scaly anteater, suggests, the pangolin lives on ants and termites, a diet that it shares with another strange African animal, the aardvark. At around 6 ft (1.8 m) long – about the same size as the pangolin – this curious creature is as at home on the ground as the other is in the trees. Thanks to its powerful, shovel-like forepaws, the aardvark can bury itself at a moment's notice, whenever the sun becomes too strong, or if it scents a nearby predator. The burrows that the aardvark leaves behind provide homes for smaller mammals and reptiles, making this improbable animal the master-builder of the savannah.

instinctively whether a lioness or leopard is hunting or merely passing through. Nowhere is this harmony more evident than at the water hole, where all must come to drink. Here the elephant lines up with the eland; the giraffe with the warthog; the lumbering buffalo with the dainty dik-dik. Not that all is necessarily peace and calm: carnivores may lie in ambush here, or assault may come from the water itself, from the terrifying lunge of a crocodile.

The hippopotamus, his eyes and nostrils, like the crocodile's, protruding unobtrusively above the water, may have an air of corpulent complacency but is actually fiercely territorial and highly aggressive towards interlopers. That mighty head can crush a canoe; a single flick can send a boat spiralling up into the air. The hippo has proved more dangerous to humans than the crocodile, but for his animal neighbours he is no threat.

Giants of the savannah

The world's largest land mammal has a huge impact on the African scene. Herds of elephants march indiscriminately through wood and grassland, devouring just about everything in their path. Weighing in at around 7 tons, an adult requires some 660 lb (300 kg) of food a day – and is not too particular where it comes from. Stripping the bark from trees, uprooting bushes and eating grass by the ton, the elephants' influence on their environment has not been entirely benign. Conservationists have learned this the hard way: having brought the elephant back from the brink of extinction, they have seen recovered populations ravaging large areas of the savannah and in many cases have been compelled to introduce selective culling to keep numbers down. The key, as so often, lies in striking a balance. The elephant's 'destructive' ways were responsible in the past for converting large areas of woodland and dense scrub to the savannah we see today. This may be to the environment's overall advantage, yet if allowed to go on unchecked, the savannah itself could ultimately be destroyed.

Rival males *For most of the year the topi is a placid animal, but in the rutting season, when the males fight for supremacy over the herd, an entirely different, violently aggressive, animal surfaces.*

An antelope with a difference

Antelopes are typically creatures of the dry savannah, but the sitatunga is an exception. Living in marshy regions such as the Okavango, it is found among dense beds of papyrus and reed, feeding while standing in up to 3 ft (1 m) of water. Its spreading hooves allow it to speed away across the shallows at the first sight of danger.

Tooth and claw

Live and let live may be the code by which the savannah's herbivores coexist, but the carnivores must kill if they are to eat. Their violent attacks may interrupt the peace, but they are ultimately a part of the same harmonious order, the final links in an elaborate food chain: in Africa's open grasslands, all flesh is grass.

***His Majesty** A full-grown lion weighs 440 lb (200 kg) or more, and stands at the apex of the savannah food chain.*

With his massive forepaws, his streaming mane and a roar that seems to shake the very earth, the male lion is a majestic sight, a 'king of beasts' indeed. Yet in the daily battle for survival on the open savannah it is the lioness which takes the lead, the role of the male in the family or 'pride' being the establishment and protection of territory.

Collective cats

The male lion's prestige within the pride cannot be doubted – he eats first from any kill; only when he is done will his lionesses and their young take over. This despite the fact that he contributes little to the day-to-day life of the group: it is the females who do most of the crucial work of hunting, their patient teamwork being especially remarkable given the solitary self-sufficiency of other cats, both wild and domestic.

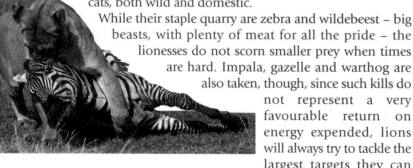

While their staple quarry are zebra and wildebeest – big beasts, with plenty of meat for all the pride – the lionesses do not scorn smaller prey when times are hard. Impala, gazelle and warthog are also taken, though, since such kills do not represent a very favourable return on energy expended, lions will always try to tackle the largest targets they can find, attacking even mighty buffalo. The hunting lionesses grow accomplished in picking out the elderly or otherwise infirm and manouevring deftly to cut them out from the sheltering safety of the herd. When their skills are on song and their collective tactics effective – and when their luck is in – the lionesses have isolated their victim before it is even aware that anything is amiss, stalking it through the long grass before erupting from the undergrowth almost at their quarry's feet. Surprise is of the essence, the only guarantee of a quick, clean kill – the lionesses cannot afford a protracted, exhausting pursuit or draining struggle.

***Skilled hunter** A lioness paralyses a zebra with a bite to the base of its skull.*

Yet if lions are sociable by cat standards, the patriarchal ruler does seem to hold himself proudly aloof from his tribe. What is often anthropomorphised as his regal haughtiness is his all-consuming preoccupation with the integrity of his own genetic line: his jealousy, his intense territoriality, both stem from this same instinct. Marking out the pride's territory with his pungent urine, he defends it fiercely – in some cases to the death – against any rival male that might seek to muscle in.

***Climbing cat** Though happy enough to hunt in open country, the leopard retires into the trees to enjoy its feast beyond the attention of scavengers.*

The all-purpose predator

Smaller than the lion, slower than the cheetah, yet more adaptable than either, the leopard is the third of Africa's big cats. Equally at home hunting by day or by night, in every habitat from desert to rain forest, it is happiest in wooded savannah, where trees provide cover. Stealth is the key to the leopard's attack: it is an accomplished stalker but needs extraordinary persistence. A leopard that was monitored through more than 60 hunts had a success rate of only 1 in 20.

Speed king

Regal though his presence may be, the lion looks ponderous beside the rakish, sinuous lines of his relative, the cheetah. This high-performance cat has been clocked at speeds of 75 mph (122 km/h), though it can maintain them only over short distances. This is not a handicap, because the cheetah has learned to work around its limitations, getting as close as possible to its grazing quarry before rushing out of the long grass in an explosive burst of speed. The Thomson's gazelle that are its primary prey are themselves fast runners, but if the cheetah has done its stalking properly and manouevred itself into close proximity before it is detected, the resulting race will be a one-sided affair. But sprinting speed is not enough: the cheetah's strong and flexible spine enables it to turn in a tight circle to track the bobbing, zigzagging flight of the terrified gazelle. Much of the cheetah's weight is concentrated along its back, which must withstand enormous forces as it accelerates, twists and turns; its long, heavy tail helps to maintain stability. Once within range, the cheetah may sweep out a forepaw to send its quarry tumbling, or sink its teeth into the gazelle's neck and drag it down. Exhausted, the cheetah will usually rest awhile before eating; once fed, it will sink into a torpor until it is time to hunt again.

Convenience food   *Often seen among vultures scavenging a ready-made meal, hyenas are, in fact, accomplished hunters in their own right.*

Nothing to laugh at

The hyena is known for its maniacal laugh and for its top-heavy appearance: its outsized head accommodates a heavy jaw capable of cracking open any bone and all but the thickest of skulls. Because of its habit of clearing up leftover carcasses, the hyena has traditionally been categorised as a scavenger. But recent research has revealed a far more fascinating animal than anyone previously thought: in particular, it has scotched the 'scavenger' image. Though the hyena does eat the leavings from a lion's kill, it is also a formidable hunter, its own efforts accounting for more than 80 per cent of what it eats and comprising such comparatively large quarry as gazelle, zebra and even wildebeest.

At around 3 ft (1 m) tall and weighing at most 175 lb (80 kg), hyenas could clearly never hope to tackle such targets individually, but they are sophisticated pack hunters. They work in close cooperation, singling out the old, young and injured in a herd. The close-knit, hierarchical groups in which hyenas live – and in which the larger females are strongly dominant – reinforce the hyena's ability to act in collaboration with its kin: the collective result is an efficient hunting machine. The fact that hyenas hunt by night, scavenging mainly by day, may account for the previous failure to appreciate this predator's true nature.

The hunting dog's social structure is even more remarkable. Each pack is built around a single 'alpha female': of all the bitches in the pack, she alone is allowed to breed, and her litters are large, 11 or more pups is not unusual. The alpha female queens it over a pack of up to 30 dogs, whose collective hunting skills, like those of the hyenas, enable them to kill much larger animals such as wildebeest and zebra. The pack moves continually in search of food. Apart from their intelligent teamwork, the hunting dogs' secret weapon is their stamina: they can maintain a speed of 25 mph (40 km/h) for hours on end.

The nearest the savannah has to the stereotypical scavenger is the jackal, though even here the truth is more complicated than it seems. In addition to snatching morsels from the kills of larger predators, the jackal kills prey of its own, though the animal is too small to take anything larger than small mammals and birds, lizards and other reptiles, and amphibians.

Diverse strategies   *Hunting dogs (above) work as a team, instinctively isolating the oldest and weakest herbivore from the herd. The cheetah (left) hunts on its own, relying on speed: this baby antelope is an easy kill.*

Wildlife in close-up

1. Still traditional Despite the pressures of modernisation, these Masai herdsmen maintain many of their ancestral ways.

2. Moving out A little indignity is a small price to pay for what may be a life-saving journey to a wildlife sanctuary.

3. Conservation college These Tanzanian students are equipping themselves to protect a natural heritage that, though still threatened, at least now has its defenders.

4. Face to face with nature The traditional African safari is now enjoyed by thousands, thanks to the modern tourist trade.

5. Doctor at large Richard Koch administers to an enormous variety of animal clients: here his men carry in a sedated lioness for treatment.

6. Africa by balloon Its burners extinguished to eliminate noise, this hot-air balloon holds its position in complete silence, the perfect platform for observing hippos in the wild.

7. Conservation war Africa's armed forces have become involved in an unrelenting and sometimes dangerous war on ivory poachers.

8. Field hospital A team of vets working in South Africa's Kruger National Park operate on a sedated elephant.

9. A friend in need Comita Walker saved this hippopotamus calf, which she found badly wounded: now she cares for it like an adoptive mother.

10. Elephant mother Daphne Sheldrick has set up an elephant orphanage outside Nairobi.

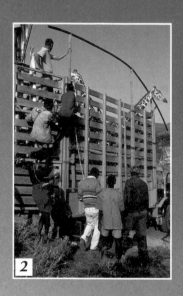

Grace in flight Flat-footed though it may be on land, the pelican is a surprisingly elegant flier, as well as an excellent swimmer and accomplished fisherman. Sometimes a group of pelicans may line up together to fish as a team, lashing the water with their wings to drive the fish towards the shallows.

King of the carrion-eaters The marabou is the largest of the stork family, growing up to 5 ft (1.5 m) tall. Unlike its more elegant cousins, it eats carrion.

Hard at work Termites have one of the most ordered and fascinating of insect societies.

Carnivorous lizard Equally at home on land and in water, the monitor is quick on its feet and an adept swimme

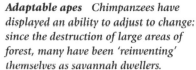

The muckraker *The yellow-billed hornbill, like others of its family, is often seen turning over elephant droppings and snatching up the dung beetles and other insects found there.*

Adaptable apes *Chimpanzees have displayed an ability to adjust to change: since the destruction of large areas of forest, many have been 'reinventing' themselves as savannah dwellers.*

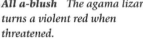

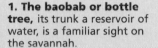

All a-blush *The agama lizard turns a violent red when threatened.*

Barefaced cheek *Descending, bold as you please, to pick over the kills of other predators, the vulture's unfeathered face and neck help protect against contamination and infection.*

Long motherhood
The female white rhino carries her young for 17 months before giving birth to it; mother and calf are then inseparable for the first few years of the young animal's life.

1. **The baobab or bottle tree,** its trunk a reservoir of water, is a familiar sight on the savannah.
2. **The sable antelope** has shapely horns that can grow up to 5 ft (1.5 m).
3. **The pelican** is one of the most efficient of all the fishing birds.
4. **Wildebeest** travel in herds in search of grass and water.
5. **A cheetah** uses a termite mound as a lookout post.
6. **The Nile crocodile** is widespread in sub-Saharan Africa, a predator of surprising speed.
7. **The aardvark's** forepaws are strong enough to break through the termite mound.
8. **The termite's mound** is a warren of passages and cells. The queen lies at its centre.
9. **The spitting cobra** blinds prey with venom, then strikes.
10. **The Thomson's gazelle** has a characteristic black band on its side.
11. **The hippopotamus** is a herbivore, but if it becomes aggressive it is one of Africa's most dangerous animals.
12. **Several flamingo species** are able to coexist because their feeding requirements are different.
13. **The hyena** uses its powerful jaws to break open the carrion bones that the lions disdain to chew.
14. **Vultures** know that scavenging is a waiting game and that patience will be rewarded when the lions finally leave.
15. **The lion** may pose as a mighty hunter, but the lioness does the work.
16. **Giraffes** love the leaves of the acacia: the two are seldom far apart.
17. **The ostrich** is the largest living bird. It can run at up to 50 mph (80 km/h).
18. **The zebra's** stripes act not only as camouflage by breaking up its outline among tall grass, they also confuse a predator trying to single out an individual from the herd.
19. **The weaverbird** makes an elaborate nest by weaving grasses together.
20. **The green mamba** lives in trees and is less deadly than its ground-dwelling cousin, the black mamba.
21. **The elephant** is quite capable of pushing over a tree to reach the foliage.
22. **Grant's gazelle,** the largest species, also has the longest horns.

Amphibious antelope
The sitatunga has adapted to life in marshy country.

On the alert *Ears pricked, a herd of impala interrupt their grazing, ready to turn and flee at the first signal.*

CHAPTER 4

AFRICAN RESOURCES, AFRICAN WAYS

The richest resource of Africa is the continent itself, its varied landscapes, its open spaces, its natural plenty. But the continent does not necessarily yield its treasures lightly. In the remotest parts of the interior, hunter-gatherers still hunt animals where they live, and gather plants where they grow; elsewhere settled villagers must coax a living from what can be an uncooperative earth. The old pastoral ways persist, nomadic tribesmen driving their herds from pasture to pasture, while modern ranchers rear stock on an industrial scale. The old colonial plantations, producing tea, coffee, sisal and sugar cane for export, now provide income for the African economies rather than for European landlords. However, the resource that first drew the colonial powers here – minerals – may yet become the engine that powers modern Africa to economic freedom.

Simple, planked boats, nets and the day's catch – familiar elements in a Lake Kivu fisherman's life.

Living off the land

Huge numbers of the region's inhabitants work on the land, some cultivating their own smallholdings while others are employed on large estates. Both groups make a vital contribution to the regional economy.

Large areas of Southern and East Africa are overwhelmingly agrarian. The statistics speak for themselves: 75 per cent of Madagascans; 80 per cent of Zimbabweans and 90 per cent of Ugandans work on the land. Despite the millions of people it employs, African agriculture is for the most part a small-scale affair, peasant farmers raising vegetables and grain for family use, with little in the way of surplus. In a typical Ugandan village of straw-roofed shacks, the harvest is housed more elaborately than its human producers, kept safe from damp and vermin in little round huts raised up on wooden piles. Cereals such as sorghum and maize are grown, as well as haricot beans, peas and sweet potatoes. What remains after everyone has been fed is traded at the market

Cape cane The temperate coastal regions of South Africa are ideal for both large and small-scale cultivation of sugar cane: the country is one of the largest producers in the world.

Economies of scale *Large-scale wheat cultivation is carried out on these vast fields beneath Mount Kenya.*

in the local town, or sold from stalls on the highway: the money buys necessities such as oil, tools and clothing. A little coffee may be grown for cash – a significant proportion of Uganda's coffee exports are produced in this way. It is a life entirely without luxury, but it has its compensations: austere it may be, but it is stable. The people know that in all essentials they live just as their ancestors did, following the same age-old rhythms of life, safely surrounded by caring kinsfolk. Similar villages exist throughout the region, though there are variations in the types of crops grown. Coconuts are grown on the tropical coasts, while the dry savannah is more suitable for cereals, and Madagascar's irrigated plateaus have been set out like Asian rice paddies. Cassava, a starchy tuber, is also widely grown.

The best traditions

What surprises visitors from Europe and North America is the intensiveness of cultivation and the amount of 'inter-cropping'. Irish travel writer Dervla Murphy was struck by this on a visit to Rwanda: 'You couldn't grow an extra onion between the bananas, sweet potatoes, sorghum, cabbages, cassava, sugar cane, ground-nuts, coffee, beans.' Apart from ensuring a wide variety of products, some for subsistence, some for cash, such varied cultivation max-imises output while putting the least possible strain on the soil.

There have been various unsuccessful attempts in recent times to 'rationalise', introducing what would at first sight appear to be sensible economies of scale. A programme introduced in the 1970s by President Nyerere of Tanzania aimed to revolutionise agriculture and provide piped water, electricity, schools and medical care for rural populations. Brought together into larger, local centres from their scattered *shambas*, the people would be able to enjoy full access to these amenities. A laudable aim, yet as Nyerere himself reflected ruefully: 'You can socialise what is not traditional. The *shamba* can't be socialised.'

Spice island

Spices account for three-quarters of Zanzibar's total export revenues. The great Swahili island port is now having to think hard about alternatives, following a collapse in the value of its products. The past ten years have seen an astonishing tenfold reduction in spice prices, while eastern importers have been economising by going into production on their own.

African corn Maize was brought from the Americas by the Portuguese and is now an important African crop.

The Cape of good wine

South African wines, long shunned by many in the outside world as part of anti-apartheid protests, have been rediscovered. Though the Cape, with its Mediterranean climate, is perfect for the cultivation of vines, the growth of this industry is still in some ways surprising. Neither the Cape Colony's original British rulers, nor the Dutch Boers who were its first main settlers, had any real tradition in growing grapes or making wine. The practice was brought by Protestant Huguenot refugees from France, fleeing the persecution of the Catholic authorities: the first grapes were pressed in 1659. Today, a wide range of grapes are grown, the harvests beginning in January with chardonnay and riesling and going on until April when the cabernet sauvignon grapes are gathered.

The colonial legacy

With an unlimited workforce to enslave, the European colonists were able to set up huge plantations for the production of coffee, tea, tobacco, sugar cane and cotton. These survived the end of colonial rule: the newly independent nations saw the large-scale production and export of these commodities as crucial to economic modernisation. Sadly, with the soaring costs of chemicals and equipment required and the collapse of prices on the international market, the main consequence has been a mountain of foreign debt. The need to keep up the cash flow has, many analysts argue, badly skewed the direction agriculture has taken. Over 98 per cent of Uganda's export revenues come from coffee alone, while Malawi makes 60 per cent of its money from the export of tobacco. A broader base is needed, a larger-scale version of the intercropping that is such a feature of African farming at village level, or the prosperous, mixed production of South Africa's southern provinces. Developed over generations under white rule and underwritten by the country's vast mineral wealth, South African agriculture has never been subject to the fearful scramble to make debt repayments. As a result its farms have been able to achieve the best of both agricultural worlds, combining diversity with high production, growing everything from citrus fruits to sugar cane.

The failure of this and other programmes was partly due to the agricultural assumptions on which they were based. While once it seemed self evident that open fields, large-scale irrigation and tractors would revolutionise African agriculture, the disappointing results have caused agriculturalists to regard the traditional methods more respectfully. So much faith did Zimbabwe invest in the work of its large-scale (and largely white) farmers in the 1980s, that when in 1984 they reported low yields of maize, the government geared up for a crisis, preparing to import enormous supplies at astronomical cost. Only afterwards did it emerge that the country's peasant farmers had been increasing their production in leaps and bounds. Practices that have stood Africa in good stead for so many centuries may, after all, be the way forward.

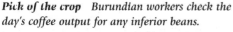

Pick of the crop *Burundian workers check the day's coffee output for any inferior beans.*

Follow the plough *After years of destructive civil war, Mozambicans are again cultivating their land and rebuilding their economy.*

Back in business

Between 1976 and 1986 the tusks of some 200 000 elephants were exported from Burundi: by 1988 only one live elephant was left in the country. In 1989 an international agreement to ban the sale of ivory was reached, but the poachers were never going to submit tamely to the loss of a lucrative trade: extensive ban-busting was soon reported. However, thanks to determined action by governments – and often the intervention of armed forces – elephant populations have grown. In some areas herds are now too large for the savannah environment, so a controversial decision was taken to permit certain countries to resume the ivory trade under strict supervision: Zimbabwe, Botswana and Namibia are now all exporting ivory.

Taking stock

A source of milk, meat and blood, the nomad's herds are the very centre of his world. But larger-scale stock-rearing is of more far-reaching significance, contributing as it does to the economy of the region as a whole.

Tall, dignified and independent, the nomadic Masai tribesman is one of the symbols of Africa. His herd is his wealth, his home, his food and drink – he has learned to draw off draughts of nourishing blood from the flanks of his cattle – and his people have ranged the East African savannah for countless generations. The nomad's flocks partake in the rhythms of the land, migrating just as the wildebeest do: he accompanies them as the egret does the buffalo. He may be more passive in his husbandry than his settled fellow Africans, but he has been more successful in maintaining his autonomy.

In recent times, however, nomads have been under pressure to modernise: their independence has often been taken as an outright affront by progressively minded leaders. Encroachment onto the savannah of large-scale ranching operations, meanwhile, has dramatically reduced the nomads' room to manoeuvre; the fencing off of much of the African interior has had serious consequences for the nomads' herds. Forced into remoter, marginal areas, their lives have become more difficult still, but they have for the most part remained loyal to their ancestral lifestyle.

Today the nomads' traditional ways are being regarded with more respect in a world where climate change and famine are forcing a reassessment of best practice. Though the nomads' small-scale pastoralism cannot begin to match the bulk output of the big new ranches, it weighs, we now see, a lot more lightly on the land. Ready to uproot and move at a moment's notice to where the grazing is, this ancient system is more responsive to the needs of the environment than its modern replacement.

Counting sheep

Yet larger-scale production may have its place in countries attempting to make their way economically in the modern world. In a nation like Namibia, where large areas are too dry for agriculture, ranching has offered a lucrative alternative. The droughts of the 1980s ravaged beef production, so Namibian agriculture has increasingly been concentrated in the raising of karakul sheep. Originally from Uzbekistan, in Central Asia, this breed has taken well to the tussocky pastures of Africa's arid regions, and the rich, black fleeces have become an invaluable export. Namibia now exports 3 million of these a year: they are used in the manufacture of astrakhan, still very much in demand on the international market.

Rationalised ranching *All the modern agriculturalist's equipment and know-how are brought to bear on beef production at this Botswana ranch.*

Barter or big business

On the little farms of the Kalahari margins, bushmen trade their labour for drink and tobacco. Meanwhile in Johannesburg, the businessman works out his tax breaks and pension plan.

Business seems brisk in the little market in Ngorongoro province, Tanzania, the babble of excited women's voices suggesting that some serious haggling is in process. The few lemons, onions and tomatoes spread out on the dusty earth are a meagre basis, the visitor might think, for so much wheeler-dealing. Similar scenes can be found in many other street markets,

Patch and press At the market in Kigali, Rwanda, all kinds of services are offered as well as goods. Here customers can have their clothes mended or ironed.

but the impression of poverty is misleading, as the traders are selling only what is surplus to their requirements; and these women – and their families – expect little in the way of luxuries. It is misleading, too, in the sense that the market is not just a mercantile centre: gossip, information, influence and favours are also traded.

Far from being business innocents, even the poorest Africans are accomplished traders: a fact clearly illustrated by the hawkers beside every highway, the yelling peddlers at every city crossroads. All sorts of goods are offered for sale, from fruit and vegetables to contraband cigarettes; so, too, are services – from photocopying to shoe-shining. Professional scribes provide help, for a small fee, with official documents, filling out forms and writing letters on behalf of the illiterate. The commercial instinct runs so deep in the cultural

character that, even in the prosperous cities of South Africa, this unofficial capitalism still functions in parallel with the official market.

Opening out

What the Ngorongoro street market is for the Tanzanian villager, the seaports are for the region as a whole: doors onto a wider world. Much of the produce is bulky raw materials – coffee, corn, meat and minerals – and almost 90 per cent of exports are sent by sea. Landlocked countries such as Zambia are at a severe disadvantage, especially during the long conflicts in the neighbouring states of Angola and Mozambique: 70 per cent of Zambia's imported supplies are still routed through South Africa. The significance of South Africa cannot be overstated: in many ways it holds the key to the region's economic future. With its multinational companies and busy stock exchange, it may prove a vital bridgehead in the world of international finance for the whole region. In the years of apartheid rule, South Africa arguably exploited this position to maintain a stranglehold on development in the 'frontline states': now, though, it could be a force for prosperity throughout Southern and East Africa.

Market day At Betafo, Madagascar, villagers trade goods and exchange gossip.

Shipping out South Africa's ports are an essential adjunct to the fruit and mining industries and a vital gateway to the rest of the world.

Riches from the ground

A majority of the 2500 minerals known to modern geology are found in Southern Africa. Many are of huge economic value, yet the benefits for ordinary Africans have been largely illusory.

The wives of wealthy nomads in what is now Zimbabwe used to adorn their wrists and ankles with copper hoops, wearing up to 30 lb (14 kg) in weight. For these pastoralist people, however, it wasn't precious metals, but cattle, that were the symbol of wealth and status. Having struggled for generations to find sustenance in the animals they hunted or raised, or the crops they grew, Africans learned the hard way not to set too much store by wealth that could not be eaten.

Fabled reserves

The first European visitors could scarcely believe the Africans' indifference to the wealth they walked upon. From the Middle Ages, stories were told of King Solomon's Mines, the great lode of gold that was thought to exist in the interior of the Dark Continent.

Bearing the brunt
South Africa's mines have traditionally been worked by black migrants from surrounding states.

Panning for gold *Workers in Rwanda's Nyungwe Forest put in back-breaking labour for negligible return.*

Generating tourism *Formed by the dammed Zambezi between Zimbabwe and Zambia, Lake Kariba has proved a big draw for foreign tourists.*

In fact the Biblical king almost certainly acquired his treasures from reserves much nearer home, in the Mediterranean and the Middle East, but the legend, once established, was not so easily dispelled. It is tempting to think that the tale gives a mythologised account of the real city of Great Zimbabwe, whose fame had spread as far afield as India and China, and first brought the Portuguese to Africa.

Buried treasure

South Africa alone is estimated to have 40 per cent of the Earth's gold reserves, while the country's diamond mines have an output of 10 million carats per year. In addition, there are major deposits of uranium, manganese and chromium, as well as large quantities of coal. The South African gold rush began in Transvaal's Witwatersrand in 1886, when a Boer teenager playing by the Orange River saw a peculiar pebble glinting in the water. Within two years gold fever had taken hold. When an 83 carat diamond, the Star of South Africa, was unearthed at Kimberley, a young Englishman named Cecil Rhodes bought out the De Beers diamond mine and built it up into a near monopoly. He then moved in on gold, founding a firm called Consolidated Gold Fields of South Africa. Rich beyond his wildest dreams, Rhodes became more famous as an empire-builder, but his vision of Anglo-Saxon world domination was from the first underwritten by African mineral resources.

As for the Africans themselves, their role has been to provide cheap labour. Migrants streamed into South Africa from the black 'homelands' and the enclave state of Lesotho, as well as from surrounding countries such as Zimbabwe and Mozambique, their lack of any legal status in apartheid South Africa enabling their employers to drive a particularly advantageous bargain over pay and conditions. These have improved since white rule ended, yet the miner's lot still scarcely seems enviable.

Runners up

No other nation can match South Africa's mineral reserves in variety or abundance, though Botswana has rich diamond reserves and Namibia manages to pay for 80 per cent of its imports with exported diamonds and uranium. Once again, however, ordinary Africans do not necessarily benefit from their countries' resources; nor, in a world of fluctuating demand, are their products necessarily

Sorting stones *After neighbouring South Africa, Botswana has the world's richest diamond mines. Here in the capital, Gaborone, women examine and evaluate gemstones.*

A royal stone

The largest diamond ever found, the Cullinan, weighed in at more than 3000 carats – several times the size of the Kohi-Noor. Discovered in South Africa in 1905, the diamond was sold to the government of Transvaal, who offered it to King Edward VII as a gift for his 66th birthday. It was broken up into smaller gems, which were added to the crown jewels. The largest gem, a pear-shaped stone, adorns the royal sceptre.

New products, new markets

With only modest mineral resources, Madagascar has been forced to find what revenues it can elsewhere. It is, for example, the world's number one producer of vanilla. In recent years another lucrative trade has been established: farming prawns, an industry that employs some 3000 people. The prawns are reared in undersea pens, then frozen for the European and Japanese markets.

Antseranana, near the island's northernmost tip, is the centre of a still more remarkable maritime trade: tuna boats come here from as far afield as France and Spain for specialist repairs.

The advanced industrialised nations of Europe, North America and latterly Asia have such a headstart in manufacturing that African countries know that they are for the most part incapable of competing. They therefore continue to concentrate on producing raw materials for export – or on exploiting their unique natural inheritance through the tourist trade. Only South Africa can hope to trade on equal terms with the outside world, its economy buttressed by mineral wealth, and – with the arrival of majority rule – buoyed up by international goodwill.

Sorting sisal *Sisal, for making rope and twine, used to be an important export, but now this plant in Madagascar supplies rug and carpet manufacturers.*

wanted. Zambia has little to show for its supposed copper wealth, for example: with an average per capita income of $500 per annum, Zambians are no better off than their neighbours in Uganda.

Water power

Hemmed in on every side by a rich South Africa, but with no significant mineral deposits to its name, the enclave state of Lesotho would have found itself high and dry, had it not been for its running water. The streams that course down from the Drakensberg have been harnessed for hydroelectric power and channelled into irrigation projects and domestic water supplies for South Africa's cities. Lesotho has not only been able to meet its own energy needs, but to sell on its surplus to South Africa at a handsome profit.

Other countries have followed Lesotho's example. Since 1975 Mozambique has sold some of the energy generated by its Cahora Bassa barrage on the Zambezi, while Zimbabwe and Zambia have shared the power produced by the dam across the Kariba gorge. This project has been doubly successful in that the artificial lake that has built up behind the dam has become a significant tourist attraction in its own right.

Fashioning a future *African countries have tried in various ways to add value to their raw exports: this picture shows a weaving factory in Madagascar.*

Bad news, good news

Famine, flood, drought, debt, poverty, war and AIDS ... Africa's problems seem to go on and on. Yet there are some rays of hope in a region whose peoples are at last being given some of the help that they need to help themselves.

Live issue

Fifteen years after Live Aid, Bob Geldof was back before the public again, speaking up not for charitable donations but for the cancellation of debt. Along with other celebrities, and 12 million signatories to a public petition, he called on the richest countries to write off the debts of the very poorest. In June 1999, the governments of the G8 industrialised countries agreed to take steps to cancel $70 million in interest payments.

Emergency assistance *The genocide in Rwanda in 1994, and the mass exodus that followed, brought a massive response from foreign agencies such as the International Red Cross.*

When cyclone Elline tore through coastal East Africa in February 2000, the accompanying floods devastated what was left of Mozambique – the country's infrastructure had already been largely destroyed by 17 years of civil war. One of the poorest countries in the world, and the most heavily in debt, Mozambique loses 190 000 children a year before they reach the age of five.

Multiple problems

In Namibia and Zambia 20 per cent of the adult population have HIV, the infection which leads to AIDS: for Zimbabwe the figure is 26 per cent. The prevalence of migrant labour in Southern and East Africa – men both married and single leaving home in large numbers and travelling long distances to find work – has helped increase the syndrome's geographical range, while the subservient role of women in traditional societies has made preventative programmes difficult.

Another problem is the crushing burden of debt these countries have carried since, buoyed up by high raw-material prices in the 1970s, they took out loans from Western governments and banks to fund modernisation efforts. The interest payments have become a millstone round the necks of the struggling

economies: money that could be spent on the treatment of AIDS is sent abroad to service debts. Organisations like Oxfam and Cafod are becoming impatient with their role as dispensers of charity. Rather than simply handing out food, workers in the field have preferred to provide assistance with infrastructure projects such as wells and roads, together with training in self-help skills from new agricultural techniques to basic medicine and bookkeeping. Even so, many workers are frustrated to see so many worthwhile projects foundering simply because their host nations are chronically short of funds. If the debt burden were to be lifted, then these countries would be better placed to make progress.

The Jubilee 2000 coalition is an alliance of aid agencies, charities and church groups formed to campaign for a wholesale cancellation of these debts. While it has not succeeded in these aims, it has certainly given the problem a greater profile in the developed world and governments have been forced by public opinion to respond.

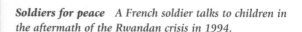

Soldiers for peace *A French soldier talks to children in the aftermath of the Rwandan crisis in 1994.*

An adventure playground in Africa

A new breed of tourists, searching for more than sun, sea and sand, have found opportunities for adventure in Southern and East Africa.

Jules Verne's Phileas Fogg went around the world in 80 days; today, it can be done in a matter of hours. But the feeling that modern communications and high-tech travel have reduced the world in some more detrimental way has led many in the developed countries to yearn for a more romantic past. Hence the tourists who, high above a muddy river in Tanzania's Serengeti National Park, drift silently across the sky in a hot-air balloon. With no noise beyond the swish of silk and the low sound of the balloon's gas flame, this makes the perfect platform from which to observe hippos at peace in their natural environment. It is also the ideal vehicle in which to make a trip back to a more adventurous age, when an unknown Africa was still waiting to be discovered. A more adventurous age, and a more gracious one, as tourists find when they land and are greeted by dinner-jacketed servants inviting them to a champagne breakfast.

White-knuckle ride *White-water rafting down the Zambezi appeals to those seeking exhilaration and excitement.*

A room with a view

No hotel in the world is more dramatically situated than the Victoria Falls Hotel, built in 1904 in the very spray of the thundering waterfall. The ultimate experience is to occupy the luxury Livingstone Suite, as King George VI did when he was a guest in 1946.

Packaging the region

While tourists need romance, Tanzania is crying out for their hard currency. With 700 000 visitors a year to its 54 wildlife parks and nature reserves, Kenya's tourist industry now raises more revenue than does coffee. The experienced native guide has always been indispensable to the African adventure, but now, rather than striding through the grass, he is more likely to be perched up high on the bonnet of a Landrover, giving directions to the driver as he spots the tracks where animals have passed. The challenge for the government is to provide efficient airports, good roads and adequate accommodation, while at the same time being aware that development of the wrong kind could damage the national heritage quickly and irreparably.

Holiday island *Waving palms, shimmering sand and a crystal blue lagoon: the tropical dream is a reality on Mauritius.*

The ultimate tropical paradise, the Seychelles are an irresistible draw for foreign tourists, yet the environment here is as fragile as it is exquisite. Great as the economic rewards may be for the Seychellois, they are all too aware of the catastrophe it would represent for them if the idyll were to end. Hence the decision to limit the number of visitors to 150 000 a year – more could not be sustained without the development of an intrusive and unsightly infrastructure. To maintain the castaway island image, the authorities have banned concrete construction anywhere near the Seychelles' ravishing beaches, and no building is allowed to dominate the islands' trademark swaying coconut palms.

The five-star train

Running through South Africa between Pretoria and Cape Town, the Blue Train offers far more than a railway journey: the luxury on board matches the stunning scenery beyond the windows. Originating in the 1920s, the train was reintroduced after World War II, and attracts travellers from all over the world.

Face to face *Tourists on safari in Kenya make the acquaintance of two utterly fearless young cheetahs.*

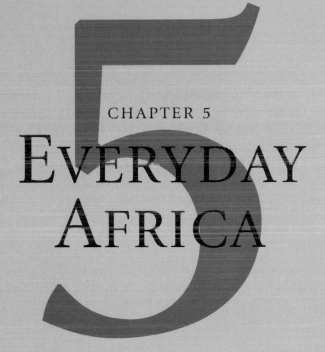

CHAPTER 5

EVERYDAY AFRICA

The region's division into nation-states is the result of the great imperial land-grab by the 19th-century colonial powers. The lines drawn so arbitrarily on the map by European statesmen do not necessarily correspond to the features on the ground, let alone to a human geography whose tribal order had established itself over countless centuries. The failure of colonial administrations to find any sort of accommodation with pre-existing traditions has had profound, and often tragic, implications in the years since independence. Yet, however slowly and painfully, the independent states of the region have been forging their own separate identities, building nationhood from a shared heritage of suffering and pride. Despite a mountain of problems, Southern and East Africa has an impressive heap of blessings as well, and today's inhabitants are growing in their awareness of their unique heritage.

This multicoloured market scene is in Burundi, one of the world's most densely populated countries.

Kenya: land of safaris

Think of East Africa and it is ten to one that a savannah scene will come to mind, all ranging lions and herds of giraffe and antelope. That stereotype is a reality in Kenya, which has one of the richest natural heritages to be found anywhere in the world – yet there is much more to this fascinating country than just its wildlife.

Islamic emblem *The minarets of this mosque in the Indian Ocean port of Mombasa serve as a vivid reminder of Kenya's cosmopolitan Swahili heritage.*

Ernest Hemingway hunted here in the 1930s, in what he called 'The Green Hills of Africa', the American writer finding in Kenya a fit setting for his self-image as a man of action. Other visitors, equally intrepid, have come here on photo safari, preferring to capture their quarry on camera rather than to kill creatures to display as cruel trophies. Times have changed then, but Kenya remains the outsiders' idea of Africa – no other country on the continent evokes such strong associations in the Anglo-Saxon mind. Between the pith-helmeted 'white hunters' on the one hand and the gin-soaked settlers of Happy Valley on the other, our sense of Kenya seems to have stuck fast in the country's colonial period.

A cosmopolitan culture

The black faces removed from that nostalgic picture in fact fought long and hard to assert themselves, the insurrection of the Mau-Mau rumbling on for the best part of a decade before independence was finally achieved in 1963. But Kenya's self-discovery as an African nation replaced one partial view with another, failing as it did to appreciate the full complexity of the hybrid heritage that was East Africa's. At the very heart of the Swahili world, Kenya's coast had historically always been in touch with cultural influences from the East (a contact renewed, ironically, by Britain's importation of Indian labourers in the 19th century). More recently, refugees from Somalia and the Sudan have flooded across the country's northern borders, bringing their own traditions to an already cosmopolitan mixture.

Not that Kenya has been without its own problems: by October 1999 a million people were in urgent need of aid, yet this remains one of the region's more attractive and prosperous countries. Kenyan tea and coffee are famous the world over, and revenue from their export together with income from the country's flourishing tourist industry are helping Kenya to cope with economic and social difficulties that remain only too daunting.

Travelling light *Thrown together quickly from skins stretched over strong branches, these nomads' tents near Lake Turkana, northern Kenya, can be dismantled and moved at a moment's notice.*

Dynasties

Following their pioneering work in the Rift Valley, Louis and Mary Leakey were acclaimed as the founding father and mother of palaeoanthropology. Yet if in the course of their excavations they discovered hominid ancestors for us all, the couple also created their own distinctively East African dynasty. For Richard Leakey, their son, was born in Kenya and decided to stay and make what contribution he could to his homeland. He was long held in suspicion by the country's new establishment. In time, however, his passion and commitment paid off: since 1999 he has had a place in his country's government.

African brew *The mark of a former British colony, Kenya's tea plantations create employment and revenues.*

Tanzania: the schoolmaster's vision

Julius Nyerere, father of modern Tanzania, was known as mwalimu, 'the schoolmaster', in Swahili. Along with a profound respect and understanding of his country's traditions, he had a strong personal sense of what its role should be in the modern world.

Isle of sultans

The legendary founder of Zanzibar was Ali, Sultan of Shiraz, in what is now Iran. One night in 975 he woke up trembling, terrified by a fearful nightmare. A giant rat with teeth of steel was chewing away at the foundations of his royal palace. The vision was frightening enough in itself, but its clear symbolic message was even more alarming: he had to leave his sultanate before it came crashing down around his ears.

So it was that he set to sea with friends and family, and a retinue of trusted servants, on a flotilla of seven little ships. As they sailed southwards, however, a mighty storm blew up and scattered the ships in all directions. Each was wrecked at a different point on the African coast, every spot becoming the site of an Arab city. The greatest of these was Zanzibar, which found fame as the great mercantile metropolis of the Swahili empire.

A rural society Women walk to the market in Marangu. Nyerere's revolution respected the essentially agrarian character of Tanzania.

A spasm of grief gripped Tanzania when Julius Nyerere died on October 14, 1999. The son of a tribal chief, Nyerere had restored to his countrymen a sense of their African identity, while at the same time marking out a way forward. An incorruptible ascetic himself, Nyerere expected the highest standards from those who served him. A lifelong pan-Africanist, he believed all Africans should strive together to solve shared problems and achieve shared aims. But while he succeeded in 1964 in uniting the colonies of Tanganyika with Zanzibar and Pemba in an independent Tanzania, his quest for a wider East African federation failed.

The socialist saint

'Africa is a beggar sitting on a mountain of gold,' said Nyerere. The words will strike a chord with anyone who cares about Black Africa, but whether Nyerere led his countrymen in the right direction has been hotly debated. With its roots partly in Christianity, partly in African tradition, Nyerere's politics of *ujamaa*, 'familyhood', caught his people's imagination. Its message of 'socialism and self-reliance' was stirring, but it was not necessarily popular – or even successful – in its actual application. Nyerere later acknowledged the damage done by his policy of 'villagisation' in the countryside. In theory a way of bringing amenities to the rural areas, in practice it uprooted communities and alienated farming folk from their land. Yet even as their founder's utopian vision ended in failure, Tanzanians remained loyal to the man, if not to his revolution. The elections of 1980 may have ended in Nyerere's supporters in government being swept away, but the *mwalimu* himself was elected as president with 95 per cent of the popular vote.

Thirty years on, Tanzania is one of the poorest countries on the planet with little to show for Nyerere's legacy. Yet, who knows? In future generations it is easy enough to imagine this prophet being honoured as the man who gave Africans back their self-respect.

Uganda: beacon of hope

After 20 years of savage oppression, Ugandans have enjoyed more than a decade of peace: their president has even restored a traditional monarchy. The land once brought to its economic knees and terrorised by the dictators Idi Amin and Milton Obote is now widely taken as a model for other states.

A blaze of colour *Here in Kasese market the textiles are a feast for the eye.*

The 'pearl of Africa', Sir Winston Churchill called it – but what should have been Uganda's first decades of freedom were marred by two of the undisputed monsters of modern African history. When King Mutesa II was replaced as head of state by his prime minister, Milton Obote, in 1966, the way was opened for more than 20 years of bloodshed and civil conflict. In 1971 Obote was overthrown by Colonel Idi Amin. More than 300 000 Ugandans were killed by Amin's dictatorship in the 1970s; 100 000 more followed after Obote's regime was restored in 1980. The death toll, grim as it is, does not tell anything like the whole story: the other great casualty of the dictatorships was Uganda's economy.

Yoweri Museveni's leftist insurrection, when it finally prevailed in 1985, did so in a country in ruins, its defeated population braced for another round of bloodletting. In the event, Museveni has proved a pragmatic and humane leader; his new Uganda – for all its continuing economic and social problems – is a beacon of real hope in a troubled region. While not abandoning his socialist beliefs – or, on the other hand, entirely embracing democratic ways where his own position is concerned – Museveni has pro-

moted what he calls 'non-party democracy'. Politicians must stand, he says, on their own character and record, not on any party platform – a sensible enough way of preventing the corrupt party machines that have vitiated so many supposed 'democracies' in sub-Saharan Africa. The transforming nature of Museveni's mild-mannered revolution was underlined when in 1993 he reinstated the monarchy overthrown by Obote three decades earlier: Mutesa's son Mutebi II has reigned as constitutional monarch ever since.

Uganda remains poor and disadvantaged, but its most acute difficulties now originate beyond its borders. The overspill of problems from the Sudanese civil war and famine have raised tensions in the north, while the Rwandan conflict has impinged on the south-western corner. Nevertheless, Ugandans are beginning to look forward to the future with comparative confidence.

Organic coffee

In the great black cloud of Uganda's years of dictatorship an unexpected silver lining appeared, resulting from the virtual collapse of the economy and infrastructure in the country. Such was the prevailing chaos that neither insecticides nor weedkillers were available, nor the chemical fertilisers on which Ugandan farmers had been learning to rely. The two-thirds of the population who made their living from growing coffee were forced by the shortages into using what we now extol as 'organic' methods. This was as true of the big plantations as it was of the small producers: chemicals were simply unavailable. Ugandan growers found they had trained themselves into 'good practice' when the vogue for organic produce took off in the 1990s.

City scene *After ten years of calm, residents of Kampala, Uganda's capital, are getting used to finding good news in the paper.*

Rwanda and Burundi: Africa's breaking heart

Hemmed in on one side by thick forest, on the other by dry savannah, Rwanda and Burundi together make a pocket of green fertility. Yet, densely populated as they are, they became a pressure cooker in which ethnic tensions boiled over into horrific violence.

Green city *Bujumbura, the capital of Burundi, is surprisingly leafy.*

Kigali and Bujumbura

Rwanda is 'the land of a thousand hills', of which Kigali is the most famous, for it is on this height that the country's capital was built and from which it takes its name. Today Kigali sprawls across several adjacent hills, the newer suburbs extending down into leafy valleys, the grand hotels and mansions of colonial times occupying the tops like defensive citadels. But the enemy they were designed to withstand was not human but bacterial: when the city was founded in 1908, malaria was rife in the valleys below.

The Burundian capital, Bujumbura, is a city of contrasts, between the grandeur of wide colonial avenues and the squalid shantytowns. With around 300 000 inhabitants, it is the country's only city of any size, the built-up area extending down to the shores of Lake Tanganyika. Though most of its people are Christian or animist, Bujumbura is dominated by its mosque.

The European powers carved up Africa without regard for ethnic divisions. The tiny states of Rwanda and Burundi have more geographical integrity than most, but it was here in 1994 that ethnic tensions boiled over into genocide, and at least half a million Tutsi were killed by the majority Hutu community. Millions more were driven into exile, causing resentments that seem set to simmer on for the foreseeable future.

Ancient enmities

The Hutu and Tutsi resemble one another closely in ethnic make-up, religion and language: it is their lifestyles that make them enemies. While the Hutu have always been settled farmers, the Tutsi have been herdsmen: two groups whose interests often came into conflict. Ironically, neither was native to the area: the original Twa pygmies found themselves increasingly marginalised into the wooded uplands as the arriving Hutu took more and more open land into cultivation some 2000 years ago. The Tutsi were comparative latecomers in the 16th century. In such a confined area, the two groups sparred, not only over land but over water resources. Even so, enmities between them might have been contained if the Belgian colonists had not sought to divide and rule their African subjects by systematically favouring the Tutsi minority.

Rich ground *Rwanda's fertile soil and tropical climate encourages cultivation.*

Lake Kivu *The fishermen of Lake Kivu, Rwanda, have followed the same lifestyle for centuries.*

A cauldron uncovered

Colonial rule kept a lid on the conflict: once that was removed, violence erupted, with thousands of Tutsi expelled from Hutu-ruled Rwanda in the 1960s. Establishing guerrilla bands in neighbouring countries, the Tutsi made raids on Hutu settlements. In Burundi, meanwhile, the Tutsi minority had contrived to take hold of the levers of state power, brutally putting down any attempt at rebellion by the Hutu. One such uprising in 1972 was punished by a massacre of 100 000 Hutu men, women and children. The scenes that appeared on our television screens in the 1990s seemed to come out of the blue, but in fact had a long and cruel incubation.

Malawi: at a new dawn

Geography – the country is landlocked – and recent history have combined to keep Malawi in an economic and political backwater. However, since the former dictator Hastings Banda was deposed in 1994, the country has started to establish itself in a wider world.

The house that NGoma built

Just outside Rumphi, in the north of Malawi, stands the house that NGoma built: bric-à-brac, car parts, old brass beds, planks and panels of all shapes and sizes make up this extraordinary palace, a monument to the serendipitous spirit of human ingenuity. The builder of this fantastic structure sits outside all day, enjoying the astonishment of passersby: he proudly shows off the postcards sent by previous visitors from many different countries. Nothing less like Banda's stable but joyless national creation could be imagined. In what has long been an introverted Malawi, NGoma looks outward to a wider world; in a land of make-do-and-mend, he has cobbled together a real architectural miracle.

The lake, life of Malawi The waters of Lake Malawi account for a quarter of the country's total territory: in economic importance, it looms even larger.

At the foot of an ancient baobab, fish lie drying on enormous rush mats. Nearby the pale, wrinkled waters of Lake Malawi stretch away to infinity. On the hillsides above are the signs of intensive cultivation: coffee, rice and cotton are all grown here. It is a pleasing, picturesque scene, yet nobody could mistake it for a prosperous one: this little, landlocked country must struggle hard to make its living. Squeezed between Zambia, Mozambique and Tanzania, Malawi – once the British colony of Nyasaland – has no mineral wealth to underwrite its agricultural economy. Of its 11 million people, 90 per cent live in the rural areas, along the shores of the lake or on the high plateaus.

Banda's repressive regime

Malawi as it is today is very much the creation of one man, its dictator for 28 years, Dr Hastings Banda. His highly individual approach to government only intensified his country's isolation. Scorning the pan-Africanism of his neighbour Julius Nyerere – and indeed the socialist sympathies of just about all the other Black African leaders – Banda's country quickly turned its back on the rest of the region. Refusing to condemn the white minority regimes of South Africa and Rhodesia, Banda seemed to be running a colonial country in all but name. Far from nationalising the big private plantations, he encouraged foreign owners to expand, forcing peasant farmers into ever-smaller plots in more marginal areas. To the poor themselves he urged hard work and contentment with the little that they had.

History will have to judge a leader whose policies left his people in the same grinding poverty in which he had found them – yet spared them the overwhelming debt and despair of so many other African societies. Banda's repressive rule gave Malawians very little in the way of political or intellectual freedom, yet the region's left-wing regimes have not necessarily distinguished themselves by their broad-minded liberalism. Since 1994 a newly democratised Malawi has taken its first small steps towards development.

A busy capital The bustling market in Lilongwe, capital of Malawi, belies the general torpor of a land that has no modern economy.

Mozambique: at peace again

From the raids of the Arab slavers to the fallout of the Cold War, the gently shelving plains of Mozambique have been the theatre for fearful conflicts: though peace has returned, the wounds of war have yet to heal.

A country under arms *Mozambique remains a militarised country, but a few years ago these young boys would have been bearing weapons themselves.*

Eight years after the first Portuguese ship landed in 1490, Vasco de Gama stopped off in Mozambique on his circumnavigation of the globe. Meeting the local Mwene Matapa chief, he gave him a pair of trousers, a shirt and a bonnet, receiving in return a chicken and a little grain. This simple exchange of gifts set the tone for the Portuguese presence in the country for several centuries: like the Arabs before them, they came not as settlers but as traders – wide rivers provided corridors to the gold and ivory of Great Zimbabwe in the interior. The Portuguese settlers built an impressive colonial capital, Maputo, but it was more a declaration of ownership than anything else: Mozambique's villagers maintained their traditional ways to the extent of still worshipping their ancestors.

From Marxism to constitutional government

Portuguese rule sat lightly on the country, so the advent of a Marxist modernity came as a painful shock. Finding no sympathy for its struggle among the Western powers, the Mozambiquan independence movement of the 1970s turned to the Soviet Union for help: it was given not only arms, but an ideology. The Mozambique Liberation Front, or Frelimo, won independence in 1975 and vowed allegiance to Marxist-Leninist ideology. A less-sensitive version of Tanzania's 'villagisation' antagonised the rural population, while in the towns anyone whose thoughts or lifestyle did not meet socialist norms was sent to one of the large-scale 're-education' camps springing up in outlying areas.

Not surprisingly, the Mozambique National Resistance (Renamo) enjoyed a groundswell of support and was helped by the Soviet Union's Cold War enemies. The civil war that resulted dragged

Colonial legacy *The station in Maputo recalls Portuguese rule.*

on for 17 miserable years, causing untold loss of life and marooning Mozambique in economic stagnation. There were no winners, though the stalemate ended in 1992 when each side agreed to recognise the outcome of multiparty elections. Now a constitutional government is headed by President Joaquim Chissano. As far as economic development is concerned, Mozambique has a lot of catching up to do, made all the more difficult by the devastating floods which have hit this low-lying country in recent years.

Power sharing

Having fought bloodily for so many years, the Frelimo ruling party and Renamo opposition confronted each other again when Mozambique went to the polls in December 1999. A massive turnout voted for continuity and peace, returning Frelimo by a decisive majority. Renamo contested the result, alleging electoral fraud, but international observers endorsed Frelimo's victory. The winning party has come under intense pressure both at home and abroad to find some sort of political accommodation with its old enemy and prevent another descent into civil war.

Old and new *Traditional fishermen against the backdrop of modern Maputo.*

Zambia: copper country

Copper is king in Zambia, accounting for 90 per cent of the country's export revenues. But what promised to be a source of prosperity has instead been the cause of anxiety since the collapse of the world copper price.

Zambia has 73 different African ethnic groups among its population. The oldest of these are comparative latecomers to the country, the Bemba and the Lozi arriving in the 14th and 15th centuries from what are now the Democratic Republic of the Congo and Angola respectively. Even then the population remained unsettled, as the farmers were nomadic, moving on every few years. They farmed by chopping down trees and burning the branches for enriching ash, then planting millet and other crops in the fertile soil. After several seasons the soil was depleted and it was time for the farmers to relocate their village elsewhere and start again.

Boom and bust

Cecil Rhodes first opened up the country for European-style development: what is now called Zambia once formed part of his personal fiefdom, 'Northern Rhodesia'. His great dream of a railway from the Cape to Cairo ran out of steam

Kuomboka's canoe

Though many Zambians live in cities, uprooted from their family traditions, certain rural communities have managed to maintain a strong identity. The Lozi take particular pride in a heritage that they celebrate annually in the ceremony of Kuomboka. At the start of the rainy season, the 'king' is borne down the Zambezi to his summer palace, paddled by 100 men in his royal canoe, the *nalikwanda*. Amid shouting and drumming, he

makes the six-hour journey wearing the traditional costume of the Lozi chieftain. Once there, he exchanges one set of finery for another, changing into the dress uniform of a Royal Navy admiral, given to his grandfather by King Edward VII in 1902.

here, but the trains came just far enough to provide an export route for a landlocked country. The start of large-scale mining in the late 19th century brought a flood of migrants, but the cycles of boom and bust meant that few felt securely settled.

The countryside could not compete with the wages in the mines. Thousands flocked to the shantytowns around the Copper Belt cities, especially Lusaka, now the nation's capital. The possession of this great resource seemed to promise Zambia a glowing future when it won its independence in 1964, yet things have not turned out as well as expected. The concentration on copper over so many years had had the effect of narrowing the Zambian economoic mind: little effort has been made, for example, to develop the country's enormous potential for tourism. Attempts to attract investment to the mineral extraction industries through privatisation programmes have, meanwhile, been hampered by bureaucracy and corruption. What was supposed to be Zambia's great national asset could yet end up dragging the whole country down.

Water carriers Frequent trips to a standpipe are a familiar part of city life for Zambia's children.

Rail artery At Lusaka station goods trains far outnumber passenger services. Without this link to the coast, the Zambian economy would wither.

A contested country These women work the land for a white proprietor, yet should they be farming it on their own account? The question goes right to the heart of Zimbabwe's problems. The contribution made by such big estates is vital to the economic life of the country, yet some claim that it helps perpetuate poverty and powerlessness among Zimbabwe's blacks.

Zimbabwe: an unresolved issue looms large

Chain of command White boss, black worker: the old hierarchy remains more or less intact – but does it actually benefit Zimbabwe as a whole?

Having come for ivory and precious minerals, Rhodesia's white settlers stayed to work the land. Now their future hangs in the balance as the country's government backs land seizures by militant black groups. The outcome is likely to have repercussions for years to come.

High on a hill not far from Masvingo, a mighty citadel stands. Even in its ruined silence, it speaks of a rich and glorious history. To the first white explorers who came to Great Zimbabwe, the implication was clear: no African people could possibly have built such a splendid civilisation. The generation of black intellectuals fighting for independence in the years of white minority rule drew the opposite conclusion, and took the name Zimbabwe, 'place of stones', for their newly independent country.

Unresolved questions

The questions 'Who really built Zimbabwe?' and 'Who really owns its land?' have still to be resolved, 20 years after the country gained independence. The white minority regime of Ian Smith managed to stay in place until 1980, thanks to support from outside powers fearing black revolution in South Africa and communist dominance in the region as a whole. Rhodesia's white farmers, having admittedly been awarded the country's choicest tracts of land, made strenuous efforts over generations to bring it to its full potential. Hence the confusion of a man like Ian Lewis, who farms 2000 acres (1000 ha) south-west of Harare, at the suggestion that, as a white man, he is somehow less than completely Zimbabwean. Far from being an opportunist, he

Shadows lengthen Workers in Bulawayo, Zimbabwe's second city, set out for home.

feels rooted in what to him might just as well be ancestral lands. Indeed, the victorious President Robert Mugabe had specifically called on the country's biggest farmers to stay and help build a nation.

Yet the Africans' anger at having been driven off the best land in their own country impelled their struggle for independence in the 1960s and 70s. The tension between the two groups has arguably impeded political and economic progress ever since: Mugabe himself has been making populist anti-white pronouncements in recent years. Surrounded by its four giant neighbours, Zimbabwe could readily enough be the peaceful, prosperous 'Switzerland of Africa' that some have imagined it. But until it resolves such basic questions, and finds an identity that all, black and white, can accept, it seems doomed to limp along, its true possibilities unrealised.

Trunk tax

Among its many glories Zimbabwe may boast the largest population of elephants in Africa. So numerous are they, that in many areas they have become a nuisance. Tired of seeing their crops and fences trampled, the local people are unsentimental in their attitude towards elephants. Under a government programme, introduced in 1989, each elephant is regarded as the property of the nearest village, to whose inhabitants the successful hunter must pay a tariff for each one shot. Not only that, but the meat of the animal now reverts by law to the local people.

Jewels of Botswana

Diamonds and livestock have both contributed to the fortunes of Botswana. Thanks to the enlightened rule of successive governments, the country has become a model of development for others in the region.

Lucky strike *Diamonds have become the principal resource of an independent Botswana.*

Mpule Kwelagobe *Campaigner in the fight against AIDS.*

In 1925, aged four, Seretse Khama inherited the crown from his father Sekgoma. Too young to succeed to his father's office, he was sent to London for his schooling. When Seretse married a young Englishwoman in 1948, the event sent shockwaves through what was then the British colony of Bechuanaland. His accession to his father's throne the following year later rocked the region as a whole, an affront in particular to South Africa, which had just instituted its apartheid system.

An unconventional country

Though his people fully supported him, Seretse was now sent into a second exile, this time by the British authorities. His presence in Africa was considered too provocative in an area whose white rulers were beginning to feel the pressure for change. But the young king never lost faith in his country or his people, nor did their love for him abate: throughout the late

1950s and early 60s he continued his campaign for a multiparty, non-racial democracy. In 1966 he became the first president of the independent Republic of Botswana. Scorning to depend on his inherited rank, the king ran for office on the basis of his political platform, yet he still saw a role for the old chiefs in the new republic: his dream was of a Botswana that brought together the best of both tradition and modernity.

Since then, the country has stood out in Southern and East Africa as a model of peaceful politics and consensual development. Its chief asset has been its leaders, a succession of moderate men of integrity and calibre. Botswana also had a stroke of luck when a rich seam of diamonds was discovered shortly after independence. This precious resource has been the basis for a balanced programme of economic modernisation, of which all Botswanans have been beneficiaries.

In the spirit of Seretse's vision, modern mineral wealth has been used to set traditional occupations, such as cattle rearing, on a firmer footing.

Capitalist capital *Barclays Bank and Finance Ministry buildings in Gaborone.*

An ambassador of hope

Winner of the Miss Universe title for 1999, Mpule Kwelagobe immediately raised the profile of a country that many TV viewers had barely heard of. Since then, she has done far more to compel their attention. In February 2000 it was announced that Mpule had been given an altogether more serious international role – as a 'Goodwill Ambassador' for the United Nations Population Fund. Expressing pride and pleasure at having her aboard, the fund's executive director Dr Nafis Sadik said: 'Mpule can be a tremendous force for change … she is a wonderful role model for women in Southern Africa and elsewhere.' Mpule sees her main task as raising awareness of AIDS in Africa and elsewhere, and attracting public interest in and support for programmes of prevention.

Namibia: where the deserts are full of promise

With some of the most haunting scenery in Africa, Namibia has been endowed with a wealth of natural beauty, but even greater riches lie hidden deep in the earth.

Old world   These Herero women wear clothes modelled on those of protestant missionaries' wives.

Sparse pasture   Bleak as it may appear, the Kaokoland in north-east Namibia affords sufficient grazing for the herds of the Himba – though these nomads have to keep moving in search of new pastures.

A culture submerged

In a dry country like Namibia, water resources are clearly vital – but how far should the authorities go to secure them, and at what price? The proposed Epupa Dam in Kaokoland in the far north-east will place an impassable barrier across an ancestral right of way. The threatened valley lies on one of the traditional droving trails of the Himba. Their nomadic way of life is already under attack from the various pressures of modernity, many young Himba moving to the cities in search of work, but will its passing impoverish Namibian culture in the long run? The abundance of water Epupa offers is obviously a tempting prospect for the government, but there may well be hidden consequences and a human price to be paid.

With fewer than 2 million inhabitants, Namibia belongs to nature. In the east lies the Kalahari, a semiarid land of sand and thorny scrub; on the Atlantic coast, the Namib Desert is one of the driest, harshest environments anywhere on Earth. Despite its barrenness, Namibia seethes with unexpected life: even the driest zones have highly specialised flora and fauna. In the northern savannah animals take the scarcity of water in their stride: lions, leopards, elephants, rhinos, giraffes, zebras, ostriches and many types of antelope are all found here. In recent years Namibia's natural beauty and wildlife has encouraged a growing tourist industry.

A small town in Germany

Formerly the German colony of South West Africa, Namibia was administered from 1920 by South Africa. In 1966 the UN voted to end South Africa's mandate, but South Africa refused to give up control. Namibia was the last country in Africa to win its independence when a long and hard-fought guerrilla war came to an end in 1990. The German influence remains: there is a Bavarian air about the architecture in the capital, Windhoek, whose public buildings were built by settlers at the beginning of the 20th century. But life at street level is emphatically African, with Bushmen and

Ovambos cheerfully rubbing shoulders with white Afrikaners and Rehobothers, the children of mixed marriages between white settlers and native Nama.

Namibia's main source of wealth is cattle-rearing, which makes good use of the vast empty areas of marginal land. Meat is an important export, but even more valuable to the overall economy is the production of diamonds and other minerals. Gold, copper and natural gas are found in the north, with uranium, tin and tungsten occurring in more central areas, while the waves that lash the southern desert coasts often turn up diamonds. Fish, which shoal in their millions in the cold Benguela Current just offshore, are another important commodity for a country with far more natural resources than may be immediately apparent.

Signs of the past   Modern Windhoek, Namibia's capital, has street signs in German and Afrikaans.

South Africa: seeking a happy ending

After the nightmare of the apartheid years came the euphoria of freedom. South Africa is now the model for a multicultural future, but the country still faces many problems, and though all races are now equal in law, economic equality remains a distant goal.

Contrast *Elegance and abject poverty exist side by side in contemporary Soweto.*

South Africa is a land of beauty and riches: 'A World in One Country', boasts the South African tourist board. From the thundering mines of the Rand to the quiet tranquillity of the Kruger National Park; from the rolling grasslands of the veldt to the pounding breakers of the Indian Ocean, this is first and foremost a land of variety – both in its many different peoples and in its diverse landscapes. But what the tourist office does not mention is that South Africa is also a land of multifarious problems, its exhilarating success story dogged by unemployment and poverty, crime and AIDS. Apartheid may have been swept triumphantly away, but bleak townships like Soweto still survive, economic segregation effectively at work in the new society.

Floral display *In August the countryside of Namaqualand in western South Africa is covered by a carpet of flowers.*

Sea, sand and city *Durban, on the east coast, is one of South Africa's leading ports.*

Diverse we stand

Few countries have been so badly wounded by their recent history as South Africa, yet not many places have the rich resources – not least demographic ones – it has at its disposal. The doctrine of 'separate development' could hardly have been more alien to the life of a country that was first established by British sailors, then settled by a wave of Dutch farming people. As the economic attraction of Cape Colony grew, Bantu and Bushmen were joined by black immigrants from elsewhere in Southern Africa, their numbers swelled by 'coloured' labourers brought in from the Asian subcontinent. The challenge that faces South Africa today is to transmute violently destructive interracial tensions into a more constructive and creative multiracial energy.

Bad habits

The abolition of apartheid did not banish injustice overnight; neither did the election of Nelson Mandela in 1994 assure instant equality. In some parts of South Africa very little appears to have changed. Throughout large areas of rural Transvaal and Natal, for instance, one could be forgiven for thinking that apartheid remained in force, so little have the realities of life altered in impoverished black villages and on white-owned farms. Even where there has been a real attempt to put majority rule into practice, its course has by no means always run smoothly: the precedents and practices of several generations are, after all, at issue.

The barbecue people

When archaeologists come to unearth the civilisation of the white South African suburbs, a thousand years from now, in all probability they will call its inhabitants the 'barbecue people'. Go into any supermarket in the country and you will see shelf after groaning shelf stacked with all the assorted paraphernalia needed for what is called the *braai*, from the Afrikaans word *braaisvleis*. Great paper sacks of charcoal, special firelighters, juicy steaks – indeed everything required for this most important of weekend rituals. As family, friends and neighbours gather round, the paterfamilias-priest makes offerings at his glowing garden altar: the dried, minced meat of *biltong*, the spicy *boerewors* sausages, and – near the Cape – the finest lobster.

A long road

Every improvement in conditions for the blacks has meant a commensurate weakening of white privilege – if not real, then at least perceived – and the majority government has had to proceed with the utmost sensitivity. The phrase 'the first' keeps recurring: the first black boss; the first coloured firm; the first black graduate of this or that prestigious 'White' university. Such arresting headlines apart, progress for the vast majority has been slow and changes have not been universally welcomed. While many blacks grow increasingly impatient with what seems to them a snail's pace of change, white South Africans feel resentment at what they see as a system of unjust and arbitrary 'reverse discrimination'. Disappointed expectations among young blacks have given rise to a wave of violent crime, which has only heightened white South Africans' sense of vulnerability. Not surprisingly, there is some nostalgia for the stark certainties of apartheid – not to mention the material benefits it brought the ruling races. South Africa has a long road to travel before such resentments are overcome and the nation's races can live side by side in true equality and trust.

Zulu traditions *The descendants of Shaka may be posing for tourists, but their independence should never be underestimated. This proud people has been a strong, if sometimes unpredictable, force in South Africa's modern history.*

An economic giant

As it sets out along that road, South Africa starts with certain advantages: few countries can match its mineral wealth or infrastructure. South Africa's mines and factories, its farms and vineyards, are served by a superb network of roads and railways; its seaports and telecommunications are the best in the continent. If it can only find a way of resolving its differences, South Africa stands poised to assume the status of a regional superpower. Leading both by authority and by example, the country could really begin to justify the ecstatic praise that has been heaped upon it by an admiring world.

Sharing *Two colours, one bench: a simple sign of South Africa's future.*

The flying witchdoctor

Perhaps South Africa's most famous doctor, Sosobala Mbatha charges more than $300 for a consultation and flies from place to place in his own helicopter. Yet Sosobala is no conventionally trained surgeon, but a *sangoma*, a traditional healer, and the contents of his medicine, or *muti*, are strictly secret. Around 85 per cent of black South Africans are thought to consult *sangomas* – often in conjunction with visits to more orthodox clinics. The inability of hospitals to fund the expensive treatments needed to deal effectively with the current AIDS pandemic has strengthened the hand of the country's 300 000 plus traditional healers. But while some are clearly charlatans, many others play a positive role. Even medical officials concede that these healers are uniquely placed to bring to many of the country's poorest people the all-important message that, where AIDS is concerned, prevention is always better than cure.

Enclave kingdoms: Lesotho and Swaziland

Dwarfed though they are by South Africa, which surrounds them, Lesotho and Swaziland have their own strong sense of identity, jealously guarded through a hundred years and more.

Pony power *Ponies are often the best way to get around in rural Lesotho.*

Lesotho's cool climate, a rarity in Africa, is the result of its lofty elevation on a mountain ridge, 3300 ft (1000 m) at its lowest level, rising to a height of 10 000 ft (3000 m). This is a country best traversed on horseback, as King Moshoeshoe I discovered when the British introduced him to riding in 1830. The pony is still the vehicle of choice for Lesotho's rural population.

The Basutoland bargain

Geographically, climatically and culturally, Lesotho is separate from South Africa, but these factors alone would never have assured its independence. The little kingdom of the Sotho people was able to maintain its integrity thanks to a deal struck in 1889 between the British, the settlers and the native chiefs of what was then called Basutoland. The deal proved enduring, though the independence it brought was not necessarily very meaningful: completely surrounded, Lesotho had no alternative but to reach accommodations with apartheid South Africa. Economically, too, Lesotho has been compelled to deal with the country that encloses it: the young men still stream westwards each year to work in the mines.

The Swazi alternative

The smallest state in Africa, Swaziland has an astonishing variety of scenery, from open savannah to tropical rain forest. Like Lesotho, its independence is the result of a three-cornered agreement, in this case made in 1890. Though not entirely enclosed by South Africa, Swaziland's border with Mozambique to the north-east was, through 17 years of civil war, a frontier on an inferno. Like Lesotho, Swaziland has had no option but to find a way of getting along in the shadow of South Africa. But as South Africa shook off the chains of apartheid, Swaziland came into its own, its young king, Mswati III, trying hard to balance tradition with modernity. His most important ceremonial function is to give his formal blessing to the harvest. At the annual festival of Incwala, after three days of festivities, the king emerges from his palace to perform a ritual dance before his assembled people. Then he takes a bite of food, giving the signal for the feasting to begin.

Stone-built dwellings *In the cool climate of Lesotho construction in stone is the norm.*

Mswati and Michael

To help Swaziland's tourist industry, King Mswati III has taken on many roles, from launching conservation projects to heading deputations to the European Investment Bank. But none of these activities seemed as strange as his meeting with the American pop star Michael Jackson in September 2000. The encounter between these two colourful characters took place in Disneyland, California, to discuss a proposed African theme park. Part of a billion-dollar Millennium Project, the park, outside the town of Manzini, is the focus of a wider scheme that aims to make the country's unique cultural and historical heritage an attraction for tourists and investors.

Swazi scene *The central plateau of Swaziland is rugged, but this small kingdom has a diversity of landscapes.*

Madagascar, a place apart

Ecologically, Madagascar is a law unto itself: a land of lemurs, civets and zebus, the island is noted also for its richly exotic flora. But most individualistic of all, perhaps, are the Madagascan people – despite the island's cultural ties with Indonesia.

Obstinately idiosyncratic, Madagascar has resisted all attempts at rationalisation since the French established a colony there in 1896. Independence from colonial rule was won in 1960 when the country became the Malagasy Republic, but following a referendum on the constitution in 1975 a military socialist government came to power, renaming the country again as the Democratic Republic of Madagascar. The philosophy of collective ownership did not fit well with so strong-minded a people, however, and by 1986 the government was forced to throw itself on the mercy of the International Monetary Fund.

Staple diet *Rice is the basic foodstuff of the Madagascans.*

The Marxist market

The IMF recommended wholesale liberalisation of the economy, which Madagascar interpreted with characteristic waywardness. But for the people the change was not fast enough, and in 1991 they deomonstrated on the streets of the capital, Antananarivo, to demand true democracy. Today the elected government proclaims the island a humanist, ecologist state, with the aims of preserving both biodiversity and national independence. Critics of both left and right accuse it of betraying their various visions, and the fact remains that many thousands of Madagascans are now living in squalid shantytowns, often scavenging from rubbish dumps or sewage outflows. More than 2500 cases of plague were reported in 1997. The ecology, too, has been feeling the pinch, large areas of land being damaged by deforestation and consequent erosion. The government can claim some success for its clampdown on traditional 'slash and burn' cultivation – though, ironically, this has been perhaps the most unpopular of its policies.

Fading style *Houses in Antananarivo recall colonial days.*

From vanilla to seafood and sapphires

There are bright spots on Madagascar's horizon, however. When the market for vanilla and then for coffee collapsed, a wholesale effort was made to start producing prawns in coastal fish farms. The industry now exports 75 000 tons a year. And this success looks set to be topped by the discovery of sapphires in the south-west of the island.

A tradition in flames

The Merina monarchy ended in 1896, when French invaders took over the royal palace and deposed the queen. The house of Merina had taken advantage of European backing to establish power over the island as a whole, so there was a certain rough justice in its coming to this end. The queen's palace continued to dominate the skyline of Antananarivo for 100 years, but the sovereigns themselves were unmourned and unremembered. Then, on the night of November 6, 1995, the palace went up in flames, and many Madagascans were shocked. The event apparently stirred ancestral memories of what may not have been a better, but was surely a prouder time, when the monarchy led a unified Madagascar onto the international stage.

Morning chore *Before they go off to school, these children must catch fish for their families in a bow-net made of reeds.*

The Comoros: a disunited archipelago

Volcanic activity brought the Comoros into being, and the islands have seen more than their share of political upheaval, too. Now the foreign powers have gone, the Comorans must find a way of working together.

Mask of beauty

If time seems to have stood still in the Comoros, so does the ageing process, thanks to the marvellous properties of a face cream that the women use. Called *msindanu*, its origins are lost in mystery and myth, but it is basically a blend of ground-up coral and sandalwood. Rubbed well into the face, it acts as an effective sun-screen, though traditionalists like to hint at more magical properties.

In the distance you can see the great oil tankers making their way down the Mozambique Channel, yet few big ships ever bother to call in here. For the fishermen of the Comoros, the wooden canoe is the rule, an appropriately traditional vessel for an ancient lifestyle. These are the waters that produced the coelacanth, a forgotten fish that brought some forgotten islands to the world's attention. The moment soon passed, however, and the Comoros slumber on once more in the cooling shade and heavy scent of their ilang-ilang trees. It may seem that nothing ever happens here, but in recent years the islands' calm has been shattered by a series of diplomatic incidents and violent coups.

Separate sisters

The Comoros islands do not embrace change easily, remaining tightly tied, even today, to their one-time colonial masters in France. After the archipelago officially gained its independence in 1975, the people of Mayotte voted to become a French 'territorial collectivity'. The rump-republic that remained was the stage for a long series of violent coups stretching through to the mid-1990s. These were followed by the secession of two of the three main islands, Nzwani and Mwali. Their inhabitants, having long cast wistful glances at the peace and prosperity prevailing in Mayotte, finally broke loose from the Grand Comoro-based republic in 1997. While Mwali, the smaller island, was quickly regained by Comoran government forces, the resentments continue to this day. As for Nzwani, it successfully

Under the volcano *Moroni, capital of the Comoros, is situated on Njazidja, at the foot of Mount Karthala, the volcanic summit of the island.*

repelled an attempted landing by government forces and remains obstinately unconquered. In the absence of international recognition, the island has an inconclusive, semi-detached status – yet the Comoran Republic is compromised in its turn, seeming incomplete, a half-formed nation. To the outsider, the Comoros seem to belong together, sharing a history, language, religion and culture. But until its peoples can find a way forward together, the troubles seem set to continue.

Mayotte: opting for dependence

The special status of Mayotte has complicated Comoran affairs throughout modern history, ever since the invading French made it their administrative headquarters in the archipelago. When, a year after independence, the islanders voted to return to the colonial fold, they were setting their faces against the wishes of their neighbours. France's accession to their demands, and the favours subsequently heaped on this *de facto* colony in the form of financial credits, exacerbated the resentment of the other islanders. So disruptive was France's continuing involvement in the area that it gave rise to concern in the international community and was condemned by a tribunal of the United Nations. Unimpressed by all the furore, the French retorted that they had merely been responding to a people's democratically expressed demands and respecting their basic human right to self-determination.

Produce for export *The majority of the people of Mayotte are involved in market gardening.*

Réunion: Europe overseas

Its flora and fauna may be exotic, its scenery verging on the outlandish, but there is something in Réunion's richly cosmopolitan culture that makes the European visitor feel instantly at home.

Rush hour *Saint-Denis, the capital of Réunion, has traffic problems that would not be out of place in a European city.*

The famous 'circus' of Mafate resembles a deep amphitheatre scooped out of the rocky heart of a virgin mountain. Its sheer sides plunge precipitously and luxuriant vegetation covers every inch of rock. This natural arena has in its day been a theatre of war, the stage on which a chapter of colonial history was enacted.

A place apart

In Réunion's spectacularly rugged interior large areas are barely accessible by land. The helicopter has opened them up to tourists, but until recently the ravines were all but unreachable, hence their appeal to the escaped slaves who flocked here and established their own little counter-colonies. Under leaders like Anchaing and Cimendef, bands of escaped slaves, or maroons, waged a long guerrilla war against their former masters, raiding the big plantations and inspiring other, still-captive slaves to join them in revolt. Punitive expeditions were launched, and Réunion's green valleys were often stained by bloodshed.

Hand work *The steep slopes of Réunion make mechanisation difficult.*

A home from home

Alongside this history of resistance Réunion has a tradition of cosmopolitan coexistence and colonial conformity. A population swollen in the latter years of the 19th century by the arrival of labourers from India and China had no alternative but to develop attitudes of racial tolerance. Identification with France has remained close, meanwhile – and not only among the island's wealthy, white settler stock: for the heirs of the maroons the country has been regarded as the cradle of revolution. Attached both emotionally and formally to France, Réunion has since 1946 been a *département* of that country – as French, in theory, as Lille or the Loire Valley. The reality has fallen short of this ideal: for a start, no European society would put up with the extraordinary inequalities of wealth that are taken for granted here. Yet Réunion remains a calm and contented annexe of the old country overseas.

Dramatic beauty *The ravishing scenery of Réunion's wild interior is best experienced, as here, by helicopter.*

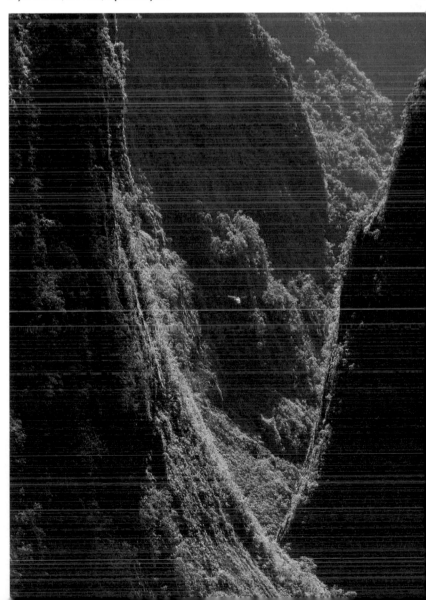

A scattering of islands

Réunion is the micrometropolis for a little empire of far-flung ocean islands. A total of ten smaller islands report to it administratively. Tromelin barely warrants the title of island at all, being little more than a glorified sandbank less than 2.5 miles (4 km) long and rising to only 23 ft (7 m) in altitude at its highest point. The chief benefit to France of such a possession is not the sand itself, but the surrounding ocean: ownership brings control over 'territorial waters' stretching for 200 miles (320 km) around it. The other islands have varying uses: scientific mission, weather station, and, in the case of Europa, military base-cum-wildlife sanctuary. Lured, perhaps, by its reassuring title, a group of settlers landed here in 1905, only to be driven off by the dry conditions and virulent mosquitoes. Since then it has for the most part been left to its natural flora and fauna.

Mauritius: almost paradise

Its natural gifts may be sublime, but Mauritius has nonetheless faced a challenging task in trying to set such beauty to work in a modern tourist economy.

Heaven on Earth *The palms of a tropical paradise wave above a tranquil blue lagoon. (Left) A multiracial bus queue in Mauritius.*

Gazing across a lagoon to shining sands and waving palms, it is hard to associate such beauty with the tribulations of the island's human history. Mauritius started its colonial history in 1638, as a staging post for Dutch East Indiamen, who abandoned it three decades later after Cape Colony had been successfully established.

Pests in paradise

What we now know as an entrancing paradise was once shunned by settlers as a rat-infested waste – and it has been home to more than just animal vermin. In September 1810, Philip Beaver, captain of the British frigate *Nisus*, set off to clear out what he described as 'a vile nest of buccaneers against our oriental commerce', but who were in fact the patriotic sailors of Napoleonic France. Under British rule Mauritius fell into the hands of a different sort of pest: the colonial treasurer Theodore Hook, who appeared

An orderly queue *At the height of the harvest, trucks line up along the road to the sugar refinery.*

to do little beyond drawing his hefty salary. It eventually transpired that he had embezzled more than £12 000 (more than £1.5 million in today's terms) in public funds. The island has for the most part been better managed over the two centuries since, but Hook himself might have raised an eyebrow when, in 1985, four Mauritian MPs were arrested for heroin-smuggling.

Demography and democracy

As in Réunion, waves of immigration from Asia in the 19th century helped give Mauritius a cosmopolitan feel: 68 per cent of islanders trace their ancestry back to the Indian subcontinent. Those of African extraction have felt marginalised both politically and economically, since independence in 1968. In 1999 their spokesman, the singer Kaya, died unaccountably in police custody, provoking large and angry demonstrations of Mauritian blacks. A troubled paradise then, but with such wonderful natural gifts at its disposal, Mauritius may be better placed than many other countries in the region to resolve its problems.

Rodrigues

Officially administered by Mauritius, the island of Rodrigues has long since had other ideas, aspiring to the same sort of status as Réunion and Mayotte as French quasi-colonies. But though the island's Gallic pedigree is indeed irreproachable, neither France itself nor its regional possessions seem much interested in what is, even by Indian Ocean standards, a remote little rock with few resources.

The allure of the Seychelles

A hundred islands, a thousand islets – and fewer than 100 000 inhabitants: the Republic of the Seychelles is one of the most remarkable little countries in the world.

Queen of the Isles Victoria, the capital, is the only significant town.

Visiting the northern Seychelles in 1609, Englishman John Jourdain wrote: 'It is a very good refreshing place for wood, water, cooker nutts, fish and fowle, without any fear or danger, except the allagartes [alligators], for you cannot discerne that ever any people had bene there before us.' Though the largest island, Mahé, with six of its neighbours, appeared on 16th-century Portuguese charts as the *Siete Irmanas*, or Seven Sisters, it was for some time one of the Indian Ocean's least-frequented areas. But its very remoteness appealed to some: by the 18th century the Seychelles had become a convenient hideout for pirates preying both on Arab and European shipping to and from the Indies.

From tortoises and timber to tourists

The first permanent settlement in the Seychelles was established in 1771, when a group of white men came with black and Indian slaves from Réunion and Mauritius; soon they were joined by Frenchmen dislodged from the Indian colonies, which Britain had taken over. After 1789, the white refugees started coming in thick and fast, as aristocrats fled the Republican Terror in Paris. The islands' earliest trades were in tortoiseshell and timber – the second

mainly for shipbuilding. The virgin forest John Jourdain had found could not hope to withstand such a sustained assault: if the islands are beautiful now, what they were like before can scarcely be imagined. Fortunately, the coconut and banana plantations that followed under French rule were themselves relatively easy on the eye.

The Seychelles were seized by the Royal Navy in 1810, Britain being primarily concerned to curtail French attacks on its shipping in the Napoleonic period. As a colonial possession, London seems to have found the Seychelles almost irksome: only in very slow stages was the status of the islands upgraded over the next one and a half centuries. But if the British were grudging masters, the Seychellois seem to have been willing subjects of the Crown: their capital was named Victoria, in honour of the queen. And however reluctant Britons may have been as governors, they have been enthusiastic holidaymakers, accounting for a significant proportion of the Seychelles' modern tourist trade.

Beyond belief *Their granite rocks shaped into improbable formations by the sea, the Seychelles offer countless scenes of natural beauty.*

Protected zones

The Seychelles' 92 named islands occupy a total area of only 175 sq miles (455 km²), but they contain two of the most exquisite – and fragile – environments on the planet. The lovely woods of the granitic northern islands and the low-lying coral reefs of the southern cluster are both remarkable in their different ways, and it will take both committed and intelligent management if they are to be protected. A longstanding concern about the effects of pollution and over-exploitation of the world's resources has found a focus in fears of global warming. International scientists working in the southern Seychelles find themselves in the front line: the reefs, with their miraculous but very vulnerable biodiversity, may be one of the first environments on Earth to register the change.

CHAPTER 6

LIVING IN SOUTHERN AND EAST AFRICA

Hunting and gathering, herding or small-scale farming – these simple economic systems served the peoples of Southern and East Africa well for generations, but became increasingly untenable in a colonised continent. Now, its history thrown into often violent fast-forward, an Africa of independent nation-states seeks to find its footing in an age of economic revolution. The world increasingly seems to be shrinking, the founding assumptions of modernity abruptly shifting as the forces of globalisation gather momentum, year on year. Malnutrition, AIDS and political repression: there is no shortage of problems, yet neither does the region lack the energy and enterprise needed to resolve them. Africa's best weapon in the fight for survival, and in the long, arduous struggle for prosperity, is the extraordinary dynamism and adaptability of her people.

Rice, originally an Asiatic crop, has been a staple food in Africa for centuries.

Prophet of freedom

*Nelson Mandela is a courageous, charismatic hero of our time. Locked away
for 26 years, he emerged to lead an imprisoned people to their freedom,
and to inspire peace and reconciliation around the world.*

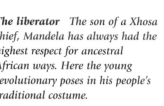

In 1971 South African journalist and civil rights activist Steve
Biko acknowledged the achievements of the developed countries, but insisted that the 'great gift' was still to come from Africa.
'It is a matter,' he said, 'of giving the world a more human face.'
Since the afternoon in 1990 when a white-haired old man took his
first steps from a South African jail, we have been able to see that
face before us in the flesh. Nelson
Mandela has transcended his South
African circumstances to become a
beacon of hope for all humanity.
The venerable symbol of a new-
born nation, this son of a Xhosa
chief has set his homeland firmly
on the march towards a far more
forward-looking and much happier
21st century.

The liberator *The son of a Xhosa
chief, Mandela has always had the
highest respect for ancestral
African ways. Here the young
revolutionary poses in his people's
traditional costume.*

Troublemaker

Mandela's African name, *Rolihlahla*,
means 'he who causes problems' – a
summation of the man that South Africa's apartheid regime would
have readily endorsed. A young firebrand in 1940, he was expelled
from university for his political activities; in 1944 he joined the
anti-government African National Congress, or ANC. As an impas-
sioned campaigner against segregation, Mandela was a tiresome
irritant to the country's white rulers, but the whole situation shifted
up a gear when policemen shot dead 69 black protestors at a peaceful demonstration. The 'Sharpeville Massacre' of 1960 caused
outrage all over the world: its back to the wall, the government
reacted with a wholesale clampdown on opposition. It was in this
uncompromising climate that Mandela led the ANC in its commitment to the 'armed struggle' – and in which he was eventually
caught and imprisoned as a terrorist in 1964.

Mandela magic

The humility and coloured shirts of *Madiba*,
'the old man', mask an iron will that saw
him through the long years of imprison-
ment. But it was his ability to set anger and
resentment aside that provided the key to
bringing about a peaceful revolution in
South Africa, creating a state that offers
democratic space for all races and traditions.
The nation still has many problems but
Mandela won the admiration of the world,
the colourful leader of what Archbishop
Desmond Tutu called 'a rainbow people'.

The hot seat

An impossible act to follow, one
might think, but Mandela's
successor has taken with apparent
ease to the role of South African
president. Once criticised for
being cold, Thabo Mbeki has
now relaxed into a more friendly
and informal style. Alternating
affably between Zulu and English,
Mbeki can be a magisterial
presence one moment and an
earnest, understanding confidant
the next. But, as with Mandela
himself, the public charm conceals
a steelier side: political opponents
have learned to respect his resolve
in negotiations. Mbeki has always
been an activist – he is the son of
an ANC militant – and is not the
instinctive compromiser his
mentor has shown himself to be.
But, as inheritor of Mandela's
country, he knows that tolerance
is the only way forward if South
Africa is to become truly a land of
equal opportunities for all.

*Nobel prizewinners Mandela's heroism is acknowledged,
but the National Party's President De Klerk deserved credit,
too, for opening negotiations with a man who was public
enemy number one to his white voters.*

Stern fathers of independence

Three decades after independence, several of the region's nations still bear the scars of the authoritarian rule of men who led their struggles for self-government.

From prison to the presidency *An active campaigner for independence, Jomo Kenyatta spent five years in prison. He subsequently ruled Kenya from 1963 until 1978.*

Mr Malawi *Hastings Banda ruled Malawi from 1966 until 1994, arguably creating the modern country, but his successors have denounced his repressive methods and reactionary views.*

'Big Man' politics

Opposed though they were in every political instinct, Banda and Nyerere nevertheless resembled one another as patriarchs of enormous authority – not to say authoritarianism. Democracy has proved a fragile flower in Africa's new nation-states: in the uncertainty that followed independence, the tendency was for strong leaders to come to the fore, often to the relief of their disorientated peoples. Jomo Kenyatta was another such man: having brought Kenya to independence in 1963, he made it his personal dependency, ruling without opposition until his death 15 years later. His skills as a mediator had seen him rise to prominence in the first place, bringing together a country riven with ethnic rivalries, but there was nothing conciliatory about the way Kenyatta clung on to power. His successor, Daniel arap Moi, turned out to be no more democratic in his ways and is still in power.

Born around 1900, the young Hastings Banda left Nyasaland on a church scholarship to the United States: a novice clergyman, he also trained as a doctor. He practised in London in the years after the Second World War, but Banda's sights were always set higher – and closer to home. In 1958 he returned to what was still the colony of Nyasaland. Politicised during his time abroad, he was elected prime minister of an independent Malawi in 1964; within three years he was the country's president and dominant political presence. A protestant pastor, Banda saw himself very much as the shepherd of his flock, imposing strict morals and repressive rule. His rule lasted 28 years until, given the chance to choose for themselves, the people of Malawi voted him out in the democratic elections of 1994.

African socialism

In Tanzania Julius Nyerere was also motivated by Christianity, but in his eagerness to 'Africanise' the businesses of the colonial companies, he came into conflict with America and Britain. Tanzania's president from 1964 to 1985, he encouraged collectivisation in agriculture, developed education, and fostered pan-African unity. Nyerere's legacy is uncertain: he won respect on the world stage, but his country was anything but utopian. His own moral rectitude may have been unquestioned, but his one-party state was corrupt. His party, the Revolutionary Party of Tanzania, still rules the country.

Father of the family *Julius Nyerere brought his own all-African version of socialism, or 'familyhood', to Tanzania. Even when his government was voted out in 1980, the people returned Nyerere himself, by a huge majority, to the presidency.*

Ramgoolam and son

The tumultuous events of India's passage to independence loomed large in the tiny island of Mauritius. Reactions differed: while some thrilled to see a colony seizing control of its own affairs, others looked on appalled at what seemed to be a disintegration into anarchy. Sir Seewoosagur Ramgoolam made his way in politics in the 1950s, as the staunch supporter of an increasingly beleaguered British administration. His reward was the leadership of a 'neo-colonial' Mauritius, a highly conservative and at times repressive regime. Defeated electorally in 1982, he was made governor-general the following year, reporting directly to the Queen until his death in 1985. Since 1990 his son Navim has been prime minister: the family firm is still very much in business.

From village to metropolis

Urban life came late to Southern and East Africa, but recent decades have seen an all but explosive expansion in the cities of the region. Africa, accordingly, has been forced to come to terms with the sort of social problems that were for a long time associated exclusively with the developed West.

Lost in time *Buildings in Ilha, Mozambique, recall the Portugal of the early 20th century.*

The earliest peoples of Southern and East Africa had no need of urban life, a mode of existence completely at odds with the mobility required by their hunter-gatherer lifestyle. Later pastoralists, too, were nomads, and though Bantu farmers did settle down, their communities were small and scattered. Most African cities were the creation of their colonial rulers. The form of these urban centres changed according to the developing needs of the imperialists, from Swahili seaports such as Mombasa and Dar es Salaam, to railway junctions like Nairobi.

African scene *The European-built centre of Befato, Madagascar, is the site of the weekly market, drawing colourful crowds.*

Though not formalised in law as it was in 20th-century South Africa, a *de facto* segregation soon prevailed in the colonial capitals. The busy commercial quarters and leafy dormitories of the white colonists extended out from the administrative districts. Indians had districts of their own, while the blacks found homes wherever they could, coming together to do business in the markets. Over time the white commercial districts have risen ever higher with their skyscraper office blocks, while black suburbs and shantytowns have sprawled across wider and wider areas as increasing numbers of the rural poor have joined the drift to the cities.

South Africa's commercial capital, Johannesburg, has the highest concentration of office space in the continent. It is not known exactly how many people live in the municipality of South Western Townships, better known as Soweto, just outside the city, but it is estimated to be somewhere between 2 and 5 million, the majority in wretched poverty. Assigned this inhospitable home during the apartheid era, the blacks have been kept here by economic inertia ever since. This juxtaposition of high finance and squalid poverty is not confined to South Africa: it is just as evident in other cities such as Harare, Lusaka and Kampala.

Development dilemmas

A world of inequality separates the air-conditioned offices of international business from a shanty of wooden pallets and corrugated iron. But the two are more closely related than they may seem: African nations must welcome and encourage foreign investors if they are to improve the condition of their poorest

The super-cities

The colonial legacy can still be seen in the old African capitals, but mostly it has been shouldered aside by the growth of the super-city in recent years. With foreign corporations building towering office blocks, and rural Africans streaming into sprawling shantytowns, the unique history of each centre has largely been eclipsed. The populations of Nairobi, Cape Town, Maputo, Johannesburg, Dar es Salaam and Lusaka had all reached a million by 1990; Pretoria, Kampala, Antananarivo and Harare followed suit by 2000. The African of the new millennium is becoming ever more urban.

Savannah city *Like some strange, futuristic termite mound rising abruptly out of the surrounding plain, Nairobi, the Kenyan capital, is now home to almost 2 million people.*

When every day was Friday

Every town has street markets, but Antananarivo has more than most, including the biggest open-air market in the world, the famous Zoma. Originally this was the Friday market – Antananarivo has Wednesday and Thursday markets, too – but such was the fame and success of the Zoma that, as far as the traders were concerned, every day became a Friday. Fruit and vegetables, meat, flowers, furniture, haberdashery, handicrafts, hardware, shoes, cigarettes, bread: you name it, you could buy it. Traders streamed into the Zoma from all over the city and surrounding countryside to set up shop in the shade of the distinctive white parasols. The entire city centre became a bustling place of commerce, with the overspill extending down adjoining streets. The sort of traffic problems that bedevilled other big cities – and which caused chaos in Antananarivo's outer zones – had no chance of arising in the Zoma district, for so completely were these streets given over to trade that no driver would ever dream of trying to take his vehicle there. Hence the concern of the municipal authorities that the Zoma phenomenon might be getting out of hand – though they were surely concerned, too, that though it was a colourful window on the cultural richness of Madagascan life, the Zoma also afforded less comfortable insights into the island republic's poverty. In 1997, the city acted to rationalise the situation, establishing separate, specialised markets in the suburbs and restoring the city centre to traffic. The conventional economy of Antananarivo has undoubtedly benefited from these changes, but it is hard not to feel that the life of the city as a whole has been the loser.

Green city The Rwandan capital, Kigali, was built on a hilltop. Its suburbs spread down slopes that remain wooded.

Pavement professions The term 'corner shop' takes on a whole new meaning in Africa: this cobbler plies his trade on a busy Johannesburg street.

Metropolitan mayhem

Most shantytowns have no clean water or electricity and only the most inadequate systems for removing sewage. Violent crime may be as endemic as disease, and drug addiction as prevalent as prostitution, but for many thousands of families, this is home. Even more affluent citizens have to put up with overcrowded streets and polluted air. Some governments have chosen to build new, more orderly capitals for their countries. Malawi has been building one such city at Lilongwe, for instance, while Tanzania has created another at Dodoma. In addition to its green-field site, this has the advantage of being in the very centre of the country. Only time will tell whether, with all its brand-new and purpose-built amenities, it will ever match the sheer 'buzz' of dirty, overcrowded old Dar es Salaam.

people. It is, however, a situation ripe for exploitation if the government is corrupt and over-willing to accommodate big business interests at the expense of the least well-off. Africa's cities stand on an economic front line on which there have been some tragic confrontations. In Nairobi in 1990, for instance, several people were reportedly killed when police moved in on the 'squatter city' of Muruoto. The land on which the inhabitants' shelters stood was required for development. Thousands were forced off the site by police so that the bulldozers could flatten their dwellings: several days of angry rioting followed the eviction.

Cape Town: the city at the end of the world

Easy-going, friendly and cosmopolitan – and with one of the most stunning settings in the world – Cape Town is the most immediately appealing of South Africa's major cities. In its dynamic, multicultural mix and its breezy, confident approach to life we glimpse the force that all South Africa might become.

Cosmopolitan city *Sprawled along the lower slopes of Table Mountain, and overlooking Table Bay, Cape Town has a spectacular setting. It is a busy port and the city where South Africa's parliament meets.*

The skyline is unmistakable: Table Mountain rears high above the bay, while the city clusters round about its base like a patterned carpet. The mountain's massive peak is sometimes set with a tablecloth of white cloud. For some, such domestic imagery does not do justice to the grandeur of the scene: they like to think that more eternal forces are at work. The Devil and St Peter play cards up there, they say, gambling for possession of the citizens' souls – and the white plumes are not clouds but the smoke that comes curling from their massive pipes. Other Capetonians are more matter-of-fact: for them, the mountain is the world's handiest weather station. A glance is enough to tell whether rain is coming, or how strongly the Cape winds are blowing.

On the waterfront *Still very much a working port, though tamed, some say, since its rumbustious heyday, the Cape Town docks are now a trendy tourist destination.*

The historic heart of Cape Town

Three centuries of architectural history can be seen on the streets of Cape Town, starting with the Castle of Good Hope, whose construction was begun in 1665. The distinctive 'Cape Dutch' style brings together 18th-century Dutch and French Huguenot styles: these buildings rub shoulders in the city centre with later constructions in which 19th-century Dutch and British Victorian influences are blended. The wrought-iron arcades of Long Street contrast with Parliament Street's elaborate art deco, but walk eastwards into Bo-Kaap ('above the Cape', in Afrikaans) and you are stepping into another world. Though the tiny artisans' cottages that line its streets seem familiar enough from European cities, the riot of gaudy colours in which they are painted renders them more exotic in Western eyes. When the Cape's Muslim Malays, brought as slaves from the Dutch East Indies, were given their freedom in the 1830s, they bought these houses and made the district their own. It is dominated even now by the minarets of mosques, and Islamic influences are apparent everywhere.

The end of the world

The road to the Cape of Good Hope winds vertiginously southwards along rocky clifftops; below, surfers scud shoreward on mighty rollers, while sunbathers share the beaches with jackass penguins, which bob and dive for fish in the waves, apparently heedless of humans. Look further out across the ocean and breaching whales can sometimes be seen. Push on to the south and finally you reach the Cape of Good Hope lighthouse. Two oceans officially meet here, though in fact the continent's southernmost point is some

Tabletop trip

Few tourists leave Cape Town without a trip to the top of Table Mountain. With 350 paths to choose from, the climb can range in difficulty from the Sunday-afternoon saunter to the all but suicidal stunt – or one can make the six-minute ride by cable car. By whatever route, half a million people a year follow in the steps of Antonio da Saldanha, the Portuguese pioneer who made the first recorded ascent in 1503. Today's visitors can avail themselves of amenities Saldanha never dreamt of, including a five-star restaurant, and a souvenir shop from which cards and letters can be sent postmarked 'Table Mountain'.

Robben Island, university of freedom

For nearly 400 years various authorities in South Africa have been building their idea of a brave new world, from the first 17th-century colonists to the 20th century's apartheid rulers. Through most of that time, any dissenting elements were banished to Robben Island along with lepers and lunatics. For much of the second half of the 20th century, Robben Island was the jail of many anti-apartheid activists, their message of multiracial democracy unwelcome in the land of white supremacy. Despite fearful conditions and crippling labour, they managed to find a 'university of freedom' in their confinement, reading avidly and talking through the ideas on which the future would one day be founded. The island's most famous alumnus is Nelson Mandela: the prison has become a shrine not only to him and his ANC comrades, but to many less celebrated predecessors who did not fit into the South African scheme of things.

Dramatic backdrop Behind Cape Town's City Hall, Table Mountain rises sheer to its level summit like a gigantic, rocky wall.

Rainbow city *Black, white and coloured sit unselfconsciously side by side. Cape Town has embraced the post-apartheid future enthusiastically.*

way to the east at Cape Agulhas. No matter – as far as tradition, symbolism and dramatic scenery are concerned, this is where Africa ends.

The colourful Cape

Cape Town was known to generations of sailors as 'The Tavern of the Seas'. Ships making the long haul out to India could stop here to take on supplies, not just of fresh water and meat, but of citrus fruits to protect against scurvy. A typical seaport, it was more outward-looking and tolerant than South Africa's other cities: the constant coming and going of mariners of all nations helped maintain its cosmopolitan feel. This reputation endures in a lively modern city with a noisy nightlife and a restaurant on every corner.

In such a relaxed and carefree setting it can easily be forgotten just how wretched a burden history once imposed on the Cape and its peoples. The freedom with which strollers of all races mingle on Cape Town's streets and in its bars and cafés; the casual way in which the students associate in the corridors and lecture halls of the city's university – what appears to be a natural multiculturalism was hard-won over years of struggle. This lively, jostling mix of races has emerged only in the past decade, since the barriers of apartheid were breached in 1990: before then this was a white preserve.

The reality today is not necessarily as upbeat as it first appears: official segregation has been replaced by what amounts to economic separation, and for many of the black inhabitants of the townships on the Cape Flats comparatively little has really changed.

The restaurants, latte bars, jazz clubs and art cinemas of Cape Town's city centre are as unattainable as they ever were for the people of the Crossroads squatter settlement, marginalised as comprehensively now by poverty as they ever were by the apartheid laws. But even if the new Cape Town falls far short of the multiracial utopia, its significance may still be far-reaching, pointing a way forward to an exciting, energetic future of diversity and tolerance.

The other Cape Town *For many Capetonians the much-vaunted multiracial South Africa exists more in words than reality; many thousands of blacks still live in squalor, as here in Crossroads.*

Johannesburg and Pretoria: contrasting neighbours

Just thirty miles separate them, but these two cities could not be more different. Quiet, sleepy Pretoria may be the country's official capital, but there is no doubt where the real power lies: in wealthy, bustling, violent Johannesburg.

Peaceful capital *The many parks and gardens of Pretoria make it one of the most restful capital cities in the world.*

Life in the leafy suburbs of Johannesburg may be privileged, but the impression visitors get is not one of comfort or ease: this is a population living in constant fear of its less affluent neighbours. Johannesburg has been marked out by violence since its foundation in the 19th century. What the Africans called *Egoli*, or City of Gold, is still the unrivalled leader of the world trade in gold, and a major marketplace for diamonds and other precious minerals, but in recent decades it has become a more general financial centre, its stock exchange a hub of international capitalism.

The 'Sleeping Beauty'

A short drive from Johannesburg, Pretoria might as well be in another world, with its august public buildings, its perfect lawns, its impeccable avenues. The administrative centre of old South Africa, this sedate city is not one to get its hands dirty in industry or commerce: it has been happy enough to leave those things to its noisy neighbour. Tucked away in a green valley surrounded on every side by rolling hills, Pretoria's white-stuccoed houses are as picturesque as its setting. Some 55 000 trees line the streets in the city centre alone: every spring the greenery bursts out in a shock of mauve as the jacarandas blossom. Imposing busts and stately statues testify to Pretoria's position as 'Voortrekker City', the Boer capital, still revered by white conservatives as a shrine to their distinct Afrikaner traditions.

Old and new *The centre of Johannesburg offers striking architectural contrasts between the present and the past.*

The new Soweto

On one side of the highway lies a sprawl of slums and shanties thrown together from empty crates and sheets of corrugated iron. On the other side stand rows of neat little newly built houses, each with its own front garden. Long famous for all the wrong reasons, Soweto is now the scene of a remarkable revolution, as the new government attempts to transform a shantytown into a prosperous suburb. If democratic rights are to mean anything to black South Africans, they need to have some economic stake in their country, too.

From the very first Jo'burg has been a magnet for fortune-hunters, and those unable to win wealth legitimately have always been tempted by the easy money to be made from violent crime. The current crime wave, fuelled by black disappointment over the meagre economic benefits of majority rule, may be more extreme than earlier crises, but it is certainly no new departure. The segregationist philosophy of apartheid only reinforced a fortress mentality that seems set to survive long after the last official trappings of white rule are stripped away. Today, as in decades past, the bustling business district empties out each night as whites drive home to their suburbs and coloureds and blacks are bussed back to their townships. They may work side by side now, but it will be a long time before they are willing or able to live together in harmony.

Infinite variety in vernacular building

Traditional dwellings across the region vary greatly in construction styles, but they all make use of materials to hand and are well-adapted to both climate and lifestyle.

Love nest Many young Comorans build houses to attract a fiancée.

A thatch of branches bound over a framework of saplings, or set above a circular mud-brick wall; a collection of skins tied over a few bent branches, ready to be taken down at a moment's notice; even, in chilly Lesotho, solid cottages of rough-hewn stone – traditional housing in Southern and East Africa comes in many forms. Whatever the building style and construction, the resulting dwelling reflects the lifestyle and needs of the occupants.

To nomadic herdsmen such as the Tsongas of Mozambique, or the Masai of Kenya, portability is all – though houses must also have brushwood palisades to protect sleeping flocks from predators and human raiders. For the settled Xhosa, on the other hand, something more permanent is required. Mud made into bricks in rough plank moulds – or simply plastered onto binding wattles of woven twigs – offers the best protection against a blistering sun, while the thatched roofs 'breathe' more effectively than any modern tiling. The curved beehive huts favoured by the Zulus have thatch not only for their roofs, but also for their walls.

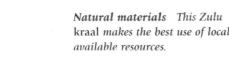

Natural materials This Zulu kraal makes the best use of locally available resources.

Tradition and taboo

In the agricultural *kraal*, as in the nomads' camp, what may seem a fortuitous layout conceals an elaborate hierarchy, the apparent crudeness of the housing masking a sophisticated social order. Nowhere is this contrast seen more clearly than in the plain rectangular dwellings of rural Madagascar. Every nuance of their layout and orientation has been arranged in accordance with tradtions, or *fady*, which govern every aspect of daily life, including building. What amounts to an ancient Madagascan *feng shui* dictates that the façade must be orientated to the west, that visitors must enter from the north, and that the north-east wall be reserved for the cult of the ancestors. Hearth, beds and even stores for rice and manioc are allocated precise spots. If the walls of a house incline to the north, the man will be master in his own house; if they lean to the south, his wife will wear the trousers.

Scented shelters

In the islands, with their balmy tropical climate, the humblest hut can seem like a beautiful bower, thanks to the practice of planting fragrant plants and flowers around every dwelling. The concrete-block and corrugated-iron constructions that in recent decades have radiated out from the urban centres, never seem as picturesque as the fine wood and canvas canopies that were once ubiquitous. In the Comoros and Zanzibar houses are built from native volcanic rocks and seem ominously dark – almost pitch black – in appearance. Many houses remain half-built for years, their owners awaiting a legacy or an advantageous marriage so that they can afford to finish them.

Blending in This settlement near Lake Turkana seems like a natural part of the arid landscape.

A Babel of tongues

With so many influences down the centuries Southern and East Africa is, not surprisingly, a region of remarkable linguistic diversity.

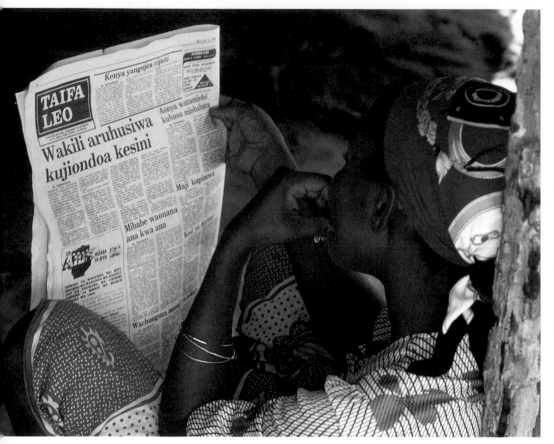

Reading matters *Rising political awareness has created a hunger for news, with newspapers published in dozens of official languages.*

While the Bantu were colonising the valley bottoms, another linguistic current was flowing over the high plateaus of East Africa, brought by nomadic herdsmen up the Nile valley from Sudan. These Nilotic languages survive in the tongues of the Turkana, the Sumburu and the Masai. These two language groups progressively marginalised the Khoisan tongues of the indigenous hunter-gatherers, which survive today only in scattered communities of Bushmen.

A lingua franca

When Arab merchants traded on the east coast 1200 years ago, many married African women and settled down in the region. Their children spoke a language that shared characteristics of Arabic and Bantu, and could be used to communicate with either. Called 'Swahili', from the Arabic *sawahil*, or 'coast', it was soon established along the coast and inland as far as the Great Lakes. Swahili is the official language only in Kenya and Tanzania, but following independence it was embraced by East Africans requiring a medium of international communication untainted by colonial subjection. Thus Swahili was given a new lease of life, a thousand years after its evolution, as a *lingua franca* for communication across national boundaries.

The role of Afrikaans in South Africa has been quite the reverse, marking out the separateness of the Dutch-descended Boers: defining them first against the country's white British colonial authorities, it now helps underscore their resistance to black majority rule.

The Bantu peoples of Southern and East Africa are named for the languages they speak, related not only to one another, but to the tongues of farming communities farther north in the Niger-Congo region. Archaeological evidence supports the view that the Bantu peoples spread slowly out from there, gradually bringing the fertile valleys of Southern and East Africa under cultivation. No fewer than 300 distinct Bantu languages have been identified, spoken by a range of peoples from the Zulus of Natal to the Kenyan Kikuyus and the Hutu of Burundi and Rwanda. The further they are from their northern roots, the more the languages seem to diverge.

Creole class *These children in the Seychelles are educated in Seselwa or Seychellois, a French creole encouraged since independence at the expense of the old official languages, French and English.*

Réunion creole, a masculine language

Creoles, languages that have developed from pidgin, have sprung up in many parts of the world. Those that have evolved on the Indian Ocean islands off East Africa have largely been based on French. Whatever their debt to the original, these languages are laws unto themselves, as can be seen from the example of Réunionnais. This creole follows French in large part, but dispenses with the notion of gender: everything here is masculine.

Facing the challenges of a new millennium

The problems of Southern and East Africa have been well-publicised in the Western media, while good news is seldom broadcast. The inhabitants of the various countries may deplore such 'Afro-pessimism', but the fact remains that the region confronts some immense challenges.

The statistic is stark and frightening: 83 per cent of the world's AIDS sufferers live in Africa, the east and south of the continent being particularly badly afflicted. Though not directly a disease of poverty, the AIDS pandemic finds it especially easy to make headway here, where people have neither the economic resources nor the education to resist it. With pitiful levels of health care by Western standards, and limited access to drugs and information on preventative measures, Africans are ill-protected against the ravages of the syndrome. Add to that the tradition of mobility in the search for work, the prevalence of a double standard which accepts that men will have multiple partners while leaving subservient women unable to exercise any control over sexual conduct, coupled with a social conservatism that stigmatises the disease and encourages denial, and all the essentials are in place for an AIDS explosion.

Two-pronged attack The war against AIDS must be fought both in the medical laboratory and in the community.

According to UN figures, more than 13 million African children have now lost one or both parents to AIDS. Any economic advances made in recent decades have largely been destroyed by a disease that strikes down men and women in their prime. Some reports suggest a 50 per cent decline in agricultural output as a result of AIDS-related deaths. Up to 70 per cent of Zimbabwe's hospital beds are occupied by patients whose problems stem from

AIDS, and the burden of caring for the sick affects the economy not only at national level but at home, in the huts and shanties of the poor. The meagre income of such families is restricted still further by the need to devote time to nursing.

A better future?

AIDS is just one of Africa's troubles, the latest chapter in a history of calamity and violence, from the trauma of slavery and the landgrab of the colonial period, to the disasters of dictatorship and tribal conflict in the years since independence. And nature has not spared the region: drought, famine and flood descend in their turn, while the tsetse fly renders large tracts of land unproductive. Yet what strikes the outsider most is the unconquerable optimism of Africa, and the indomitable will that has brought its peoples through so many adversities.

Tide of refugees Ethnic conflict and political violence have plagued Africa since independence. The uprooting of populations is inherently destabilising.

Mama Daktari

By the time she came to Africa in her early thirties, Anne Spoerry had already lived a full and dramatic life, having fought in the French Resistance and almost starved to death in a Nazi concentration camp. After the war she worked as a doctor in the remote villages of North Kenya. On independence in 1964, the farm that had been her base was confiscated, so she joined the new African Medical Research Foundation (AMREF) as a flying doctor. As *Mama Daktari* ('Mother Doctor' in Swahili) she became a legendary figure and was still working at the age of 80. She lived long enough to see the start of the AIDS catastrophe, but never despaired of her adoptive continent; at her death in 1999 she remained full of hope for the future.

The decline of the Masai warrior

No other African people has had quite the glamour of the Masai warriors – most famous of the savannah nomads. Tall, handsome, proud and fiercely independent, they have come to symbolise a free and untamed humanity, but recent decades have seen them being increasingly domesticated by circumstances.

In 1910 anthropologists W.S. and K. Routledge published their recollections of their time among the Masai. 'Nothing more romantic can be pictured than the return of a raiding party,' they wrote. 'Far away behind some undulation of the ground is heard the first faint refrain of the Blood Song. Everybody rushes out wild with excitement. The captured cattle gradually come into view, with here and there a guard tending them. Then the warriors appear in a compact body of regular formation, moving very slowly with measured tread. The rhythm of the song is marked by slightly throwing the spear vertically up into the air, making it spin, and catching it again. As the spears are bright as silver, and the blades four feet long, they throw back the sun's rays like so many revolving mirrors.'

Paragons or pests?

Not everyone shared this romantic view: a people prized for their wildness may all too easily be branded wild animals. Sir Charles Eliot, British Commissioner in Kenya in the early years of the 20th century, denounced what he regarded as an irredeemably immoral, bloodthirsty and savage race. To an official who saw the future for Kenya as lying in 'white settlement', all black Africans were perhaps subhuman, but the settled Bantu could at

A promised land?

In 1903, after a pogrom in Tsarist Russia, Zionist leaders lobbied for a Jewish homeland. Britain's Secretary of State for the Colonies, Joseph Chamberlain, offered the movement a grant of 5000 sq miles (13 000 km²) of 'empty' East African savannah. Three Jewish commissioners were escorted by colonial officials to the Uasin Gishu plateau, and after a long and arduous trek inland, made their camp deep in the interior, where they passed a restless night to the sound of trumpeting elephants and roaring lions. By day the scene seemed more welcoming, and they walked onwards in much better heart until, all of a sudden, they found themselves facing a Masai warband in full regalia. Though the ferocious warriors were persuaded to back off, they withdrew only a short distance before getting down to a noisy war dance, all whooping cries and flashing spears. In great consternation, the visitors beat a retreat with all the dignity they could muster: any idea of an African Zion died that day.

Living capital The Masai's livestock are important not only for their material usefulness and exchangeable value, but as a mark of status and as a link between the herdsman and his ancestors.

least be confined to their villages and conscripted as labour. The Masai, on the other hand, ranged the open country at will, entirely heedless of imperial authority: they were not merely animals but troublesome vermin.

The commissioner's racist contempt seems abhorrent to us now, but the idealisation of the Masai is just as inaccurate. It is not romantic wanderlust that drives the Masai on, but the seasonal dictates of a demanding landscape, for theirs is a life at the margins of survival. There have been easier times: in the 19th century the Masai occupied rich pasturelands all the way down the central plateaus of the Great Rift Valley. With their herds of cattle and flocks of sheep and goats, the nomads had the potential to be self-sufficient: their livestock provided milk, yoghurt, butter, cheese and meat for food, hide for harness and wool for clothing. They had also learned over time how to draw off safe quantities of blood from their living cattle to be drunk neat or mixed with milk, or added to meat stews as a thickener.

Killing cousins The Samburu are close kin to the Masai, but the two have been sworn enemies for as long as anyone can remember.

Rain dance *Leaping high above the ground, these young men fall back to earth like the rain they hope will fall in response to the ceremony.*

Nomadic treasures *Portability is everything for a people on the move: the best possessions can walk by themselves; after that come the rich trappings that can be carried on one's person.*

The making of a Masai

Of all the traditional lifestyles, nomadic pastoralism is the most precarious. In good times the Masai had surpluses of meat and skins to trade, but in bad times they had to raid. Hence the warrior ethos that is so central to Masai tradition: though young boys and girls tend their father's flocks together, from the moment of his circumcision, the boy becomes a *moran*, a Masai warrior, and must keep only male company. Inducted into manhood along with other youths of his age, he learns the skills of herding livestock and making war. His body streaked with ochre earth mixed with beef tallow, his plaited hair piled high on his head, his arms ringed in copper or gold, ankles hooped in the snowy fur of colobus monkeys, strings of brightly coloured beads around his neck and a bright red cloak draped round his shoulders, the *moran* in full accoutrement, armed for battle with spear and shield, was one of the most fearsome sights of

Instant removals *Here the herdsmen's hut of skins has been placed next to the animals' rough stockade: both home and pen can be dismantled and moved on at a moment's notice.*

Africa. It is a stirring spectacle still, but now reserved for ceremonial occasions, for the warlike heyday of the Masai has long since passed.

The function of the Masai woman was decorative and domestic, her value not so different from that of a prestigious piece of livestock. The young girl's rites of passage are analogous to those of her brothers: she, too, is circumcised before being initiated into the skills of women's work. Dressed up in her full finery, she is as impressive a sight as a warrior, adorned with beaded necklaces, earrings, bracelets and anklets. Given in marriage at the age of 12, she is allotted her own hut in the *manyatta* in accordance with her rank – for the man with many cattle, sheep and goats will have several wives.

Decline and fall

By the end of the 20th century the Masai were a sadly depleted people, decimated first by disease, then increasingly sidelined by the march of history. Efforts made by white settlers to respect the land rights of established black farmers did not extend to the apparently empty tracts of Masai territory. Independence did nothing for them, as the leaders of the new nations shared Eliot's prejudices regarding the apparent 'primitiveness' of the Masai lifestyle. The nomads' rootless ways fitted ill with ideas of nationhood, while their readiness to follow the rhythms of nature were an affront to a modernising mentality bent on bringing in economies of scale and maximising agricultural output. Today, few Masai live as nomads: those who have not drifted into dead-end jobs in the cities work as stockmen and drovers on big cattle stations.

Guardians of the desert

From the Bushmen of the Kalahari to the Rendile nomads of north-east Kenya, a number of peoples have adapted their ways of life so as to be able to thrive in arid conditions.

Clash of styles *The spear has been the weapon of the Samburu warrior for generations; the greatcoat belongs to a different military tradition.*

It is now 30 000 years since the first Bushmen populated the Kalahari Desert. Increasingly driven into drier zones by the Bantu, a few survive there still, pursuing the stone-age lifestyle of our ancestors. Living in extended family groups of up to 30, the Bushmen have no chiefs or headmen, but instead reach decisions through collective discussion, governed by a system of what anthropologists call 'dispersed leadership'. Nomadic hunters, without beasts of burden, they have no means of carrying large numbers of possessions – nor, beyond bows and arrows, digging sticks and the odd utensil, do they need them. Their wealth is a knowledge of the countryside and skill in exploiting its resources. They take sustenance from around 100 different animals and 150 plants. When they can, the men hunt antelope using arrows coated with a poisonous chemical extracted from beetles. More often, though, they have to content themselves with smaller mammals, birds and reptiles.

Hunter-gatherers *Once all humans must have lived this way; now the Kalahari Bushmen are members of a minuscule minority.*

The !Kung have an encyclopedic knowledge of their territory's water supplies. When surface water dries up, they know where moisture can be sucked from underground reserves through hollow, tubular stems, or found stored in certain spongy roots.

Desert nomads

The deserts of northern Kenya are home to the Rendile, one of the Nilotic group of nomadic-pastoralist peoples that includes the Turkana, Samburu and Masai. Their possession of the one-humped camel, or dromedary, as well as the usual sheep and goats, gives their culture a distinctly North African feel – some 19th-century commentators were convinced that they were lost survivors from ancient Egypt. Though less grandiose than the civilisation of the pharaohs, their culture is nonetheless well suited to the environment. Their homes are huts of sisal matting stretched over arcing wooden frames, which can easily be transported on camels, and they carry their wealth on their bodies in the form of jewellery.

Art in the open

On the walls of caves all down the Drakensberg, and on boulders and outcrops in the Kalahari and elsewhere, the Bushmen ancestors of the San and !Kung hunter-gatherers have left a pictorial record of the region's wildlife and their own ritual history. The works, in rich red and ochres from the earth, have been found at 15 000 sites so far, and South African researchers are working to complete the catalogue begun in the early 20th century by the French palaeontologist-priest Henri Breuil. With each passing year, their task becomes more urgent. Exposed as they are to the elements, the paintings are slowly being worn away: the race is on to record them before they vanish for ever.

Moving on *The Rendile nomads of northern Kenya transport their goods on camels.*

Tradition and change

The countries of Southern and East Africa have not been exempt from the globalising trends of recent years, yet there are still places where life seems to have changed very little in several centuries.

Reading the signs
A Madagascan soothsayer casts lots in order to divine the future.

Among the Tsonga of Zambia, the wake when somebody dies goes on for days, the young men of the village dancing, accompanied by the chanting of old men, women and children. Some keep time with beating drums or blow antelope-horn trumpets in a ritual cacophony aimed at keeping the restless spirits of the dead at a distance from those still living. The purpose of the ceremony may be to mediate mystically between a people and its ancestors, but it also contributes to social cohesiveness and order. Bound by common rituals, a community is better placed to meet the more immediate challenges of day-to-day living.

Rites of passage

Collective rites are a way of underlining the integration of the individual with his or her community, hence the importance of rites of passage in indigenous societies. Several hundred men may be involved in the ceremony of *Eunoto*, by which a young boy is initiated into Masai manhood. As the men dance and chant in full *moran* regalia, they are urged on by their wives, richly painted and dressed in jewellery – the whole community turns out to welcome its own child to adult status. Potent mead, distilled from honey, and narcotic herbal broths are drunk: soon all are reeling in a kind of collective euphoria. As the festivities reach their climax, the boy's braided locks are shorn and he stands uncovered as a man, ready to carry on the traditions of his people into another generation.

A wealth of wives

Polygamy, the practice of having several wives, was for many centuries a vital part of native African tradition. It survived well into the modern era, despite the best efforts of Christian missionaries to stamp it out. Its decline is being brought about by changing economic realities and aspirations. Few African men are wealthy or powerful enough now to keep more than one household. Meanwhile, global TV and other media have bombarded Africa with images of a very different way of life, in which the Westernised nuclear family is the norm.

Coming of age *All the girls who have reached marriageable age come together in celebration in the Kwazulu Bamboo Ceremony in South Africa.*

Keeping time *Whether whipping up excitement, creating a mood of mystery or setting a solemn tone, music is an essential accompaniment to important social rituals. These musicians belong to the Shona people of Zimbabwe.*

The lion's mane

For the Masai of East Africa the lion is a symbol of male strength and mastery. The lion hunt is a traditional ritual in Masai life, an opportunity to test masculine courage and prowess to the limits. There are sound practical reasons for it, too: left unchecked, the lion represents a danger both to life and livelihood, its depredations over time a major drain on precious resources. But there is much more to the hunt than pest control: armed as for battle with a human foe, the *moran* go into action with their shields and long spears at the ready; they scorn to stalk their quarry, but walk out to meet it in brazen challenge. The first man to plant his spear in the lion's body will have the mane when it has been killed, a coveted headdress that marks out the wearer as a man of special skill and bravery.

Side by side, faith by faith

Just as other cultural traditions have survived European influence, so ancestral religious beliefs have made their peace with Christianity. The region has proved open-minded in embracing the new without renouncing the old.

Sorcery *Traditional religious practices have succeeded in reaching an accommodation with the imported religions.*

Our lady of the islands *The cult of the Virgin Mary is very strong in the Mascarenes: her statue is a familiar sight by rural waysides and, as here in the Seychelles, in grander city shrines.*

Elusive animism

A varied miscellany of traditions and tribal taboos are lumped together by anthropologists under the name of 'animism'. So multifarious a creed is difficult to formulate in terms that Western theology comprehends: scholars talk vaguely of 'traditional healers' and 'ancestor worship'. This elusiveness has made it all but impossible to mount a sustained challenge: with no institutions to be attacked, no official scripture to be denounced, the traditions have continued to exist at village level untouched by changing governments or official ideologies. Adherence to traditional practices does not appear to have affected the people's readiness to accept the beliefs of their conquerors, so most sensible rulers have decided upon tolerance. In Madagascar, for example, the official Christian churches are followed with genuine devotion, but sorcerers, healers and soothsayers are also widely revered.

Nowhere is this more clearly the case than in the offshore islands of Réunion, Mauritius and the Seychelles, where forcibly converted slaves secretly kept up the traditions of their forefathers. Now Catholicism is freely embraced – but so, too, are more mysterious African rituals akin to the voodoo practised in Haiti and other parts of the Caribbean. As interpreted by sorcerers and healers, the key Catholic saints take on dual roles, standing simultaneously for Christian figures and for ancestral deities – proving that a faithful Christian may yet honour the cult of his ancestors.

The melting pot

Important as Christianity has been in Southern and East Africa, it has never enjoyed the monopoly it achieved in other areas colonised by Europeans. Islam was a vital presence in East Africa and several of the islands long before Christianity had any real foothold there, while Indian immigrants gave Hinduism a special spiritual authority in Mauritius. Given the resilience of pre-existing 'folk' religions, none of these imported religions has been able to impose itself to the exclusion of the rest: like it or not, the region has had tolerance thrust upon it.

Though imposed under the authority of the colonial powers, the various brands of Christianity brought to Southern and East Africa by missionaries nonetheless won the adherence of countless ordinary Africans. The Gospel of Christ may have been the religion of the master race, but its committed opposition to the slave trade earned great respect, while its doctrines seemed to speak to those who lived in poverty. Thanks to a combination of Christian tolerance and imperialistic arrogance, however, the churches never took a complete hold over believers' hearts and minds: there was always a little spiritual space where white religion did not venture. Under the noses of priests, nuns and ministers, Africans managed to maintain their ancestral rites in quiet coexistence with sincerely held Christian beliefs and practices.

Islamic influence *Muslims gather in the M'tsapere mosque, Mayotte, in the Comoros. Arab merchants brought the Muslim message.*

Minibus madness
A popular form of transport in many African cities, minibuses throng a street in the Ugandan capital, Kampala.

A *different pace of travel*

Difficult terrain and inadequate transport networks can make travel a slow business: experienced European travellers learn the African virtues of patience and good humour.

Travellers, peddlers, pickpockets and idlers jostle and throng in the great barn of the bus station, the air thick with fumes and the rafters ringing with raised voices and unsilenced engines. It will be a long and uncomfortable journey, so it makes sense to stock up with snacks and drinks from one of the hawkers who accost you at every step through the milling confusion. The best-maintained suspension will make heavy weather of an African road cratered with huge potholes; the springs on the bus evidently gave up the ghost some decades ago. So it is with an air of resignation that everyone makes their way to a seat – to have a place to sit down at all is for many African passengers an unimaginable luxury.

Crammed into a solid mass in the furnace-like heat, thrown bodily together as the bus lurches painfully along, the passengers on a long journey are destined to make each other's very close acquaintance. A ride in the back of a lorry may be a better-ventilated experience, but it makes still fewer concessions to comfort, and none to safety. Thrown this way and that as the truck careers along unmetalled roads, it is a rough-and-ready mode of travel.

British railways

Those who can afford it travel by train, a more comfortable option, but not necessarily a fast one. The 280 mile (450 km) journey from Nairobi to Mombasa takes 13 hours, but the luxurious leather seats of the first-class carriages and the liveried stewards of the restaurant car recall the elegant excesses of the British Empire, and panoramic views of East Africa can be enjoyed as the train makes its leisurely way across vast expanses of open savannah. However, those in a hurry may prefer to fly.

By boat and on foot

One might expect that the great rivers of the region, like the Limpopo and Zambezi, would provide perfect routes for long-distance transport, but their tortuous twists and turns, and tumultuous rapids, render them unnavigable except for short stretches. Lakes such as Victoria are crisscrossed by frequent ferries, while other ships ply up and down the coast of the Indian Ocean.

When all else fails (as, in Africa, it often does), the traveller is compelled to fall back on shanks's pony: along many routes, the walkers far outnumber the vehicles.

River crossing *Flat barges ferry vehicles and pedestrians across sluggish sections of the Zambezi.*

A stopping service

Plying up and down the western side of Lake Malawi between Monkey Bay and Chilumba, the *Ilala II* stops off at 12 towns in its three-day voyage. The ferry makes slow progress, its decks thronged with happily chattering passengers. Some of the villages served are too small and insignificant to have landing stages: here the crew simply drop anchor, and goods and people are picked up by canoe.

Finding a single voice

Except for South Africa, none of the countries of the region could hope to make much economic or political impact internationally – hence their growing recognition of the need to form alliances and act cooperatively.

In the years after independence, some called for a pan-African confederation that would transcend petty national self-interests. Others dismissed such aspirations as being at best utopian, at worst a recipe for Soviet-style totalitarianism. Whatever the objections, the arguments in favour of cooperation are overwhelming, given the relative weakness of so many of the region's states. Only South Africa could hope to cut much of a figure on the international stage, and even so would benefit from the support of regional allies.

Trading partners France's President Chirac with the leaders of Madagascar, the Seychelles, the Comoros and Mauritius.

not sound catchy, but it is music to the ears of peoples for too long mired in poverty. With its own trade and development bank and re-insurance company in Nairobi and a communal clearing house in Harare, the community has established financial institutions with the sort of monetary muscle that will allow member states to gain a genuine piece of the global market.

Freedom through free trade

Several African states took tentative steps towards economic partnership in 1981, when the Preferential Trade Area (PTA) was founded. By 1994, this union had hardened into a Common Market of East and Southern Africa (COMESA), including 21 countries with a collective population of 385 million, and a total import bill of over US$32 billion per annum. 'Economic prosperity through regional integration' is COMESA's current motto: it may

Where three continents meet

Since 1997 the states of Southern and East Africa have been participants in an exciting international economic venture. The Indian Ocean Commission (IOC) brings into being an enormous free-trade area, involving countries all along the Indian Ocean Rim. Its trading territory roughly triangular in shape, with apex ports at Durban, Madras and Perth offering ready access to giant markets in Africa, India and Australia respectively, the commission has its official centre in Port Louis, Mauritius, a point roughly equidistant between the three continents.

Cup winners A multiracial South African football team celebrates its victory in the 1996 African Cup of Nations, the ultimate endorsement of the tournament's ideal of friendship and racial harmony.

A world made familiar by the camera

Makers of documentaries and movies have given shape to the imaginings of audiences about this region, recording the struggles of its wildlife and human inhabitants.

A bottle from the blue *Appearing out of nowhere, a Coca-Cola bottle brings consternation to the Bushman's world.*

When Danish countess Karen Blixen published *Out of Africa* in 1937, she little knew that she would one day be represented to international filmgoers by Meryl Streep. Sydney Pollack's film of her book won several Oscars on its release in 1985. As many critics remarked at the time, though it may have been a Hollywood movie, it was Africa and its people who were the real stars. For several talented local actors the film was their ticket out of Africa, giving them the opportunity to appear on a wider stage. It also brought Africa to the world, presenting the beauty of the savannah scenery and the richness of its culture on the movie screen. Many millions saw for the first time the magnificent Masai and the warlike Kikuyu, and learned a little about the incredible human diversity that is Africa.

Out of Africa was not the first Hollywood blockbuster to be set in the wilds of Africa: John Huston's *African Queen* was made in 1951. It is a memorable movie, but this is due less to its evocation of the African scene than to the dramatic pairing of Humphrey Bogart and Katherine Hepburn. Another classic director, John Ford, made *Mogambo* (1953) on location in Kenya and Uganda, but critics sneered that stars such as Grace Kelly, Ava Gardner and Clark Gable were out-acted by the local apes that were given walk-on parts.

The Bushman and the Bottle

Jamie Uys's *The Gods Must Be Crazy* (1980) co-stars a Kalahari Bushman and an empty Coca-Cola bottle, a completely alien object which the hunter concludes must have fallen from the sky. The catalogue of errors and misunderstandings that results when the modern world and the Stone Age meet are considered in a dazzling comedy of culture-clash, which also has its more serious side. Uys's concern is to explore the ironies of the situation, not to cover up the often brutal facts. Some films engage more straightforwardly with recent African history, notably Richard Attenborough's *Cry Freedom* (1987), which tells the tragic true story of the black South African anti-apartheid activist Steve Biko.

Primates on parade

The gorilla has been a familiar presence on our cinema screens since 1933, when audiences thrilled to the sight of King Kong astride the Empire State Building. More recently, Hollywood has returned to the subject in a more realistic frame of mind. In Michael Apted's movie *Gorillas in the Mist* (1988) Sigourney Weaver stars as scientist Dian Fossey, whose researches in the mountains of Rwanda revolutionised our understanding of these complex primates.

Co-stars *Sigourney Weaver admitted to being completely won over by the personality of her fellow-actors in Gorillas in the Mist.*

From black and white to full colour *The story of the long war against apartheid has given South African film-makers the ultimate challenge.*

Well-documented

Fictional films set in Africa may be few, but the continent has long fascinated documentary makers. The lion lazing in the savannah sun, the hurtling cheetah, the wallowing hippo: these are familiar sights in every suburban living-room. Among so many marvellous productions, the selection of outstanding examples is difficult, but German director Bernhard Grzimek's *Serengeti Shall Not Die* (1959) is a classic. Apart from their entertainment value, documentaries have played a vital role in educating opinion in the industrialised world, raising awareness of ecological issues and driving home the message that Africa's wildlife is the common heritage of us all.

Kenyan super-athletes

For some years now Kenya has dominated international competition in distance running. Sports scientists have tried to find an explanation for Kenya's success in such events, and the answer seems to come down to the gruelling realities of life on the Kenyan high plateaus.

When the organisers of the annual 10 000 m 'Bolder Boulder' road-race introduced new rules to restrict runners to three per country, no one was in any doubt which particular nation they had in mind. American sports journalist Don Doxsie put it bluntly: the Colorado committee was making an attempt to 'de-Kenya' the competition. An extreme, even vindictive reaction to a poorer country's richly deserved athletic success? Perhaps – but the organisers were in a difficult position. In a comparable road-race elsewhere in America, Kenyan runners had just taken the first 17 places; no non-Kenyan has won the Boston Marathon since 1990. The Men's World Cross Country championship has become a battle for second place; since 1986 the title has belonged to Kenya.

Winning form *The 3000 m steeplechase, with Kenyans in first, second and third places at the 1999 World Championships in Seville.*

A crowded field

An astonishing number of winners have come from Kenya since Kipchoge 'Kip' Keino burst upon the athletics scene in the mid-1960s, trouncing American favourite Jim Ryun in the 1500 m at the Mexico City Olympics of 1968. Keino and his teammate Ben Jipcho were followed by men like Paul Kipkoech, John Ngugi, Daniel Komen, Paul Tergat and Noah Ngeny. Kenya's women have lagged behind, but since 3000 m runner Pauline Kongo came to prominence at the 1996 Atlanta Olympics, all eyes have been on the women to see whether they can match the achievements of the men.

How to explain this extraordinary dominance? It seems that a hard life led at high altitude near the Equator has toughened up Kenyans and given them the special qualities needed for success in distance running. Few families have a car, and even buses are thin on the ground: every morning and afternoon the red dirt roads fill up with straggling lines of children making their way between home and school. And there is more to distance running than physical stamina: Kenyans also score highly in mental discipline and stoical endurance. Though international coaches have done much in recent years to put Kenyan athletics on a scientific footing, they admit that sophisticated training methods are merely fine-tuning the Kenyans' enormous natural talents.

Football mad *All it takes is a ball, a bit of ground, and children with energy to burn: football is the passion of the poor worldwide, and Africa is no exception.*

Medals prove elusive

Wilson Kipketer was born in Kenya but in 1997 took citizenship of Denmark, where he was a student. Kenya could ill afford to lose a runner of his quality. It seems likely that Sebastian Coe's 800 m Olympic record survived the 1996 Games in Atlanta only because IOC doubts over Kipketer's nationality prevented his taking part – he beat the Briton's record time for the event at other meetings the following year. Kipketer's career has been haunted by ups and downs: malaria contracted during a trip home to Kenya disrupted his 1998 season. Though he seemed back on peak form in 1999, what should have been his triumphant Olympic debut in Sydney, in 2000, did not quite go according to plan. The firm favourite for gold in the 800 m, he was beaten into second place by the German, Nils Schumann.

Sporting potential yet to be realised

The people of the region inherited rugby and cricket from the British, but it could be in that most internationally popular of sports, soccer, that they will make their greatest mark.

Playing the game   *Cricket was bequeathed by the British.*

Every region has its sporting heroes: Southern Africa's idol is a Namibian sprinter named Frankie Fredericks, who has proved a match for the world's greatest athletes. Though not always a winner, he has had his share of international success, casting reflected glory on a region that has otherwise had little to boast of. The astonishing achievements of Black North American and European athletes have not yet been matched by their peers in Africa itself. A long string of Kenyans apart, Fredericks is one of the few exceptions that prove the rule: Southern and East Africa has underachieved in the sporting arena. The reasons are almost certainly economic: with so many other problems, there have been no resources to spare for intensive – and expensive – training programmes. The barefoot boys of Kenya were fortunate enough to find themselves equipped by lifestyle factors that

Mancala   *In this traditional game, players compete to acquire wealth in the form of tablets, or 'cows'.*

enabled them to achieve world-beating form in long-distance running: sporting success does not normally fall into place so easily.

White rugby, Black football

The coastline of South Africa has some of the best beaches in the world for pounding surf, but the apartheid government set harsh restrictions on areas open to Black or Asian-descended 'Coloured' citizens. An informal system of segregation is still to some extent in force, rugby union and cricket belonging very much to the old White élite. The new majority government has applied pressure on the governing bodies of these games to increase access – and they appear to have been making genuine efforts to comply – but the reality is that they remain minority interests.

Another game introduced by the British, association football, has become not just the game of choice but the fierce passion of the ordinary people. In the space of a few short years, the African Cup of Nations has gone from being an international sporting joke to being one of the world's most prestigious and eagerly awaited football competitions. Scouts from leading European clubs flock to see the up-and-coming stars of Africa brought together by a tournament in which the dominance of North and West Africa is increasingly being threatened by more southerly countries.

Flying feet   *Namibia's Frankie Fredericks is the greatest sprinter to ever come out of an African country. He is the perfect sporting ambassador for Southern Africa.*

Good sport?

Nothing could be more English than a game of cricket: the slap of leather on willow; the desultory applause of spectators; the leisurely succession of overs through a summer afternoon. For generations of Englishmen who built the empire in the 19th century, 'sportsmanship' was about much more than sport – it was more an all-embracing philosophy of 'fair play'. But fairness did not extend to members of the subject races: not until 1921 did the first team of Kenyan Asians take the field. Almost a decade after the boycott on South African cricket was lifted, allegations of racial discrimination are still being made. Black Africans have never really taken to what has always been regarded as the sporting preserve of the whites, but the reason for this may be quite simple: what game currently stands any chance of matching the international glamour of football?

Stirring the melting pot

Brought to the region in the 19th century as labourers, the Asians of Southern and East Africa carved out a niche as traders. Through their hard work, enterprise and imagination they have made enormous contributions, culturally and economically, to the entire region.

Asian faces *Immigrants from China and India, brought in to work the sugar plantations of the Mascarenes, have had a profound impact.*

The experience of 80 000 Ugandan Asians expelled by Idi Amin in 1972 brutally underlines the fact that a long tenure in a country does not necessarily imply acceptance. Amin's actions were those of a tyrannical dictator, but the prejudice from which they sprang seems to have been shared by many black Africans.

Prejudice and persecution

The first shipload of Asian labour arrived in Mombasa in 1896, to work on the railway being built to link Lake Victoria with the Kenyan coast. By 1901 the task was completed, albeit with the loss of 2500 lives. Prepared by education and the work ethic for something more demanding than heavy manual labour, Indians found the way to preferment in the colonial administrations blocked by racist regulations. The most mediocre white took precedence over the best-qualified black or coloured candidate, while non-whites were similarly barred from owning land in the richer areas: hence the growth of the *duka*, the all-purpose local shop, and the *dukawallah*, its Asian owner. The Asian community found itself regarded with disdain by the ruling élite, and with suspicion – or outright hatred – by the indigenous people. Amin's state-sponsored pogrom was the most outrageous of a number of persecutions: Asian

businesses were, it has been suggested, singled out vindictively in the wave of nationalisations that followed the foundation of Tanzania in 1964. In Madagascar, vague and largely unfounded suspicions of involvement in smuggling led to large-scale confiscation of Asian property.

Caught uncomfortably between Whites and Blacks, some of South Africa's Coloureds were bought off by the apartheid regime and given their own, admittedly impotent, chamber in Parliament. Others followed the lead of Mahatma Gandhi in campaigning against racial injustice of every kind. Whether the great advocate of nonviolence would have approved of the career-choice of Yegan Moodley must be in doubt, but he would certainly have felt that his appointment to the command of the South African navy's strike craft, the SAS *Jan Smuts*, in 1994, represented progress of a sort.

As post-apartheid South Africa plays a more positive regional role, members of its Indian community have been well to the fore in furthering progressive causes. In 1999 the appointment of Navanethem Pillay to the Presidency of the International Criminal Tribunal for Rwanda (ICTR) was doubly significant, marking an important advance not only for a South African of Indian descent, but for a woman working in a patriarchal African government.

Islamic aid

In the West the Aga Khan is known as a racehorse-owner and socialite, but he has a more serious side as a religious leader and philanthropist. The Aga Khan Development Network organises educational and economic development projects in Muslim communities throughout the Third World: countries such as Tanzania, Uganda, Kenya, Mozambique and Madagascar have all benefited. The richly endowed foundation has been especially important in underwriting Ismaili enterprise in the sphere of business, helping would-be entrepreneurs with banking facilities, financial and legal advice and other assistance.

Ugandan, again *Driven out in 1972, Uganda's Asians have been slowly re-establishing a presence in the country: their return underlines not only their resilience but the new-found stability and tolerance of the Museveni regime.*

OOM SAMIE SE WINKEL
DORPSTRAAT 84 • TEL: 70797

SELL

ALGEME

Out of time *The Dutch-descended Afrikaners have no other homeland than South Africa, their ancestors having arrived here as long ago as the 17th century.*

Set apart

Sandton is perhaps the richest, most exclusive suburb this side of Beverly Hills, its Sandton Centre boasting what may well be the most expensive shops outside Rodeo Drive. What the street market is to women from poorer communities, this shopping mall is to Johannesburg's wealthiest matrons, who emerge from their high-walled compounds to stroll, exchange gossip – and of course shop in its ritzy precincts. White rule may have been and gone, but whites still control much of South Africa's wealth: the nation's essential power-relations have, some allege, remained substantially unaltered. Whatever the truth of such claims, it is only too easy to believe them here: any black face would stick out a mile among the expensively maintained complexions on display in Sandton's glamorous boutiques.

Staying on

White rule may have ended in Southern and East Africa, but whites remain a significant, if discreet, presence, their influence stronger and more far-reaching than their numbers might imply.

Television audiences in the West looked on in horror as, through the early months of 2000, white-owned farms in Zimbabwe were attacked by angry mobs, their black employees intimidated, their proprietors harassed and expelled – and in some cases killed. What deepened the dismay of those in the world outside was the role of the president, Robert Mugabe, who, far from damping down the flames of discontent, seemed to be fanning them deliberately.

Despite the protests of foreign governments and of educated urban opinion at home, Mugabe's campaign struck a chord with electors in rural areas. There was undoubtedly some truth in the claim that a few wealthy white farmers had been allotted the best land at the expense of Zimbabwe's blacks – Mugabe himself had pleaded with the richest whites to stay on and help build a successful agrarian economy. Mugabe's violent *volte-face* is an extreme example of the profound ambivalence felt towards whites throughout what is now known as 'Black Africa': that the wealth of the European élite was wrested from those indigenous peoples to whom it should rightly have belonged does not alter the fact that the whites remain crucial to the economic well-being of the region.

One world *A healthworker from* Médecins sans Frontières *administers to an AIDS patient in a Kenyan hospital.*

A lingering memory *The old colonial values live on at the Nairobi Jockey Club in Kenya, the social hub of a still-influential white minority.*

The white tribe

White families caught up in the troubles in Zimbabwe wept at the thought of having to go 'home' to a Britain whose every aspect, from climate to culture, seemed strange and alien. The sort of 'Britishness' represented by the elegant gatherings of the Nairobi jockey club may find few parallels in Britain itself, but that does not diminish its sincerity. This is all the more true of South Africa's Afrikaners, descendants of the Dutch settlers, whose only national identity is with a white South African state that no longer exists and whose memory is despised. Fortunately, a new and very different breed of whites, young aid workers inspired by idealism rather than acquisitiveness, have been helping Africans deal with their adversities. If the whites of the past have much to answer for, their descendants are beginning to make amends.

CHAPTER 7

7

ARTS AND TRADITIONS

Dismissed as 'primitive' by colonialists steeped in European values, African art has been appreciated only in the past few decades. It took the great modernist revolutionary Pablo Picasso to sense the boldness and freedom of African art, its utter independence of the conventions of the Western mainstream. In African art, ancestral tradition and innovation, old and new, are brought together with an unselfconscious ease. Painting and sculpture are not shut away in the reverential silence of a gallery; nor are music and dance divorced from the rhythms of everyday existence – the African is surrounded by creative outpourings from the cradle to the grave. How well these artistic traditions will survive current trends towards globalisation remains to be seen.

Hoops, squares and jagged angularity jostle in an Ndebele artistic tradition.

Body adornment

For nomadic populations always on the move, the body is by far the best canvas for artistic expression. Jewellery serves a dual function, as both ornament and sign of status.

Every strand tells a story *These colourful necklaces are not just a display of finery, but an indication of the Masai woman's social status.*

A community of farmers or urban craftsmen can express their creative energies in anything from architecture to monumental sculpture, but nomads have to be able to pick up and carry their entire possessions at a moment's notice – so they have developed a way of making artworks of their own bodies, painting on pigments, fashioning extravagant coiffures and decking themselves with bracelets, armlets, anklets and extravagant necklaces. His face and body painted in red ochre, his hair dressed with a mixture of butter and russet earth, and the whole effect set off by oversized earrings and rich bead jewellery, the young Samburu male proclaims his masculinity and pride – his desirability, in short, as a marriage prospect for the similarly adorned maiden of his people.

Talking trinkets

What outsiders may see merely as a splendid show can actually signify a great deal more: the red pigment with which the Samburu male coats himself, for example, traditionally suggests blood, fire and sexual potency. The beaded necklaces that festoon the Masai woman indicate her marital status, her rank, and the number and age of her children.

The pastoralists are not the only ones with a taste for jewellery: Bantu villagers also love body adornments, which may, at the same time, speak eloquently to the initiated. While the heavyweight earlobe-extending earrings beloved of Kenya's Kikuyu simply exaggerate what is seen as a desirable trait, and the copper rings with which women from various Bantu communities like to adorn their arms, legs and necks are badges of wealth, other jewellery sends more particular messages. In part, at least, it is a matter of different coloured beading: for Africans, white represents purity; black is a mark of death or evil and, more positively, marriage; deep blue is the colour of fidelity.

Love letters can be created with multicoloured beads threaded on to little tassels. The young man receiving such a missive must ask the sender to interpret it for him: this gives her the opportunity to tell of feelings that might not find expression any other way. It would be improper to utter her desires directly, but no blame attaches to her reading aloud what she finds 'written' in the beads.

An integrated art *The multifarious skills of painting, jewellery, costume, music and dance come together in the climactic scene of a village festival: centuries of tradition distilled into a moment of communal excitement.*

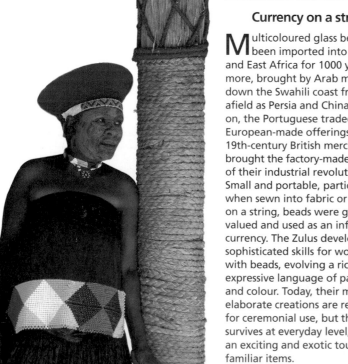

Currency on a string

Multicoloured glass beads have been imported into Southern and East Africa for 1000 years or more, brought by Arab merchants down the Swahili coast from as far afield as Persia and China. Later on, the Portuguese traded their European-made offerings, while 19th-century British merchants brought the factory-made products of their industrial revolution. Small and portable, particularly when sewn into fabric or threaded on a string, beads were greatly valued and used as an informal currency. The Zulus developed sophisticated skills for working with beads, evolving a richly expressive language of pattern and colour. Today, their most elaborate creations are reserved for ceremonial use, but the art still survives at everyday level, lending an exciting and exotic touch to familiar items.

A musical heart beats in perfect rhythm

The music of the region is as ancient as the ancestors, as up-to-date as this week's hit record. Brought to a wider audience in the West by the 'World Music' boom of the 1980s and 1990s, it has provided a unique way into the region's culture.

When American singer-songwriter Paul Simon released his *Graceland* album in 1986, he brought the music of South Africa to a wider public. Written and recorded in collaboration with Joseph Shabalala and his band Ladysmith Black Mambazo, it won critical acclaim worldwide. Other South African musicians benefited immeasurably from the interest that followed: from old stagers such as Miriam Makeba, who returned to her homeland in 1990 after 38 years in exile, to Yvonne Chaka Chaka, 'The Princess of Africa'. It also played a vital role in educating an influential section of the Western public – the young – on the richness of African culture and the moral bankruptcy of the apartheid regime.

Beyond the boom

The whole of Southern and East Africa is rich in musical traditions that, far from being overshadowed by South Africa's success, have been brought into international focus by the furore. More enterprising fans abroad have ransacked the music stores in search of exotic sounds, such as the haunting voice of Uganda's Geoffrey Oryema. The music of Madagascar is as unusual as one might expect from the hybrid cultural traditions of the island, drawing alike on the rhythms of Africa and the oriental harmonies of Indonesia. An all-African sound of jangling electric guitars against a pulsating, percussive beat, the *watcha watcha* of the west coast closely resembles Kenyan *benga*. Almost as weird to Western ears is the *taareb* of Zanzibar: a distinctively Swahili sound, part African and part Arabic.

Once a mystic priest, now a secular star, the musician has always had a special place in African society. Tanzania's Remmy Ongala sees his adulation as a responsibility rather

The drummers of Burundi
Spectacle is just as crucial as sound to the Burundian royal drummers' performance.

Real roots music

The quest for 'real' or 'pure' African music is in a sense the search for something that could never be: great music has always been an evolving, adapting art open to outside influences. Traditional African music is just one strand in a complex combination of dance and drumming, chant and costume: abstracted from this context, it may sound shapeless and monotonous – it is as part of the whole spectacle that it comes triumphantly into its own. The true power of traditional African music is experienced at a village feast or communal gathering. Here, flesh tingling, the visitor may encounter the languid rhythms of the python dance, a sinuous celebration of fertility and sex, or the terrifying thunder of the Zulu drums of war.

African queen *After almost 40 years in exile, Miriam Makeba returned in triumph to find the multiracial South Africa for which she had so long campaigned beginning to take shape: an international diva for decades, she was welcomed home as a queen.*

than a privilege. In addition to witty raps and tender lyrics, he likes to explore important themes of the day in his songs: in *Mambo kwa soksi* he encourages his people to use condoms. The scourge of contemporary life in sub-Saharan Africa, AIDS has certainly not spared the region's musicians, claiming the lives of key members of the great Zimbabwean band, the Bhundu Boys. Though the band still limps on, it is the merest shadow of the group that once produced what British DJ John Peel described as 'the most flowing natural music I can remember hearing'.

Stone fragments of a golden empire

As mysterious as it is majestic, the citadel of Great Zimbabwe has haunted the imagination of Westerners for centuries. Now it inspires a new generation of African idealists.

Enduring mystery *The ruins of Great Zimbabwe remain in many respects inexplicable to archaeologists.*

Stone totem *Beautifully fashioned in stone, this bird figure is believed to be the emblem of the Rozwi, one of the great dynasties that reigned in the citadel at Great Zimbabwe. A museum near the site displays the most important finds from the ruins.*

Long before the first European settlers brought 'civilisation' to the Dark Continent, a mighty empire ruled much of Southern Africa, uniting the Bantu villages under a single imperial authority. Chieftains were only vassals, reporting to the divinely appointed monarch at the ancient capital of Great Zimbabwe, near modern-day Masvingo. Though the word *zimbabwe* literally means 'place of stones', it does not do justice to the monumental scale or austere beauty of a citadel that, even in its ruined state, is still grand enough to awe visitors. Nor does it suggest the splendour of an empire that was founded on the fabulous wealth of the African interior.

A realm of riches

European dreams of an African Eldorado were not so far wide of the mark, to judge by the evidence uncovered at the site by modern archaeologists. Built around the summit of a hill, Great Zimbabwe was a military stronghold, a living city and a shrine for honouring generations of departed kings. Their spirits endured, not only in the living monarch, but in the fire that burned continuously for several centuries to symbolise the sacred life of the ancestors and their blessings on the current ruler.

In its heyday, between about 1250 and 1450, Great Zimbabwe seems to have had anything between 10 000 and 20 000 inhabitants – a considerable number by the standards of the day and unheard of in sub-Saharan Africa. The circular huts with their thatched roofs retained the stamp of the small village from which the settlement had grown, but there was nothing rustic about the drystone battlements that ringed the city. Nor did Zimbabwe's rulers live like peasants: excavations have uncovered artefacts of copper, gold and ivory. Indian glass and Chinese porcelain was obtained in exchange for gold, ivory and slaves. Thanks to an efficient bureaucracy and a ruthlessly effective army, the Shona élite who were masters in the city had control over the resources of the entire region. There is no evidence that they were great travellers, preferring to deal with the outside world through Arab merchants from the coast, but they formed one end of an extensive trading network with contacts in many countries.

Lords of the mines

Since the earliest explorations of the Portuguese there were tales of a great black emperor, Monomotapa, who ruled the African interior from his capital built on a vast mountain of gold. That so grand a city as Great Zimbabwe could have been built by blacks was unthinkable to white theorists. Elaborate and arcane suggestions were offered to explain its establishment by Phoenician merchants who had strayed far from their normal stamping ground. In John Buchan's novel *Prester John* (1910), a lost kingdom in Southern Africa is ruled by a white emperor, while H. Rider Haggard's *King Solomon's Mines* (1885) has fictional fun with similar ideas.

Place of ruins *Only stones survive, but from these ruins the visitor gets a sense of grandeur, military might and complex social organisation.*

Long live the dead!

The belief that the ancestors live on among their mortal descendants is found in many parts of Africa. In Madagascar, the cult of the dead celebrates the passing of mortal life as the start of an immortal existence that is the real point of living.

When the dead complain of cold

Between four and seven years after burial, in the cool, dry season, the dead begin to appear in their descendants' dreams: they are cold, they say, and feeling neglected by their families. This is a signal for the famous Malagasy funeral rites, the *famadihana*, or 'turning of the bones'. Kinsfolk of the departed are present as the corpse is taken from its resting place, given a fresh shroud, or *lamba*, and paraded around the tomb. The body is then interred for a second time: only now has its bodily existence truly ended and its spirit life begun. The *famadihana* is a joyful occasion, well lubricated with alcohol, the living taking the opportunity to bring the departed up-to-date with all the news. It is of crucial significance in Malagasy life, more important in its way than the original funeral.

Link to the departed
In a stony burial ground in Madagascar, the dead are marked by aloalos. But these are more than 'gravestones': they have a spiritual function, connecting the living with those in the afterlife. Each aloalo is crowned with a symbol of its owner's profession – many of those buried here were cattle farmers.

In Madagascar the dead were traditionally housed in stone; for the living, wooden structures were deemed quite adequate. Why waste more permanent materials on a mortal existence that was doomed to be finite, even fleeting? True life would be lived in the spirit realm, once death had unburdened the soul of its breathing, suffering body. Far from representing an end, death was the doorway to the life that would last forever.

Links with the living

The immortal ancestors are ever-present in Malagasy life, not only as shadowy spirits but as a vast body of rules and sacred sayings, called *fady*, which rank somewhere between everyday superstitions and profound taboos. Among the Merina of the Highlands, for example, it is forbidden by *fady* for a person to hand an egg directly to another: it must be set down first, and then picked up by its recipient.

As is only to be expected, the dead have strong views on the treatment of graves: they must not, according to another *fady*, be dug with a spade that has a tightly fitting handle – that would create too close a connection between the living and the dead, whereas a loose handle helps ensure a break between the two levels of existence.

Dwellings for the dead

Impressive tombs are found throughout Madagascar: the most elaborate are those built by the Mahafaly of the southern interior. Their name for tomb, *fanesy*, means 'your eternal home': they are certainly built to last, and scrupulously cared for. Traditionally, zebu were killed as an offering for the dead, the richer the departed the grander the funeral and the larger the sacrifice.

More striking still are the carved and painted wooden poles planted in the earth around the tomb. These show not only the appearance of the dead in life, but their social status and occupation, their families – even their erotic relationships. Among the Sakalava of western Madagascar, these *aloalo* are regarded as sacrifices in themselves: after all the money and care lavished on their creation, they are simply left to moulder.

Voyager *An exquisitely carved aloalo marks out its departed owner as a fisherman and seafarer.*

A spicy cuisine

Reflecting the region's long history of migrations, its rich mix of cultures and an abundance of exotic spices, Southern and East Africa has all the ingredients for tasty and exciting regional dishes.

Though a European-style omelette may be eaten by the urban middle class, Africans for the most part prefer their eggs cooked in a piquant curry sauce. This rich and cosmopolitan culture has little taste for blandness, though not all dishes are searingly hot. A famous fish recipe from the Swahili coast, *samaki wa kupaka*, uses coconut milk as a foil for more tangy flavours. To an abundance of fish from the Indian Ocean, East Africa can add a variety of exotic meats, from fine zebu beef and buffalo to such rarefied delights as antelope and ostrich.

Imported tastes

Some 70 different types of curry grace the tables of the East African coastal countries – a method of cooking brought to Africa by Indian immigrants in the 19th century. Arab merchants were the first to introduce spicy cuisine, bringing foods and flavourings from the coastal cities of southern Asia.

Zanzibar's status as world capital of cloves is a comparatively recent phenomenon, the plant having been brought to Tanzania, via French Mauritius, in the early 19th century. Its introduction is said to have been politically motivated, French agents having worked in secret to get the seeds that would enable them to break the monopoly held by the Dutch colonies of the East Indies.

In South Africa the cuisine reflects the well-established Indian population, but Dutch and Anglo-Saxon influence remains strong alongside it. The north-European emphasis on plain and sturdy fare is evident in the grilled meat or *braaivleis* that takes pride of place at suburban barbecues.

Island accents

In the Comoros home-grown staples such as manioc and plantains are supplemented with imported rice, with odd bits of fish and meat for protein, served with lightly spiced coconut sauces. The former French colonies of Mauritius and Réunion are influenced by three continents: a wide range of ingredients was brought by the old European planters, their African slaves and by a later Asian immigrant workforce. All now make their distinct contribution to one of the most intriguing and appetising cuisines in the world.

> ### Rice with everything
>
> Not only is rice eaten at every meal in Madagascar, for many poor families it forms the major part of the diet. Where possible, it is augmented with greens or other vegetables, or supplemented with scraps of meat – but for most Madagascans, for most of the year, the rule is rice with everything. Most Madagascan foods are not indigenous: rice was brought to the island with the first settlers from the East Indies. Generally cooked without salt, it appears on Malagasy plates as a sticky, tasteless mass; its function is to provide a simple stodge for the hungry or, in richer kitchens, a neutral sop for spicy sauces. This applies even to those festive occasions when the Malagasy national dish is served: *romazava*, a meat and vegetable stew, seasoned with hot ginger and strong-tasting *brèdes*, native greens.

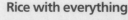

Conservation Recycled plastic bottles help preserve both the environment and a batch of fruit.

Cooking al fresco In Zanzibar, cooking traditionally takes place on outdoor fires, ringed with rough hearths of large stones that help keep in the heat.

African literature: finding a voice

A predominantly oral culture slowed the start of literature in Africa, but now the region's writers grow in confidence and there are signs that the outside world is ready to hear.

Changing times *Once this painter's works would have had clear ceremonial functions, now for the most part they are created with the tourist trade in mind.*

The book *Bwana Myombekere na Bibi Bugonoka* (*The Children of the Rainmaker*) is the work of Tanzanian novelist Aniceti Kitereza. Though written some 60 years ago, it has yet to appear in English translation. A family saga set in a small community on the island of Ukerewe, Lake Victoria, the novel did not find a publisher in any language in Kitereza's lifetime. In 1981, as he lay dying, the first Swahili edition was being printed in China: copies arrived in Dar es Salaam two weeks too late for their author to see them. Since then German and French editions have brought Kitereza to the attention of a wider world, but his achievements remain neglected in English-speaking countries.

Writing as resistance

Not surprisingly, given such treatment, many African writers have written in a spirit of anger, seeing European indifference as a mark of colonialist contempt. Many in the French-speaking countries have united behind the banner of *Négritude*, a movement that rejects all white influences as inherently oppressive, striving instead for a literature that will be all-African, not only in its themes, but in its imagery and language. The Kenyan novelist

and playwright Ngugi wa Thiong'o has declared that his literary career has been a sustained attempt to 'decolonise the mind' – his own and his fellow Africans'. His rage against white authority has not necessarily made him a comfortable companion for the rulers of post-colonial Kenya: jailed from 1977 to 1978, he has since then lived in exile. Mozambican poet José Craveirinha was twice imprisoned by his country's Portuguese rulers, before being enthroned as its bard of national independence.

No such happy ending lay in store for the black South African poet Bessie Head, who lived much of her life in exile in Burundi and died there in 1986. She was in any case overshadowed by the long line of liberal white writers who followed Alan Paton, author of the classic 1948 novel, *Cry the Beloved Country*. The fiction of André Brink, J.M. Coetzee and Nadine Gordimer bore witness to the wrongs of a South Africa under white minority rule.

Old or new? *All bold, bright colours and geometric shapes, the Ndebele have been creating 'modern art' for generations.*

Graphic display *Dolls made by the Ndebele exhibit the same fusion of graphic forms as their makers' fashions and building decorations.*

Arts ancient and modern

The influences of the past are very visible in today's African art. This has made the discovery of African art such an exhilarating experience for artists reared in a European tradition where each generation has 'progressed' from the one that went before. In the 'folk' painting of South Africa's Ndebele, for example, we see not just the traditional geometric designs of ancient times, but also stylised versions of street lights, road signs and office blocks that belong to the modern age. Conversely, the Zulu Sizakele Mchunu uses the conventions of native beadcraft as a starting point for works of cutting-edge contemporary art. Zimbabwean sculptor Bernard Matemera has received international acclaim and his work is exhibited in collections at home and abroad.

MAPS, FACTS AND FIGURES

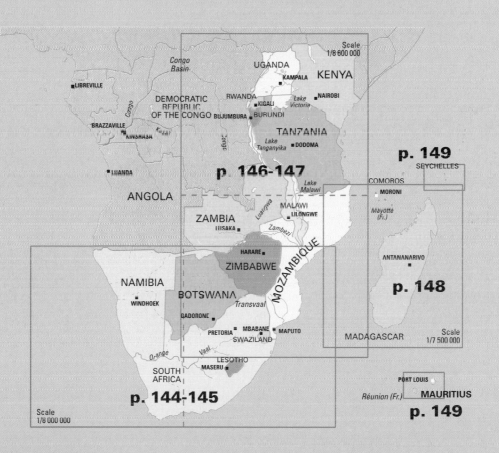

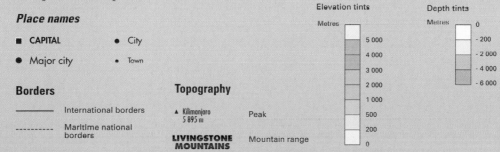

Key to Maps

Place names

- ■ CAPITAL
- ● Major city
- ● City
- ● Town

Borders

| —— | International borders |
| ------- | Maritime national borders |

Topography

▲ Kilimanjaro
5 895 m — Peak

**LIVINGSTONE
MOUNTAINS** — Mountain range

Elevation tints

Metres
- 5 000
- 4 000
- 3 000
- 2 000
- 1 000
- 500
- 200
- 0

Depth tints

Metres
- 0
- -200
- -2 000
- -4 000
- -6 000

A B C D

7

Foz do Cunene
Cunene
Ruacana
Cubango
Cuangar
Rundu
Caprivi Strip

Opuwo
Ondangwa
Ovamboland
Okavango
Shakawe
Kaudom Reserve ★

Cape Fria
Kaokoland
Oshivelo
Kaudom
Reserve ★
Moram
Wildlife
Reserv
Rocky Point
Etosha ★
Okaukuejo
Etosha Pan
Tsumeb
Okavango
Mt Aha
▲ 1 070 m
Okavango
Delta Shore
Maun

Kamanjab
Otavi
Grootfontein

20°
Palgrave
Point
Damaraland
Outjo
Tsao

Otjiwarongo
Waterberg Plateau ★
Lake Nga

Skeleton Coast ★
Mt Brandberg
▲ 2 579 m
Mt Etjo
▲ 2 085 m
Hereroland

Cape Cross
Mt Erongo
2 305 m ▲
NAMIBIA
Ghanzi

Khan
Okahandja

8

Swakop
Swakopmund
Usakos
Swakop
WINDHOEK ■
Gobabis
Okwa

Walvis Bay
Walvis Bay
Kuiseb
Gamsberg
▲ 2334 m
Rehoboth
Leonardville
Nossob
Aminuis

Tropic of Capricorn
Nauchas
Okwa

24°
Conception Bay
Tshane

Namib- Naukluft ★
Hardap
Dam ▼
Mariental
Kokor

Maltahöhe
Olifants
Khakhea

Spencer Bay
Great Namaland
Asab
Mt Brukkaros
▲ 1586 m
Koes
Kalahari Gemsbok ★
Tshabong

Hottentots Pt
Aus
Keetmanshoop
Aroab
Auob
Kuruman

9

Lüderitz
**GREAT
KARAS
MOUNTAINS**
Molopo
Kuruman

Elizabeth Bay

28°
Grünau
Karasburg
Swartmodder

A T L A N T I C
Richtersveld ★
Warmbad
Upington
Augrabies Falls ★
Kakamas

Oranjemund
Orange
Alexander Bay

O C E A N
Port Nolloth
Namaqualand
Pofadder
Kenhardt
Orange

Springbok
Prieska

10

Hoakdoorn
Brandvlei
S O U T H

Garies

Bitterfontein
Carnarvon

Calvinia
Williston

32°
Lambert's Bay
Olifants
Doring
Tankwa-Karroo ★
Sutherland
Karroo ★ Beaufort W

St Helena Bay
GREAT KARO

Cape Columbine
Saldanha
Saldanha Bay
Groot Berg
Mt Winterhoek
▲ 2078 m
Laingsburg
Uniond

LITTLE KAROO
George

11

Malmesbury
Worcester
Paarl
Stellenbosch
Franschhoek
Somerset West
Strand
Fish
Gouritz
Oudtshoorn
Kny

Cape Town
Table Mountain 1 087 m ▲
Hermanus
Bredasdorp
De Hoop
Nature Reserve ★
Mossel Bay

Cape of Good Hope
Cape Point
Cape Agulhas

0   50   100 miles
0   100   200 km

A B C D

E F G H

ZIMBABWE

BOTSWANA

MOZAMBIQUE

Lake Kariba

Sesheke
Livingstone (Maramba)
Victoria Falls
Kasane
Chobe
Victoria Falls
Zimba
Binga
Hwange
Dete
Gerufa
Hwange
Nxai Pan
Kanyu
Odiakwe
Nata
Makgadikgadi Pans
Lake Xau
Makgadikgadi Pans
alahari
Serule
Sebina
Plumtree
Francistown
Orapa
Mahalapye
Serowe
Selebi-Phikwe
Shoshe
odimo
Desert
Letlhakeng
Molepolole
GABORONE
Kanye
Lobatse
Mmabatho
Zeerust
Rustenburg
Mochudi
neng

Mulusodona
Karoi
Chinhoyi
Copper Queen
HARARE
Chitungwiza
Chegutu
Kadoma
Marondera
Kwekwe
Gweru
Shurugwi
Gutu
Gwayi
ZIMBABWE
Bulawayo
Rhodes Matopos
Gwanda
West Nicholson
Zvishavane
Masvingo
Zimbabwe
Chiredzi
Nuanetsi
Mazunga
Tokwe
Gonarezhou
Beitbridge
Messina
Mapai
Limpopo
Louis Trichardt
Pietersburg
Potgietersrus
Nylstroom
Warmbad

Mutoko
Luenha
Chemba
Zambezi
Mocuba
Mucubela
Moma
Morrumbala
Campo
Nacurra
Pebane
Caia
Quelimane
Catandica
Macossa
Macossa
Marromeu
Chinde
Mt Inyangani 2 592 m
Macheke
Manica
Chimoio
Gorongosa
Dondo
Beira
Mutare
Revue
Chimanimani
Búzi
Sabi
Chipinge
Búzi
ILHA BUENE
ILHA CHILOANE
ILHA MACAU
Save
Luido
ILHA DO BAZARUTO
ILHA BENGUERUA
Mabote
Vilanculos
Ponta São Sebastião
Ponta da Barra Falsa
Changane
Massinga
Tropic of Capricorn
Inhambane
Ponta de Barra
Massingir
Chókwe
Limpopo
Chibuto
Ponta Zavora
Magude
Inharrime
Xai-Xai

PRETORIA
Witbank
Middelburg
Barberton
Nelspruit
Krugersdorp
Roodepoort
Soweto
Johannesburg
Springs
Lichtenburg
Vanderbijlpark
Vereeniging
Bethal
Ermelo
MBABANE
SWAZILAND
Potchefstroom
Klerksdorp
Parys
Standerton
Orkney
Heilbron
Catuane
Lavumisa
MAPUTO
Baia de Maputo
ILHAS DA INHACA

Gauteng

Vryburg
Harts
Bloemhof Dam
Vaal
Kroonstad
Reitz
Utrecht
Vryheid
Mkuze
Lake St Lucia
Warrenton
Welkom
Virginia
Odendaalsrus
Bethlehem
Dundee
Kimberley
Modder
Orange
Mt-aux-Sources 3 289 m
Ladysmith
Kwazulu
Cape Saint Lucia
Bloemfontein
Champagne Castle 3 375 m
Empangeni
Natal
Tugela
Richards Bay
Ladybrand
MASERU
Mt Thabana-Ntlenyana 3482 m
Stanger
Riet
LESOTHO
Edendale
Pietermaritzburg
Mafeteng
Drakensberg
Durban
FRICA
Quthing
Caledon
Orange
Amanzimtoti
Aar
Gariep Dam
Aliwal North
Kokstad
Port Shepstone
Burgersdorp
Margate
Daddy Coast
Middelburg
Umtata
Port St Johns
Mt Kompasberg 2504 m
Queenstown
Mountain Zebra
Reinet
Cradock
Cathcart
Great Kei
Wild Coast
Fort Beaufort
Great Fish
King William's Town
Mdantsane
Grahamstown
East London
Groot
Sundays
Zuurberg
Uitenhage
Port Elizabeth
Algoa Bay
Cape Recife
St Francis Bay

INDIAN

OCEAN

7

20°

8

21°

9

28°

10

32°

11

ETHIOPIA

Wabé Gestro
Wabé Mena
Ganale Wenz
Dawa
Oro
Lake Abaya
Chénch'a
Boko
Gurar

SUDAN

Akobo
White Nile
Uele
Oubangui
Bangassou
Obo
Niangara
Bomokandi
Isiro
Wamba
Faradje
Watsa
Dungu
Aba
Nimula
Juba
Aswa

CENTRAL AFRICAN REPUBLIC

DEMOCRATIC REPUBLIC OF CONGO

Bondo
Bumba
Basoko
Congo
Bombesa
Buta
Yangambi
Kisangani
Aruwimi
Lindi
Ituri
Maiko
Lubutu
Ubundu
Opala
Lomami
Lowa
Ulindi
Kindu
Kibombo
Lomela
Tshuapa
Lodja
Sankuru
Lukeni
Mbuji-Mayi
Kabinda
Lubefu
Lubefu
Lusambo
Kamina
Kabalo
Kitabu
Kongolo
Lac Upemba
Malemba Nkulu
Miwoba
Parc Nat. de l'Upemba
Etila
Luama
Kabambare
Kasongo
Congo
Kongolo

UGANDA

Lokitaung
Lodwar
Gulu
Agago
Okok
Nabalach
Mt Moroto 3 083 m
L. Bisina
Mt Elgon 4 321 m
Pager
Lake Kyoga
Scroti
Mbale
Tororo
Kitale
Kakamega
Kisumu
Victoria Nile
Jinja
Owen Falls
Kabalega Falls (Murchison Falls)
Murchison Falls
KAMPALA
Entebbe
Mayanja
Kafu
Nkusi
Fort Portal
Kasese
Katonga
Katwe
Lake Albert
Lake Edward
Mt Ruwenzori 5 109 m
Bunia
Butembo
Goma
Nyiragongo 3 470 m
Lake Kivu
KIBUYE
Bukavu
Uvira
Albert Nile
Arua
Bembembo

KENYA

Wajir
Lagh Bor
Lagh Dima
Lagh Dera
Gurar
Lagh Bogal
Milgi
Chalbi Desert
Marsabit
Lake Turkana
Suguta
Kerio
Turkwel
Tarach
Eldoret
L. Baringo
L. Bogoria
Nakuru
L. Nakuru
L. Elmenteita
L. Naivasha
Meru
Mt Kenya 5199 m
Embu
Muranga
Thika
NAIROBI
Machakos
Mt Magadi
ABERDARE RANGE
Ewaso Ngiro
Ewaso Ngiro
Tula
Kathua
Thua
Galana
Voi
Tsavo
Athi
Yata Plateau
Garissa
Tana
Garsen
Malindi
Kilifi
Mombasa
Lamu
PATE I.
Kipini
Ungwana Bay
Equator

RIFT

TANZANIA

Musoma
Tarime
Mara
Mbalageti
Grumeti
Serengeti
Serengeti Plain
Oldivai Gorge
L. Natron
Ngorongoro Crater
Mt Meru 4 565 m
Arusha
Lake Manyara
L. Amboseli
Mt Kilimanjaro 5 895 m
Moshi
Koroygwe
Mkata
Mjrigasi
Wami
Morogoro
Tanga
Pangani
Msangasi
Kwale
Wete
PEMBA ISLAND
ZANZIBAR ISLAND
Zanzibar
Dar es Salaam
MAFIA I.
Mafia Channel
Rufiji
Matandu
Kilwa Masoko
Kilwa Kivinje
Kilpandoni
Lukombero
Mahenge
UKA MTS
Mikumi
Iringa
Kilombero
Little Ruaha
Great Ruaha
Great Ruaha
Njombe
Igula
Ruaha
Kinyasung
DODOMA
Kungani
Singida
Manyoni
Wembere
Nyahua
Kisigo
Yssev
Igombe
Kisigo
Tabora
Ilunde
Nzega
Mwanza
Shinyanga
Semu
L. Eyasi
Sibiti
Siniya
Kula
Mjgor
Kisii
Kakamega
Lake Victoria
UKARA I.
UKEREWE I.
SESE Is.
KOME I.
I. MFANGANU
RUBONDO I.
Bukoba
Kagera
Kibondo
Masaka
Kasulu
Kigoma
Ujiji
Kigosi
Nikonga
Moyowosi
Ugalla
L. Sogara
Uvinza
Kasulu
Lake Tanganyika
Karema
Kipili
Mbala
Kasanga
Sumbawanga
Mbeya
Ngomba
Piti
L. Rukwa
Lake Rukwa
Rungwa
Kavu
Kigosi
Kabambare
Kalemié
Kapona
Karema
Sumbu
Pweto
Lake Mweru

RWANDA
Parc Nat. de la Kagera
Ngororero
Mt Karisimbi
Gisenyi
KIGALI
Butaré
VIRUNGA MTS

BURUNDI
Gitega
Kibondo
Muyinga
BUJUMBURA
Mt Ugoma 2 981 m
CHAÎNE MITUMBA

L. George
Queen Elizabeth
Mbarara
Bukoba

Mozambique Channel

ANGOLA

ZAMBIA

MALAWI

ZIMBABWE

MOZAMBIQUE

BOTSWANA

Kalahari Desert

Tropic of Capricorn

MUCHINGA ESCARPMENT

Lake Bangweulu

Lake Malawi (Lake Nyasa)

Lake Chilwa

Lake Kariba

Lake Xau

Lake Ngami

Okavango Delta

Makgadikgadi Pans

Caprivi Strip

Zambezi

Limpopo

Mt Namuli ▲ 2419 m

Mt Mulanje 3000 m

Mt Inyangani ▲ 2592 m

Jeci 1836 m ▲

Major towns and places:
Mtwara, Pemba, Nacala, Moçimboa da Praia, Montepuez, Nampula, Mocuba, Quelimane, Beira, Mecula, Lichinga, Songea, Tunduru, Mbamba Bay, Nkhata, LILONGWE, Zomba, Blantyre, Chiromo, Tete, Cahora Bassa Dam, HARARE, Mutare, Chimoio, Gorongosa, Dondo, Bazi, Inhambane, Massinga, Vilanculos, Xai-Xai, MAPUTO, MBABANE, PRETORIA, Johannesburg, Soweto, Springs, Witbank, Messina, Beitbridge, Bulawayo, Gweru, Kwekwe, Great Zimbabwe, LUSAKA, Kabwe, Kafue, Mazabuka, Choma, Livingstone (Maramba), Victoria Falls, Kasane, Hwange, Francistown, Serowe, GABORONE, Lobatse, Kanye, Jwaneng, Maun, Ghanzi, Lubumbashi, Kolwezi, Likasi, Kasama, Mansa (Fort Roseberry), Mpika, Kasempa, Solwezi, Mongu, Senanga

Mozambique Channel

100 miles
200 km
0   50   100   150

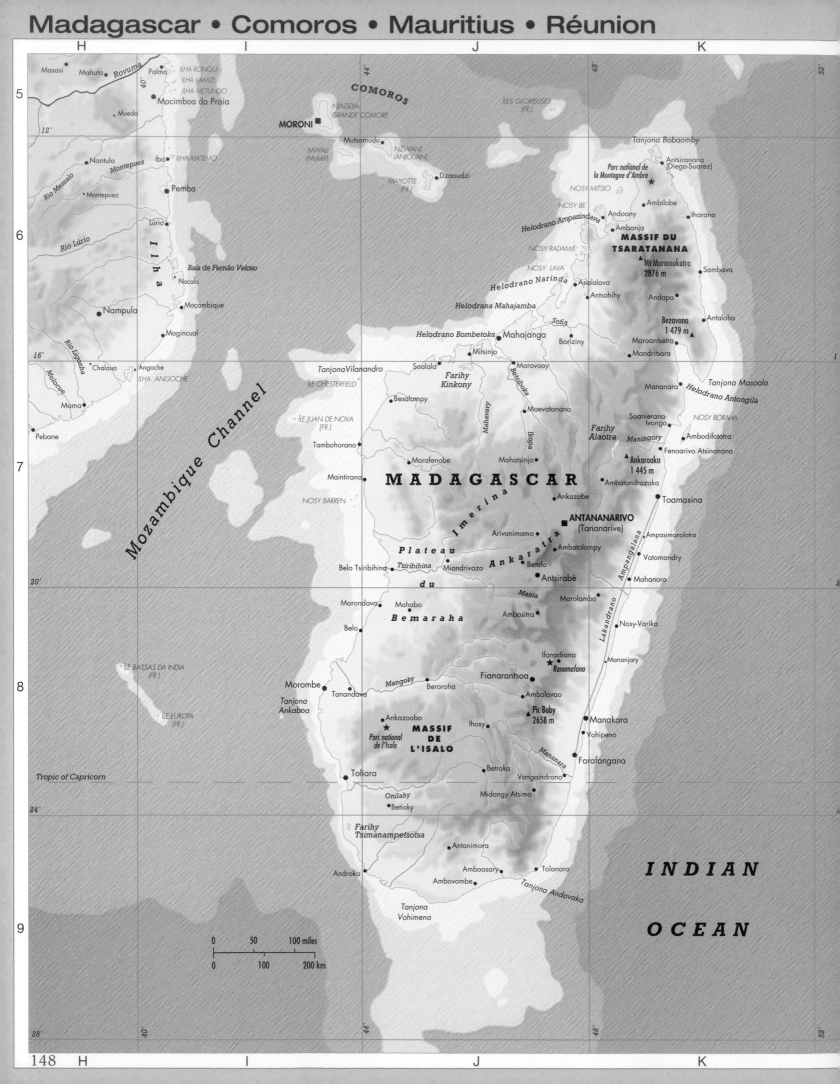

Masasi • Mahuta Rovuma Palma
• ILHA RONGUI
• Mueda ILHA VAMIZI
ILHA METUNDO
Mocimboa da Praia

COMOROS

NJAZIDJA
GRANDE COMORE
MORONI

Mutsamudu

NZWANI
(ANJOUAN)
MWALI
(Mohéli)

MAYOTTE
(FR.) Dzaoudzi

ÎLES GLORIEUSES
(FR.)

Tanjona Bobaomby

Antsiranana
(Diego-Suarez)

Parc national de
la Montagne d'Ambre
NOSY MITSIO

Nantulo
Montepuez
Rio Messalo
• Montepuez
Pemba

Lúrio
Rio Lúrio

Nacala
Baia de Fernão Veloso

Moçambique
Nampula

Mogincual

NOSY BE
NOSY RADAMA
Helodrano Ampasindava
Andoany
Ambanja
Ambilobe
Iharana

MASSIF DU
TSARATANANA

NOSY LAVA
Helodrano Narinda
Analalava
Antsohihy
Mt Maromokotro
2876 m

Sambava

Andapa
Bezavona
1 479 m
Antalaha

Chalaua
Angoche
ILHA ANGOCHE
Moma
Rio Ligonha
Motecue
Pebane

Helodrana Mahajamba
Mahajanga
Helodrano Bombetoka
Mitsinjo
Marovoay
Soalala
Besiboka
Sofia
Boriziny
Maroantsetra
Mandritsara

Tanjona Masoala
Mananara
Helodrano Antongila

TanjonaVilanandro
ÎLE CHESTERFIELD
Farihy
Kinkony
Besalampy

Maevatanana
Mahavavy
Farihy
Alaotra
NOSY BORAHA
Soanierana-
Ivongo
Maningory
Ambodifototra
Fenoarivo Atsinanana

ÎLE JUAN DE NOVA
[FR.]
Tambohorano
Morafenobe
Mahatsinjo
Ikopa

Maintirano
NOSY BARREN

MADAGASCAR
Imerina
Ankaroaka
1 445 m
Ambatondrazaka

Toamasina

Mozambique Channel

Ankazobe
ANTANANARIVO
(Tananarive)
Arivonimamo
Ambatolampy

Ampasimanolotra
Ampangalana
Vatomandry
Mahanoro

Plateau
Ankaratra

Belo Tsiribihina
Tsiribihina
Miandrivaza
Betafo
Antsirabé

du
Mania
Marolambo
Lakandrano

Morondava
Mahabo
Bemaraha
Belo
Ambositra
Nosy-Varika

ÎLE BASSAS DA INDIA
(FR.)

Ifanadiana
Ranomafana
Fianarantsoa
Mananjary

Morombe
Tanjona
Ankaboa
Tanandava
Mangoky
Beroroha
Ambalavao

ÎLE EUROPA
(FR.)

Ankazoabo
Pic Boby
2658 m
Manakara
Vohipeno

Parc national
de l'Isalo
MASSIF
DE
L'ISALO
Ihosy
Mananara
Farafangana

Toliara
Betroka
Vangaindrano
Tropic of Capricorn
Onilahy
Betioky
Midongy Atsimo

Farihy
Tsimanampetsotsa
Antanimora
INDIAN

Androka
Antimora
Amboasary
Tolanaro
Ambovombe
Tanjona Andavaka
OCEAN

Tanjona
Vohimena

0   50   100 miles
0   100   200 km

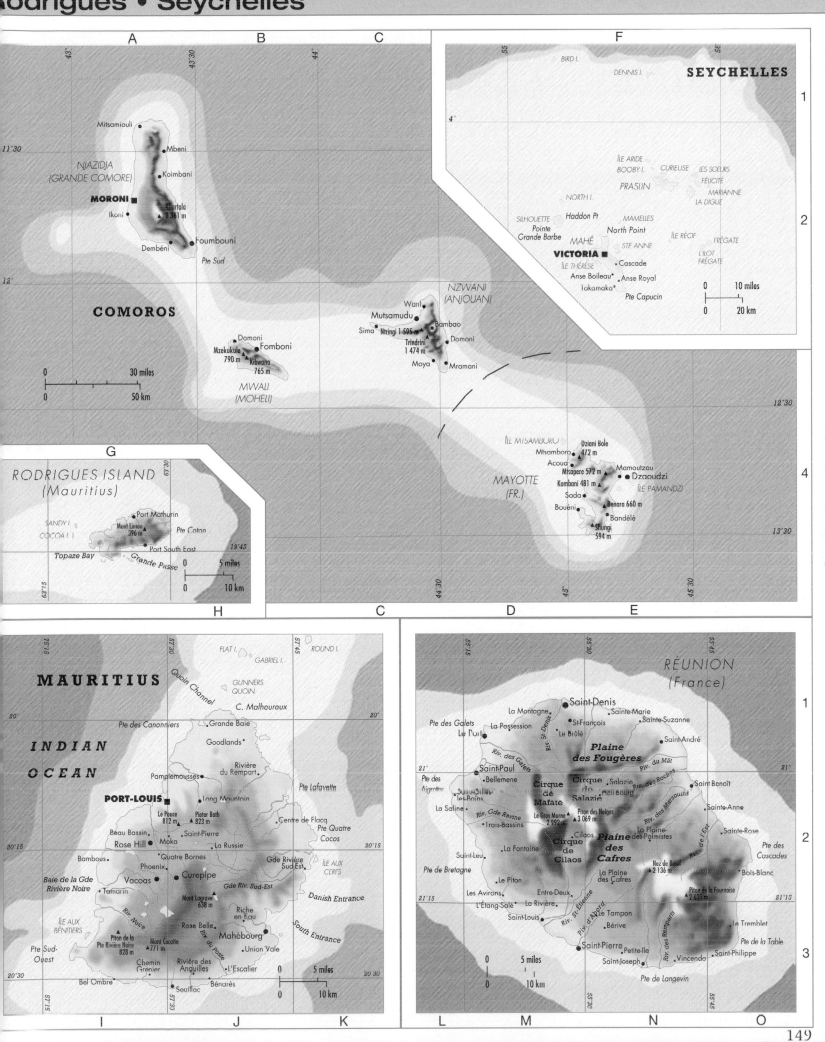

Countries of Southern and East Africa

States of all shapes and sizes make up Southern and East Africa and the offshore Indian Ocean islands. Though united in natural splendour, they could hardly be more different in their human geography, their political outlook or their economies.

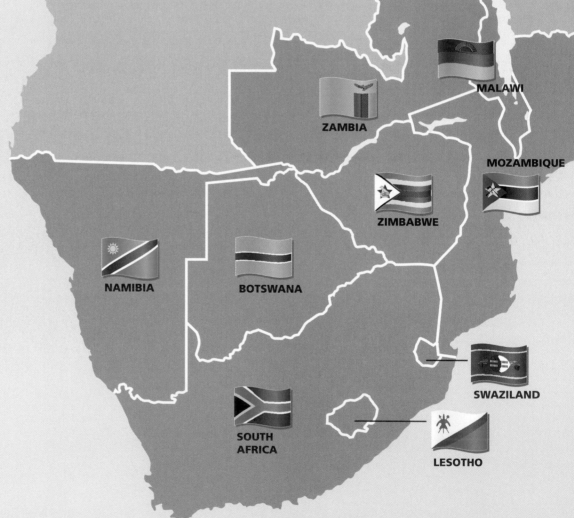

UGANDA

RWANDA

BURUNDI

KENYA

TANZANIA

MALAWI

ZAMBIA

MOZAMBIQUE

ZIMBABWE

NAMIBIA

BOTSWANA

SWAZILAND

SOUTH AFRICA

LESOTHO

EAST AFRICA

BURUNDI
Area: 10 745 sq miles (27 830 km²)
Capital: Bujumbura
Currency: Burundian Franc
Population: 6 300 000
Status: Republic
Languages: French, Kirundi, Swahili

UGANDA
Area: 93 104 sq miles (241 139 km²)
Capital: Kampala
Currency: Ugandan Shilling
Population: 21 030 000
Status: Republic
Languages: English, Luganda

KENYA
Area: 224 080 sq miles (580 367 km²)
Capital: Nairobi
Currency: Kenyan Shilling
Population: 29 010 000
Status: Republic
Languages: Kiswahili, English, Kikuyu, Luo

RWANDA
Area: 101 70 sq miles (26 340 km²)
Capital: Kigali
Currency: Rwandan Franc
Population: 6 600 000
Status: Republic
Languages: Kinyarwanda, English, French, Kiswahili

SOUTHERN AFRICA

SOUTH AFRICA
Area: 470 689 sq miles (1 219 080 km²)
Capital: Pretoria
Currency: Rand
Population: 42 130 000
Status: Republic
Languages: English, Afrikaans, and 9 African languages

BOTSWANA
Area: 224 607 sq miles (581 730 km²)
Capital: Gaborone
Currency: Pula
Population: 1 570 000
Status: Republic
Languages: English, Setswana

LESOTHO
Area: 11 718 sq miles (30 350 km²)
Capital: Maseru
Currency: Loti
Population: 2 060 000
Status: Constitutional Monarchy
Languages: English, Sesotho

MALAWI
Area: 45 747 sq miles (118 484 km²)
Capital: Lilongwe
Currency: Malayan Kwacha
Population: 10 350 000
Status: Republic
Languages: English, Chichewa

MOZAMBIQUE
Area: 308 641 sq miles (799 380 km²)
Capital: Maputo
Currency: Metical
Population: 16 920 000
Status: Republic
Language: Portuguese

NAMIBIA
Area: 318 261 sq miles (824 292 km²)
Capital: Windhoek
Currency: Namibian Dollar
Population: 1 660 000
Status: Republic
Languages: English, Afrikaans, German

SWAZILAND
Area: 6703 sq miles (17 360 km²)
Capital: Mbabane
Currency: Lilangeni
Population: 950 000
Status: Constitutional Monarchy
Languages: SiSwati, English

ZAMBIA
Area: 290 586 sq miles (752 614 km²)
Capital: Lusaka
Currency: Zambian Kwacha
Population: 8 780 000
Status: Republic
Language: English

ZIMBABWE
Area: 150 873 sq miles (390 759 km²)
Capital: Harare
Currency: Zimbabwean Dollar
Population: 12 680 000
Status: Republic
Languages: English and six other major local languages

SEYCHELLES

COMOROS

MAURITIUS

MADAGASCAR

RÉUNION

ISLANDS OF THE INDIAN OCEAN

COMOROS
Area: 719 sq miles (1862 km²)
Capital: Moroni
Currency: Comoran Franc
Population: 660 000
Status: Federal Islamic Republic
Languages: Arabic, French, Swahili

MADAGASCAR
Area: 226 656 sq miles (587 040 km²)
Capital: Antananarivo
Currency: Malagasy Franc
Population: 15 060 000
Status: Republic
Languages: Malagasy, French

MAURITIUS
Area: 788 sq miles (2040 km²)
Capital: Port Louis
Currency: Mauritian Rupee
Population: 1 160 000
Status: Republic
Languages: English, Creole

RÉUNION
Area: 969 sq miles (2 510 km²)
Administrative Centre: Saint-Denis
Currency: French Franc
Population: 717 000
Status: Overseas department of France
Language: French

TANZANIA
Area: 364 898 sq miles (945 087 km²)
Capital: Dodoma
Currency: Tanzanian Shilling
Population: 32 100 000
Status: Republic
Languages: Swahili, English

SEYCHELLES
Area: 176 sq miles (455 km²)
Capital: Victoria
Currency: Seychelles Rupee
Population: 80 000
Status: Republic
Languages: English, Seychellois (Creole), French

The lie of the land

The region of Southern and East Africa comprises less than a quarter of the continent, which covers more than 11.5 million sq miles (30 million km²), but it is still a place of staggering spaces – vast plains and plateaus, extensive deserts and mountain ranges. Cloven by rift valleys down its eastern side, its empty interior punctuated by spuming volcanoes and jagged escarpments, its landscape is as dramatic as it is immense.

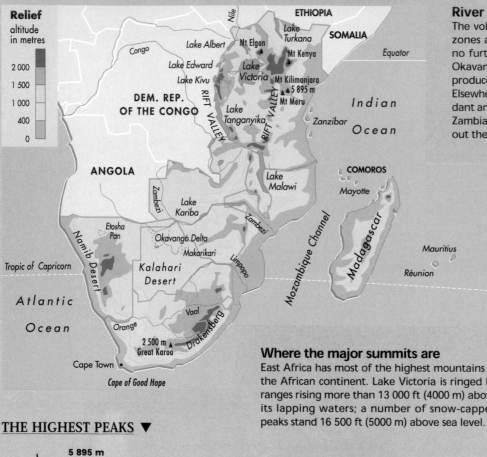

Relief
altitude in metres

2 000
1 500
1 000
400
0

River resources

The volume and flow of Africa's rivers depends on the climatic zones and terrains that they cross. Rising in Angola but with no further rainfall to supplement its evaporating waters, the Okavango comes to an end in an inland delta, sprawling out to produce a vast area of wetland at the arid heart of the Kalahari. Elsewhere, more regular precipitation levels lead to a more abundant and regular flow. Springing in the cool uplands of northern Zambia, the Zambezi enjoys a more or less steady flow throughout the year.

Where the major summits are

East Africa has most of the highest mountains in the African continent. Lake Victoria is ringed by ranges rising more than 13 000 ft (4000 m) above its lapping waters; a number of snow-capped peaks stand 16 500 ft (5000 m) above sea level.

Ecological zones

- Mediterranean
- Desert
- Semidesert
- Dry savannah and scrub
- Wooded savannah
- Forest
- Alpine
- Mangrove

THE HIGHEST PEAKS ▼

5 895 m Kilimanjaro
5 199 m Mount Kenya
5 119 m Ruwenzori
4 507 m Karisimbi
3 408 m Injasuti
3 069 m Piton des Neiges
2 876 m Tsaratanana
2 361 m Kartala
905 m Morne Seychelles

6 000
5 000
4 000
3 000
2 000
1 000
0

- Tanzania
- Uganda
- South Africa
- Madagascar
- Seychelles
- Kenya
- Rwanda
- Réunion
- Comoros

A range of climates

The region of Southern and East Africa falls for the most part into four distinct climatic zones.

- Equatorial: high, largely constant temperatures averaging around 26°C (78.8°F).
- Tropical: two separate seasons, one rainy and the other dry.
- Desert and semidesert: a very dry zone with no more than 4 in (100 mm) annual rainfall, and a considerable difference between overnight and midday temperatures.
- Mountain: a zone in which latitude is to a greater or lesser extent rendered irrelevant by altitudes of above 8000 ft (2500 m), which may bring humidity (mists) or, at the highest levels, permanent ice and snow.

Generally speaking, the farther from the Equator, the more arid the conditions become. The driest areas (Namib and Kalahari deserts) are in Southern Africa along the Tropic of Capricorn. Shielded by mountains from the rain-bearing westerly winds, equatorial East Africa receives a quarter of the rainfall of equatorial West Africa.

Population, religion and standard of living

Faced with an apparently never-ending round of catastrophes, from drought and famine to epidemic and armed conflict, the countries of Southern and East Africa seem precariously placed at the start of the new millennium.

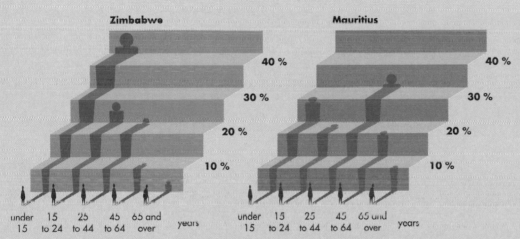

Zimbabwe — Mauritius

40 % 30 % 20 % 10 %

under 15 / 15 to 24 / 25 to 44 / 45 to 64 / 65 and over / years

Population density

Southern and East Africa remains sparsely populated overall, with an average density of fewer than 20 people per sq km. But this average masks profound disparities: 37 per cent of the total population of the continent lives in East Africa, with only 8 per cent in Southern Africa and the islands of the Indian Ocean. The greatest demographic concentrations are to be found in the areas around the great lakes (Victoria, Kivu and Tanganyika), along the eastern seaboard (Kenya, Tanzania), in Madagascar, in Zimbabwe (Shona country) and in South Africa (especially Transvaal and the Orange Free State). In the interior, by contrast, levels of population density are much lower: large areas here have fewer than five inhabitants per sq km.

Despite a catalogue of calamities, the population in Southern and East Africa keeps on growing, thanks to a birthrate that, though showing some signs of slowing, remains high. Average income per head of population has been rising only very slowly: for the poorest it has actually been falling in recent years. In the long term, a higher population should help boost economic performance and facilitate the development and management of resources. But, due to the ravages of AIDS, the youthful population that might have been the region's great resource threatens to become the millstone that drags these nations down into disaster.

The age pyramid

Almost half of all Africans are under 15 years of age. While infant mortality rates have plummeted, the birthrate has fallen only slowly, particularly in the countryside. The chief cause of demographic change in the rural areas has not in fact been the (comparatively meagre) success of large-scale birth-control campaigns, but a drift to the cities – which has introduced social problems of its own.

AGE PYRAMID ▲

LIFE EXPECTANCY ▼ ▶
(average, in years)

The countries where life expectancy is lowest

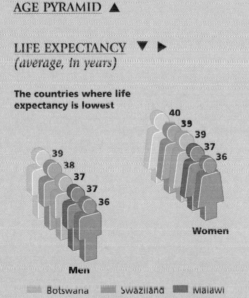

39 38 37 37 36

Men

40 39 39 37 36

Women

Botswana — Swaziland — Malawi
Zimbabwe — Zambia

The countries where life expectancy is highest

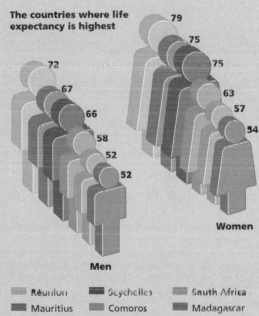

72 67 66 58 52 52

Men

79 75 75 63 57 54

Women

Réunion — Seychelles — South Africa
Mauritius — Comoros — Madagascar

Why islanders live longer

Throughout the countries of Southern and East Africa, life expectancy remains well below the world average. Even the richest country in the region, South Africa, currently has an average life expectancy of only 55. The life expectancy rate is rather higher in the offshore islands, where the development of successful tourist industries has raised standards of living in general and levels of sanitation in particular, and whose isolation from the mainland seems to have afforded the inhabitants some protection against epidemics – most notably from AIDS.

LITERACY AND LEVELS OF PRIMARY EDUCATION

The average literacy level in the region has risen to 66 per cent for men and 50 per cent for women. But progress has been disappointing compared with that in other areas of the world composed of developing countries, where literacy levels are as high as 86 per cent. There are also major discrepancies in educational opportunities for boys and girls, notably in Burundi and Mozambique, where less than a quarter of girls have access even to primary schooling.

	THE LEAST EDUCATED			THE MOST EDUCATED	
	Boys	Girls		Boys	Girls
Burundi	49.3%	22.5%	South Africa	81.9%	81.7%
Namibia	45.0%	31.0%	Mauritius	87.1%	78.8%
Mozambique	57.7%	23.3%	Zimbabwe	90.0%	80.0%

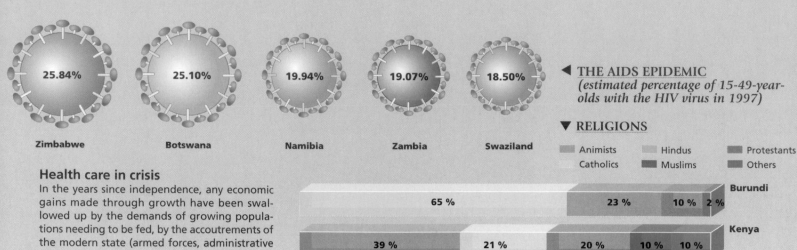

25.84%	**25.10%**	**19.94%**	**19.07%**	**18.50%**	
Zimbabwe	Botswana	Namibia	Zambia	Swaziland	

◀ **THE AIDS EPIDEMIC**
(estimated percentage of 15-49-year-olds with the HIV virus in 1997)

▼ **RELIGIONS**

Animists　Hindus　Protestants
Catholics　Muslims　Others

Health care in crisis

In the years since independence, any economic gains made through growth have been swallowed up by the demands of growing populations needing to be fed, by the accoutrements of the modern state (armed forces, administrative institutions and economic infrastructures), and the servicing of international debts. The proportion of GDP set aside for health care has fallen steadily, leaving Africa ill-equipped to deal with the AIDS epidemic. Young adults have been the most hard hit, with fearful consequences for society as a whole. The absence of any vaccine, the costs of medication and care, the lack of the resources required to develop programmes of education: all these factors have militated against effective action. The spread of AIDS has been made worse by a vicious circle in which women whose families are afflicted, and who have therefore lost their income, resort to prostitution, which helps to spread it further.

Burundi　65 %　23 %　10 %　2 %
Kenya　39 %　21 %　20 %　10 %　10 %
Madagascar　50 %　25 %　20 %　5 %
Mauritius　52 %　32 %　13 %　3 %

A multiplicity of faiths

Visited by Arab traders for more than a millennium, and later colonised in earnest by the European powers, Southern and East Africa has been exposed to a wide range of outside religious influences. The collection of indigenous beliefs referred to under the general heading of 'animism' has not so much been displaced as overlayered by the introduction of foreign monotheisms such as Islam and Christianity, with traditional beliefs and practices frequently flourishing just beneath the surface. Later waves of immigration brought polytheistic faiths from Asia – notably Hinduism.

ETHNIC COMPOSITION OF THREE STATES ▼

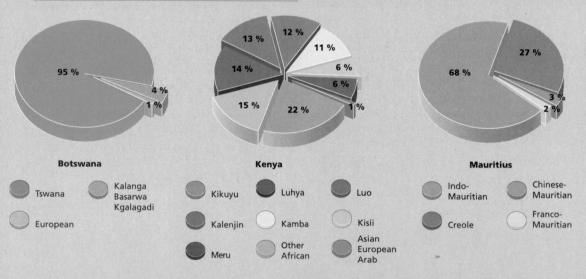

Botswana　95 %　4 %　1 %

Tswana
Kalanga Basarwa Kgalagadi
European

Kenya　12 %　11 %　6 %　6 %　1 %　22 %　15 %　14 %　13 %

Kikuyu　Luhya　Luo
Kalenjin　Kamba　Kisii
Meru　Other African　Asian European Arab

Mauritius　68 %　27 %　3 %　2 %

Indo-Mauritian　Chinese-Mauritian
Creole　Franco-Mauritian

The linguistic patchwork

The diversity of languages spoken in Southern and East Africa bears witness to the richness of the region's history, and to the inexhaustible adaptability of its peoples. The official languages, often those of the old colonists, may still be favoured for legal and other formal uses, but those of the main indigenous ethnic groups are promoted vigorously in both schools and in the media. While English may be the language of international big business, many millions in East Africa speak Swahili. An accretion of Arabic and other vocabularies upon a basic structure of Bantu, this historic tongue of traders has been finding a new lease of life as a *lingua franca*, or language of exchange.

Source of conflict

Created by the cartographers of the colonial era, the political and administrative boundaries of the region's nations are for the most part arbitrarily drawn, making few concessions to demographic realities on the ground and dividing peoples who were originally united. The tragic consequence for the countries concerned has been half a century of ethnic tension, at times flaring up into violent conflict. The difficulties experienced by neighbouring states in absorbing the large numbers of refugees produced by such crises has often had a destabilising effect on these countries in their turn. All human costs apart, these ethnic troubles have been a running sore upon the region, a drain on resources and a barrier to economic development.

TOWN AND COUNTRY

The second half of the 20th century saw a population explosion in Southern and East Africa, marked by a wholesale drift to the towns and cities. Less than 4 per cent of the population of the region lived in urban areas in 1920: the figure currently stands at more than 35 per cent. Despite this shift in demographic emphasis, the proportion of the population living in urban areas remains low compared with levels prevailing in countries of the developed world.

THE MOST URBANISED	Town	Country	THE LEAST URBANISED	Town	Country
Zimbabwe	33%	67%	Rwanda	6%	94%
Mauritius	41%	59%	Burundi	8%	92%
South Africa	51%	49%	Uganda	13%	87%
Botswana	63%	37%	Malawi	14%	86%

All change in the region's economy

In most of the countries of Southern and East Africa economic growth is either matching rises in population or slightly outstripping them. All sectors have made their contribution to this modest increase in wealth: most exciting of all has been an upsurge in small businesses, which hold out hopes of better times ahead for a part of the world too long economically overshadowed by others. The great state-socialist experiments have for the most part been abandoned, and governments in the region are doing their best to create an entrepreneurial climate in which energy and talent can thrive, to the benefit of all.

Mineral resources
- copper
- diamonds
- iron
- gold
- uranium
- coal

▼ GROSS NATIONAL PRODUCTS, GREAT AND SMALL: SOME EXAMPLES
(per capita, in US dollars)

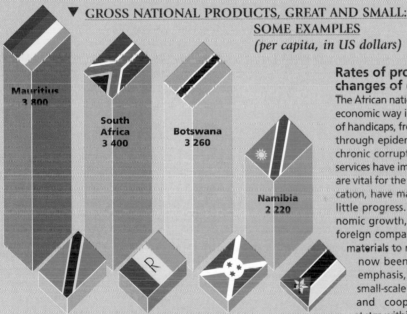

Mauritius 3 800
South Africa 3 400
Botswana 3 260
Namibia 2 220
Tanzania 210
Rwanda 210
Burundi 180
Mozambique 90

Rates of progress, changes of emphasis

The African nations must make their economic way in the face of a host of handicaps, from adverse climates through epidemics to conflict and chronic corruption. Though some services have improved, others that are vital for the future, such as education, have made disappointingly little progress. The drive for economic growth, once entrusted to foreign companies exporting raw materials to richer countries, has now been given a different emphasis, with a focus on small-scale African enterprises and cooperation between states within the region.

Women at work

The 'domestic' and 'economic' spheres, so clearly distinct in Western countries, are more difficult to distinguish in Southern and East Africa. Despite great changes in recent years, comparatively few of the inhabitants clock on in factories or commute to offices: most still cultivate the soil, or busy themselves in workshops in or around their homes. In what for most is not a cash economy, it is hard to put a monetary value on work or its products: often, goods and services are exchanged for other goods and services. Men, women and children all make economic contributions, but it is women who do the bulk of the work. As far as the figures are concerned, however, their efforts are all but invisible, since they take place overwhelmingly in the informal, unsalaried sector.

THE WORKING DAY FOR WOMEN ▼ AND MEN: HOW THEY COMPARE IN HOURS
(average per day)

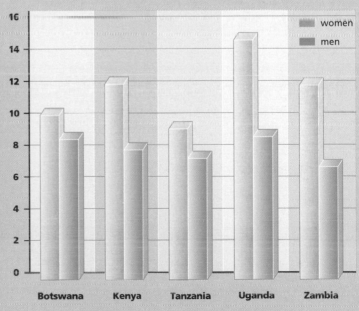

women
men

Botswana   Kenya   Tanzania   Uganda   Zambia

DIVISION OF LABOUR: HOW GENDER DETERMINES JOB OPPORTUNITIES IN UGANDA

The traditional differentiation between men's and women's work remains pronounced in Uganda, with strong specialisation between different spheres of labour. Work in agriculture, for example, belongs very much in the woman's domain: they carry out almost 90 per cent of the tillage, 90 per cent of the sowing and 60 per cent of the harvesting. The service and industrial sectors, by contrast, belong overwhelmingly to men, in everything from schoolteaching to textiles and small businesses.

SECTOR	% of GDP	% of EXPORTS	DIVISION OF PRODUCTION Women	Men
Agriculture	49.1%	99%	75%	25%
Industry	14.3%	1%	15%	85%
Services	36.6%	0%	32%	68%
Total/average	100%	100%	50.6%	49.4%

(From Elson & Evers, 1997.)

Agriculture and industry

Despite providing work for two-thirds of the working population, agriculture still faces enormous problems. Harsh, arid climates, poor soils and erosion due to deforestation have all made life difficult for farmers, and while traditional techniques have struggled to produce enough to support steadily growing populations, modern methods have all too often damaged the environment without producing the hoped-for increases in yield.

Most of the countries in the region have attempted to prioritise industry, but relatively few have had tangible benefits to show for their efforts. South Africa was always a special case, and Kenya, Zimbabwe and Mauritius have made modest progress; but for most of their neighbours inadequate infrastructure, government interference or corruption, and low educational levels make the work of the would-be entrepreneur difficult.

The export trade

Ninety per cent of the region's export revenues are generated by the trade in raw materials. Agricultural produce (cocoa, coffee, cotton) and minerals (copper, diamonds, gold) all have to be sold on the international markets where, subject to the vagaries of global supply and demand, prices can fluctuate wildly, with ruinous consequences.

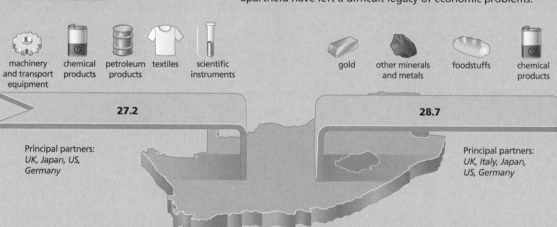

AFRICA AS A WHOLE
Agriculture: 66%
Industry: 12%
Services: 22%

SERVICES
Botswana: 51%
Burundi: 24%
Kenya: 54%
Zimbabwe: 40%

INDUSTRY
Botswana: 45%
(35% mining)
Burundi: 18%
Kenya: 17%
Zimbabwe: 32%

AGRICULTURE
Botswana: 4%
Burundi: 58%
Kenya: 29%
Zimbabwe: 28%

IMPORTS AND EXPORTS IN THREE STATES ▼
(Inward-pointing arrows indicate imports, those pointing outwards represent exports – both expressed in millions of US dollars)

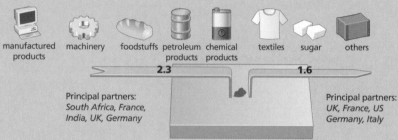

manufactured products | machinery | foodstuffs | petroleum products | chemical products | textiles | sugar | others

2.3

1.6

Principal partners:
South Africa, France, India, UK, Germany

Principal partners:
UK, France, US Germany, Italy

DISTRIBUTION OF THE WORKING POPULATION ▲

South Africa: abundant resources ▼

South Africa is privileged in having both a modern infrastructure and superb transport; its stock exchange is one of the top ten in the world. Yet growth is still not sufficient to absorb the 30 per cent of its workers who remain unemployed, while the politics of apartheid have left a difficult legacy of economic problems.

Mauritius: going for growth ▲

The past 30 years have seen a complete transformation in a Mauritian economy that has developed from one of subsistence agriculture to one in which fast-growing industrial, financial and tourist sectors all have their part to play. Throughout this period, growth has been 5-6 per cent a year. Accounting for 90 per cent of all cultivated land, sugar is practically a monoculture on Mauritius: the crop represents almost a quarter of the island's total exports, but net receipts are lower than one might expect, given the high cost of maintaining and updating essential equipment.

machinery and transport equipment | chemical products | petroleum products | textiles | scientific instruments | | gold | other minerals and metals | foodstuffs | chemical products

27.2

28.7

Principal partners:
UK, Japan, US, Germany

Principal partners:
UK, Italy, Japan, US, Germany

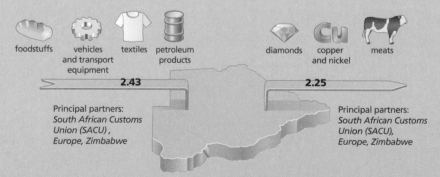

foodstuffs | vehicles and transport equipment | textiles | petroleum products | | diamonds | copper and nickel | meats

2.43

2.25

Principal partners:
South African Customs Union (SACU), Europe, Zimbabwe

Principal partners:
South African Customs Union (SACU), Europe, Zimbabwe

Botswana: a model economy ▲

The World Bank places Botswana in the first rank of countries in terms of industrial growth and strength. Good luck and good management of natural resources have gone hand-in-hand in its recent economic history.

With fewer than 2 million inhabitants to support, and the products of fabulous diamond mines to sustain them, Botswana is uniquely blessed among the nations of Southern and East Africa.

MILITARY SPENDING

South Africa and Botswana intervene in Lesotho while Zimbabwe, Angola and Namibia fight to suppress a Congolese rebellion that is backed in its turn by Rwanda and Uganda. War looms large in the budgets of nations who can scarcely manage their foreign debt repayments, let alone spend significant sums on health and education.

PERCENTAGE OF GDP THAT GOES ON MILITARY SPENDING

THE LEAST WELL-ARMED		THE MOST WELL-ARMED	
Tanzania	0.2%	South Africa	2.2%
Mauritius	0.4%	Burundi	2.6%
Malawi	0.8%	Namibia	2.6%
Madagascar	1.0%	Rwanda	3.8%
		Zimbabwe	4.6%
		Mozambique	4.7%

Index

Page numbers in *italics* denote illustrations. The letter and number references
in brackets are the co-ordinates for places in the map section, pp. 144-149

Acknowledgments

Abbreviations: t = top, m = middle, b = bottom, l = left, r = right.

FRONT COVER: *Elephants in Kenya*: PHONE/J.-P. Ferrero - J.-M. Labat. BACK COVER: *Women walk to market in Marangu, Tanzania*: HOA QUI/J.-D. Joubert

Pages 4/5: HOA QUI/P. Duval; 6: COSMOS/SPL; 8t: PHONE/ J.-P. Ferrero - J.-M. Labat; 8b: PHONE/J.-M. Labat; 9: PHONE/ J.-P. Ferrero - J.-M. Labat; 10l: HOA QUI/M. Denis-Huot; 10r, 11tr: HOA QUI/Krafft; 12t: RAPHO/G. Sioen; 12b: HOA QUI/Ph. Bourseiller; 13r: COSMOS/ANZENBERGER/ C. Sattlberger; 14t, b: HOA QUI/Jouan-Rius; 15: BIOS/Klein-Hubert; 16l: HOA QUI/S. Grandadam; 16r: HOA QUI/C. Pavard; 17b: HOA QUI/STOCKSHOOTER; 18t, m: COSMOS/SPL/ J. Reader; 18b: HOA QUI/Jouan-Rius; 19t: BRIDGEMAN ART LIBRARY/*Hottentot village on the left bank of the Orange river* by Samuel Daniell; 19m: HOA QUI/M. Denis-Huot; 19b: BRIDGEMAN ART LIBRARY/*Dodo* by George Edwards/ Natural History Museum, London; 20tl: HOA QUI/Jouan-Rius; 20tr: ROGER-VIOLLET; 20bl: HOA QUI/P. de Wilde; 21tr: HOA QUI/J.D. Joubert; 21m: ROGER-VIOLLET; 21bl: HOA QUI/ M. Denis-Huot; 21br: ROGER-VIOLLET; 22t: BRIDGEMAN ART LIBRARY/*Vasco de Gama* by Pedro Barretti de Resende/British Library, London; 22m: ROGER-VIOLLET; 23tl: GAMMA/SAOLA/ Hodalic-Brecelj; 23tr: BRIDGEMAN ART LIBRARY/The Stapleton Collection/*Le Grand Seigneur* by Philippe Simonneau; 23bl: BRIDGEMAN ART LIBRARY/*Map of Africa* by J. Beaue/Royal Geographical Society, London; 23br: HARLINGUE-VIOLLET; 24t: BRIDGEMAN ART LIBRARY/*Group of prisoners* by Josiah Wood Whymper; 24m: RMN/J. G. Berizzi/*Emancipation of Réunion* by A. Garreau/Musée des arts d'Afrique et d'Océanie, Paris; 24b: HOA QUI/Ch. Vaisse; 25t: Jean-Loup CHARMET; 25m: ROGER-VIOLLET; 26tl: BRIDGEMAN ART LIBRARY/The Stapleton Collection/*Zulu warrior*; 26tr: BRIDGEMAN ART LIBRARY/*Battle of Blauwktantz* by Thomas Baine/Afrikaner Museum, Johannesburg; 26m: BRIDGEMAN ART LIBRARY/*Cecil Rhodes* by Howard Davie; 26b: BRIDGEMAN ART LIBRARY/ The Stapleton Collection/*Zulu village, Natal*; 27tl: BRIDGEMAN ART LIBRARY/*Genadendal* by George French Angas; 27tr, b, 28t: ROGER-VIOLLET; 28l: GAMMA/LIAISON/P. Jordan; 28r: GAMMA/ N. Quidu; 28b: GAMMA/LIAISON/P. Magubane; 29tl: EXPLORER/ G. Boutin; 29tr: BRIDGEMAN ART LIBRARY/*Spion Kop*, lithograph by Neuman/Afrikaner Museum, Johannesburg; 30/31: HOA QUI/NF/H. Bertiau; 32: ALTITUDE/Y. Arthus-Bertrand; 34t: EXPLORER/Louglet-Theurer; 34b: ALTITUDE/ Y. Arthus-Bertrand; 35l: HOA QUI/Jouan-Rius; 35r: HOA QUI/ S. Grandadam; 36l: HOA QUI/M. Denis-Huot; 36r: COSMOS/ AURORA/R. Caputo; 37tr: HOA QUI/P. de Wilde; 37b: EXPLORER/ J. Brun; 38tl: HOA QUI/Ch. Vaisse; 38tr: HOA QUI/P. de Wilde; 38b: HOA QUI/Ph. Bourseiller; 39t: PHONE/Labat-Jardel; 39b: HOA QUI/P. de Wilde; 40tl: RAPHO/G. Gerster; 40tr: PHONE/J.-M. Labat - J.-P. Ferrero; 40b: RAPHO/G. Sioen; 41t: GAMMA/T. White; 42t: COSMOS/P. Maitre; 42m: PHONE/ J.-M. Labat - J.-P. Ferrero; 42b: PHONE/J.-M. Labat; 43m: HOA QUI/J.-D. Joubert; 44t: HOA QUI/P. de Wilde; 44m: Yvette LAVAUX; 44bl: PHONE/Cl. Jardel; 44br: HOA QUI/P. de Wilde; 45r: HOA QUI/E. Valentin; 46: HOA QUI/J.-D. Joubert; 48t: COSMOS/AURORA/R. Caputo; 48b: HOA QUI/Images and Volcanoes; 49t: ALTITUDE/Ph. Bourseiller; 49m: HOA QUI/ Krafft; 50t: ALTITUDE/Ph. Bourseiller-B. Durieux; 50b: ALTITUDE/ Ph. Bourseiller; 51m: BIOS; 51b, 52t: HOA QUI/M. Denis-Huot; 52m: HOA QUI/Ch. Vaisse; 52b: GAMMA/A. Lafargue; 53b: BIOS/ Seitre; 54ml, b: BIOS/N. Dennis; 55t: HOA QUI/Jouan-Rius; 55b: PHONE/R. Valter; 56t: BIOS/R. de La Harpe; 56m: BIOS/ A. Van den Berg; 56b: PHONE/A. le Toquin; 57t: BIOS/N. Dennis; 57b: BIOS/Klein-Hubert; 58: PHONE/Cl. Jardel; 60tl: HOA QUI/C. Farhi; 60t: PHONE/R. Valter; 60m: HOA QUI/Jouan-Rius; 60b: HOA QUI/Ph. Bourseiller; 61b: HOA QUI/Ch. Vaisse;

62ml: PHONE/R. Valter; 62b, 63t: PHONE/J. J.-M. Labat - J.-P. Ferrero; 63m: BIOS/D. Heuclin; 64tl, ml, mr, 65t: PHONE/ J.-M. Labat - J.-P. Ferrero; 65b: PHONE/Y. Vallier; 66t: PHONE/ J.-M. Labat - C. Jardel; 66m: PHONE/R. Valter; 66b: HOA QUI/ C. Pavard; 67t: PHONE/R. Valter; 67bm: BIOS/M. Gunther; 67br: HOA QUI/Jouan-Rius; 68t: BIOS/G. Martin; 68bl: BIOS/ Y. Lefevre; 68br: PHONE/A. Visage; 69m: BIOS/F. Bavendam; 69b: BIOS/Y. Tavernier; 70t: PHONE/J.-M. Labat; 70m: BIOS/F. Bruemmer; 70b, 71t,mr: PHONE/J.-M. Labat - J.-P. Ferrero; 72t: PHONE/R. Valter; 72ml: PHONE/J.-M. Labat; 72br, 73t, bm, 74/79: PHONE/J.-M. Labat - J.-P. Ferrero; 74tr: HOA QUI/ J.-D. Joubert; 74tl: GAMMA/P. Landmann; 74mr: GAMMA/ D. Simon; 74bl: GAMMA/LIAISON/J. Leachman; 74br: GAMMA/ D. Barritt; 75tl, bl: PHONE/J.-M. Labat - J.-P. Ferrero; 75tr: PHONE/J.-M. Labat; 75br: PHONE/J.-F. Hellio.N. Van Ingen; 75bm: PHONE/J.-M. Labat; 75/76t, 76t: PHONE/J.-M. Labat - J.-P. Ferrero; 76bl: BIOS/M&C Denis-Huot; 77tl, tr: PHONE/J.-M. Labat - J.-P. Ferrero; 77bl: PHONE/P. Goetgheluck; 77br, 78tl, mt: PHONE/J. M. Labat-J. P. Ferrero; 78tr: PHONE/ J.-M. Labat - J.-P. Ferrero; 78mtr: PHONE/J. M. Labat-J. P. Ferrero; 78mbr: BIOS/Klein-Hubert; 78bl: PHONE/R. Valter; 78br: PHONE/J.-M. Labat - J.-P. Ferrero; 79tl: HOA QUI/ C. Farhi; 79tr: GAMMA/LIAISON/J. Leachman; 79mr: HOA QUI/M. Denis-Huot; 79bl: GAMMA/A. Denize; 79br: GAMMA/ LIAISON/Guerrini; 80: GAMMA/N. Quidu; 82t: HOA QUI/ Y. Gellié; 82m: COSMOS/AURORA/R. Caputo; 82b: HOA QUI/ M. Huet, 83bl HOA QUI/C. Pavard; 83br: COSMOS/AURORA/ R. Caputo; 84t: HOA QUI/ALTITUDE/Y. Arthus-Bertrand; 84b: HOA QUI/Y. Gellié; 85t: HOA QUI/H. Ruiz; 85m: HOA QUI/Ph. Renault; 85b: HOA QUI/J.-D. Joubert; 86m: COSMOS/ P. Maitre; 86m: HOA QUI/N. Launay; 87tl: GAMMA/N. Quidu; 87tr: HOA QUI/Y. Gellié; 87bl, br: HOA QUI/C. Pavard; 88t, b: GAMMA/LIAISON/Peterson; 89ml: GAMMA/Th. White; 89mr: HOA QUI/J.-D. Joubert; 89b: HOA QUI/M. Denis-Huot; 90: GAMMA/B. de Hogues; 92t: HOA QUI/Ph. Roy; 92m: HOA QUI/J.-L. Manaud; 92b: HOA QUI/M. Denis-Huot; 93l: HOA QUI/J.-D. Joubert; 93r: HOA QUI/C. Pavard; 94t: HOA QUI/ M. Denis-Huot; 94b: GAMMA/LIAISON/Linton; 95t: HOA QUI/ C. Pavard; 95m: COSMOS/P. Maitre; 95b: GAMMA/N. Quidu; 96t: HOA QUI/A. Gérard; 96b: HOA QUI/Ch. Delu; 97t: COSMOS/P. Maitre; 97m: HOA QUI/C. Pavard; 97b: GAMMA/Spooner-Diffidenti; 98tl, tr, b: GAMMA/Th. White; 99t: COSMOS/G. Buthaud; 99m: GAMMA/Reynard-Figaro Magazine; 99b: HOA QUI/M. Dovic; 100t: HOA QUI/Y. Gellié; 100m: GAMMA/LIAISON/Agostini; 100b: EXPLORER/G. Boutin; 101t: HOA QUI/Ch. Vaisse; 101m: HOA QUI/Jouan-Rius; 101b: HOA QUI/P. de Wilde; 102t: HOA QUI/N. Launay; 102b: HOA QUI/P. de Wilde; 102m: HOA QUI/Ch. Vaisse; 103t: EXPLORER/S. Frances; 103m: HOA QUI/P. de Wilde; 104t, m: HOA QUI/G. Boutin; 104b: EXPLORER/P. Le Floch; 105t: GAMMA/D. Austen; 105ml: HOA QUI/N. Thibaut; 105b: GAMMA/D. Austen; 106t: HOA QUI/C. Pavard; 106b: HOA QUI/Ch. Vaisse; 107t: EXPLORER/Le Tourneur; 107m: HOA QUI/S. Grandadam; 107b: HOA QUI/ALTITUDE/Y. Arthus-Bertrand; 108t, m: HOA QUI/Ch. Vaisse; 108b: HOA QUI/ C. Pavard; 109t, b: HOA QUI/M. Renaudeau; 110: HOA QUI/ N. Thibaut; 112t: GAMMA; 112m: GAMMA/UK PRESS/de Keerle; 112b: GAMMA/S. Tait; 113t: GAMMA/Chambeau; 113mt: GAMMA/ Camerapix; 113mb: GAMMA/B. Inverson; 113b: GAMMA/Abbas; 114t: HOA QUI/C. Pavard; 114m: HOA QUI/J.-D. Joubert; 114b: HOA QUI/M. Denis-Huot; 115t: GAMMA/N. Quidu; 115m: GAMMA/Spooner-B. Alistair; 116t, b: COSMOS/ G. Buthaud; 117tr: GAMMA; 117m: COSMOS/G. Buthaud; 117b: GAMMA/M. Graham; 118t: HOA QUI/H. Collart; 118m: COSMOS/ASPEN/Aaronson; 118b: HOA QUI/M. Dovic; 119t: HOA QUI/Ch. Vaisse; 119m: EXPLORER/S. Frances;

119b: HOA QUI/J.-L. Manaud; 120t: HOA QUI/P. de Wilde; 120b: HOA QUI/C. Pavard; 121t: GAMMA/N. Quidu; 121m: GAMMA; 121b: GAMMA/J.-M. Turpin; 122t: HOA QUI/ ALTITUDE/Y. Arthus-Bertrand; 122m: HOA QUI/M. Denis-Huot; 122b: COSMOS/Visum; 123t: EXPLORER/PHOTO RESEARCHERS/Holton; 123b: HOA QUI/J.-D. Joubert; 124t: HOA QUI/J.-L. Manaud; 124m: HOA QUI/Jouan-Rius; 124b: HOA QUI/M. Denis-Huot; 125t: HOA QUI/Jouan-Rius; 125m: HOA QUI/Y. Gellié; 125b, 126t: HOA QUI/Ch. Vaisse; 126m: HOA QUI/C. Pavard; 126b: HOA QUI/Ch. Vaisse; 127t: COSMOS/P. Maitre; 127b: GAMMA/P. Lages; 128t: CORBIS-SYGMA/R. Bouhet; 128b: GAMMA; 129t: Collection KIPA/Film *The Gods Must be Crazy*; 129bl: Collection KIPA/Film *Gorillas in the Mist*; 129br: Collection KIPA/Film *A World Apart*; 130t: GAMMA/ LIAISON/Chalasani; 130b: VANDYSTADT; 131t: GAMMA/ Renault-Rieger; 131mt: HOA QUI/C. Pavard; 131mb: GAMMA/ Pool J.O. Atlanta 96; 131b: GAMMA/T. White; 132t: HOA QUI/Ch. Vaisse; 132b: GAMMA/LIAISON/Peterson; 133t: HOA QUI/P. de Wilde; 133m: GAMMA/A. Nosten; 133b: COSMOS/ P. Maitre; 134: HOA QUI/P. de Wilde; 136t: HOA QUI/ M. Renaudeau; 136bl: HOA QUI/P. de Wilde; 136br: HOA QUI/M. Denis-Huot; 137t: HOA QUI/D. Simon; 137b: HOA QUI/C. Pavard; 138t: HOA QUI/G. Boutin; 138m: BRIDGEMAN ART LIBRARY/*Statue of a bird, Zimbabwe*; 138b: HOA QUI; 139t: COSMOS/C. Portal; 139m: COSMOS/Robert-Bergerot; 139b: HOA QUI/C. Pavard; 140t: EXPLORER/J. Brun; 140b: GAMMA/SAOLA/Hodalic-Brecelj; 141t: GAMMA/T. White; 141m: HOA QUI/Courtney-Clarck; 141b: GAMMA/F. Reglain; 142/143: HOA QUI/M. Denis-Huot.

Printing and binding: Printer Industria Gráfica S.A., Barcelona
Colour separations: Station Graphique, Ivry-sur-Seine
Paper: Perigord-Condat, France